Seer Stone
v.
Urim & Thummim

Book of Mormon Translation on Trial

There have been some who have belittled him, but I would like to say that those who have done so will be forgotten and their remains will go back to mother earth, if they have not already gone, and the odor of their infamy will never die, while the glory and honor and majesty and courage and fidelity manifested by the Prophet Joseph Smith will attach to his name forever.

So we have no apologies to make.

— *President George Albert Smith*

Joseph Smith Foundation Documentaries

www.JosephSmithFoundation.org

Statesmen & Symbols: Prelude to the Restoration (DVD)

What do LDS temples have in common with the Great Pyramid of Giza, Stonehenge and the Hopewell mounds in North America? Why are some of the sacred symbols used by the Founding Fathers, also found on tapestries in China that date to the time of the flood? What are the details of American Founding Father Benjamin Rush's vision concerning Thomas Jefferson and John Adams?

Unlocking the Mystery of the Two Prophets: Revelation 11 (DVD)

Who are the two prophets in Revelation 11? The two messengers who lie dead in the great city? An assassination by enemies, a forbidden burial by persecutors, and bodies lying in the street for three and a half days are only a few of the clues found in scripture revealing their identity. The two prophets have generally been shrouded in mystery . . . until now.

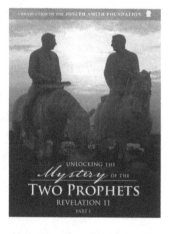

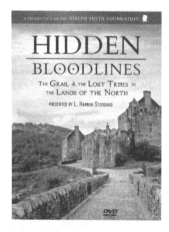

Hidden Bloodlines: The Grail & the Lost Tribes in the Lands of the North (DVD)

The legendary search for the Holy Grail has resonated with millions for centuries! What is the Holy Grail, and why is this legendary symbol important to the lives of Joseph Smith and the Son of God? Was Jesus Christ married and did He have children? Discover your own heritage, your own royal birthright, in a way you may never have imagined!

SEER STONE
v.
URIM & THUMMIM
Book of Mormon Translation on Trial

L. Hannah Stoddard
James F. Stoddard III

To Grandma Stoddard for her persistent encouragement,
support and help in making this project possible

ASSISTANT WRITERS:

Russell H. Barlow
Margaret J. Stoddard
Kimberly W. Smith
Lee H. Pearson, Ph.D.

ASSISTANT EDITORS:

Leah M. Stoddard
Moriah E. Barlow
G. Lee Andersen
Cory D. Schmidt

Joseph Smith Foundation®

Seer Stone
v.
Urim & Thummim
Book of Mormon Translation on Trial

L. Hannah Stoddard

James F. Stoddard III

👤 Joseph Smith Foundation®

Joseph Smith Foundation is an organization focused on supporting and contributing to projects founded in the words of Jesus Christ. Those contributing to *Joseph Smith Foundation* projects are members of The Church of Jesus Christ of Latter-day Saints, but the foundation is not sponsored by the Church. *Joseph Smith Foundation* projects include documentary films, Latter-day Answers, ZionTube, InspiraWiki, FAQs, Papers, Audio, Ebooks and much more.
www.JosephSmithFoundation.org

Published by:
Joseph Smith Foundation®
Salem, UT, USA

2nd printing

Interior Design: Leah M. Stoddard, Isaiah M. Stoddard, Ephraim J. Stoddard, Mary D. Stoddard, Ezra B. Stoddard
Cover Design: Leah M. Stoddard, James F. Stoddard III
Thanks & Contribution: Ephraim J. Stoddard, Julie A. Smith, Amber E. Schmidt, William H. Burns, Threesa L. Cummings

Library of Congress Control Number: 2019902608
ISBN: 978-164467011-8
Printed in the USA

CONTENTS

Foreword

I cannot express fully my appreciation for the work that went into this project, and for the truth it embraces. Like many members of The Church of Jesus Christ of Latter-day Saints, I love the Prophet Joseph Smith, but the degree to which I came to know him as I worked with his testimony and the testimonies of his loyal supporters has blessed my life immeasurably. The adversary has always waged war on the truth, but perhaps more than ever before in the history of the Earth, Satan has sought to undermine every vestige of our society, especially in our schools, using our own historians. In addition to strengthening our resolve to seek knowledge about significant events in Church history, this book restores confidence in the translation of the *Book of Mormon*, it affirms the prominence of the Prophet Joseph Smith in the annals of world history, and it brings peace to the soul. In all solemnity I add my own testimony of Joseph Smith, his divine calling as prophet, seer, and revelator of this, the last dispensation, his righteous character, and eternal significance to the authors of this book. I testify that the Holy Spirit has borne sacred witness to me of the translation of the *Book of Mormon* through the ancient instrument, the Urim and Thummim, from actual plates delivered to him by Moroni. I invite the reader to obtain that same witness.

Russell H. Barlow, *Universal Model* Editor in Chief, March 2019

INTRODUCTION

To our progressive and non-believing friends—

For non-believing historians of Mormon studies, this book will seem antiquated and perhaps frustrating. The book was not written for agnostic academics. We apologize that, at present, there is no way to accommodate your needs. No attempts have been made to adjust the language and approach to fit our cynical, politically correct climate. When one of the authors was preparing to begin work toward a Ph.D. in history, the author had an interesting visit with a distinguished professor at Brigham Young University. The professor advised that for the next dozen or so years all opinions, feelings, and beliefs not agreeable to the secular humanist and liberal academic climate should be hidden or smothered to allow for educational progress and success. No attempt has been made in that direction in this work.

For those who fit into the believing, progressive camp of Mormon historians, this book may seem "unscholarly" for the above reasons. Please remember that you are approaching the subject matter from a disparate paradigm. Both you and we believe this discussion is a struggle for the continuance and even the existence of our faith. We have been direct in our approach because of the seriousness of the subject matter, and do not desire to offend but rather to build faith and testimony. We understand that you, like we, are moving the narrative discussion in the direction believed best. We, the authors, after thousands of conversations with those in, or supporting those in, faith crisis believe that open discussion on these matters, on both sides, is the answer. Most members and many leaders of the Church have an extremely limited understanding of these issues. Open dialog, without fear and condemnation, is the answer. All sides must be presented, allowing individuals choice and agency.

The essence of the debate surrounding the new narrative is the character of Joseph Smith. For progressives and modernists, the character of any historical figure is a shade of grey. For progressives, Joseph Smith is a flawed, weak instrument that should be removed from the pedestal upon which he has been placed by past Latter-day Saints and leaders. Progressives cannot conceive a Godlike Joseph

Smith. Conversely, for many traditionalists, as well as the authors of this book, the Prophet stands next to the Lord himself in character and faithfulness. The distinction between progressives and traditionalists is the interpretation of historical sources. Traditionalists for the past several decades have increasingly been accused of covering up or ignoring history. We, the authors, conversely approach historical conflict by scrutinizing all sources and employing open dialog on all points.

We believe that the *Book of Mormon* itself is the model for good history and that the Prophet Mormon is the model for true historians. The "bias" toward the Nephites as opposed to the Lamanites is essential in depicting true history. *Book of Mormon* heroes are portrayed as heroes without shades of grey. Faith is never demeaned and wickedness is never trivialized. Good and bad, light and darkness are contrasted rather that melded together. Mormon, the compiler and editor, was directed by God through revelation to produce what we believe to be the most correct book. Contemporary historians could learn a great deal from Mormon's approach to history.

Historians and observers, in general, for the past 200 years have attempted to superimpose their personal and cultural character upon the prophets in the *Book of Mormon* and early Church history. These prophets, however, were real heroes with character traits inconceivable to our contemporary mind. Only virtue can perceive virtue. The Prophet Joseph Smith said, "You don't know me— you never knew my heart . . ."[1] This is more true today than when stated in 1844.

---

1 Joseph Smith History, 1838–1856, volume E-1, 1979, The Joseph Smith Papers.

1

TWO CONFLICTING NARRATIVES

"Take away the Book of Mormon, and the revelations, and where is our religion? We have none . . ." (Joseph Smith, traditionalist)[1]

"It seems safe to assume that without the Book of Mormon, there would be no Mormonism." (Grant Hardy, progressive)[2]

Upon one point, we seem to all agree. Yes, the believers, the unbelievers, the traditionalists, and the progressives. We all share this lonely, yet paradisical, island of common ground. Without the *Book of Mormon*, there is no Restoration, and for true believers, there is no foundation for the Gospel of Jesus Christ. Therefore, the *Book of Mormon* is the central focus for both progressives, as well as traditionalists. This Book of books is the battleline.

For 190 years The Church of Jesus Christ of Latter-day Saints and its leaders have put forth the overwhelmingly dominant and consistent position that Joseph Smith translated Nephite characters engraven on ancient plates from whence came the *Book of Mormon*. Faithful leaders and members have agreed that the Nephites and Lamanites were actual people who dwelt on this the American continent and that their prophets produced physical, tangible records, which were abridged by the prophet-historian, Mormon, who engraved characters upon metal plates "hav[ing] the appearance of gold."[3]

---

1   Joseph Smith, Minute Book 1, 21 April 1834, 44, The Joseph Smith Papers; capitalization modernized.

2   Grant Hardy, "Textual Criticism and the Book of Mormon," in *Foundational Texts of Mormonism* (New York: Oxford University Press, 2018), 37.

3   Joseph Smith, "Church History," *Times and Seasons* 3 (March 1, 1842): 707.

In the traditional narrative, the characters engraven on the plates represented the written language of the ancient Nephites (reformed Egyptian[4]). These characters were translated into the English language by the Prophet Joseph, who used the Nephite interpreters, called the Urim and Thummim. For nearly 200 years, our official Church history never promoted the seer stone hypothesis. Since its inception, the official history of the Church describes the Prophet Joseph Smith and his family as coming from worthy, hard-working, and God-devoted New England stock.[5] The Smith family was honest, industrious, pure-minded, and holy. For them, treasure seeking, folk and ritual magic, alcoholism, and other unworthy practices and pursuits were unthinkable.

We the authors, over the past several years, in meeting with and talking to thousands of members, members just like you, have noted a shift. A shift from confidence and faith in our religious tradition to countless stories of heartache, even heartbreak. Stories of confusion, frustration, doubt, disillusionment and even anger. Have I been lied to? What can I hold on to? Who is telling the truth? Does anyone have answers? Why is the story changing?

What has sparked this wildfire? Since before the publication of the *Book of Mormon*, there have always been detractors and those antagonistic toward the Prophet Joseph Smith who have promoted a different narrative. In one flavor or another, all of these detractors have certain elements in common. According to their viewpoint:

1. The Nephite nation may, or may not, have existed; no one knows with any certainty.

2. There either were no plates, the Prophet fabricated plates, or there were authentic plates, but those plates were rarely, if ever, used during the translation process.

3. Critics of the traditional Restoration narrative have also portrayed the Prophet's father, Joseph Smith Sr., as an

---

4   See Mormon 9:32; emphasis added. "And now, behold, we [Mormon and Moroni] have written this record according to our knowledge, in the characters which are called among us the *reformed Egyptian*, being handed down and altered by us, according to our manner of speech."

5   Joseph Fielding Smith, *Essentials in Church History* (Deseret Book, 1960), 25-31.

unmoored, indolent treasure digger who descended from a superstitious, magic-ridden ancestry.[6] They claim the Smith family was unprincipled, deceptive, wandering, and average; simply a reflection of the lower elements of their culture.[7]

4. Joseph Smith Jr. allegedly continued the "family tradition" by acting as the "village seer"[8] and by engaging in magic, treasure digging, and other occultic practices. These activities led him on a "pathway to prophethood."[9]

5. Finally, Joseph Smith did not use, or rarely used, the Urim and Thummim (or Jaredite—Nephite interpreters) preferring instead the use of an occultic[10] seer stone.

A Major Shift

For nearly two hundred years these two narratives stood in stark contrast to one another. However, over the past decade a major shift has prompted many Latter-day Saints to abandon the "traditional narrative," as many progressive intellectuals call for a "new narrative."

Ironically, this "new narrative" is not "new" at all. Many progressive scholars and intellectuals believe that the new narrative is reinforced by "new information," "new sources," and "new understanding." However, in regard to the translation of the *Book of Mormon*, no historical source has been discovered that substantially alters our understanding. In fact, there are no new sources, only new interpretations or a return to previous anti-interpretations of the same data.

---

6   Richard L. Bushman and Jed Woodworth, *Joseph Smith: Rough Stone Rolling* (Alfred A. Knopf, 2005), 26-27, 42, 48-52, 54-55, 57, 69. See also, "Was Joseph Smith Sr. a Weak and Failed Father? A *'Rough Stone Rolling'* Response," Latter-day Answers, February 17, 2017, accessed December 2018, http://ldsanswers.org/was-joseph-smith-sr-a-weak-and-failed-father-a-rough-stone-rolling-response/.

7   E. D. Howe, *Mormonism Unvailed* (Painesville: E. D. Howe, 1834), 11-13.

8   Ronald W. Walker, "Joseph Smith: The Palmyra Seer," *BYU Studies Quarterly* 24, no. 4 (1984), https://scholarsarchive.byu.edu/byusq/vol24/iss4/5.

9   Mark Ashurst-McGee, *A Pathway to Prophethood: Joseph Smith Junior as Rodsman, Village Seer, and Judeo-Christian Prophet,* Master's thesis (2000).

10   Occultic activities are those "relating to magical powers and activities, such as those of witchcraft and astrology" ("OCCULT | Definition in the Cambridge English Dictionary," Cambridge Dictionary, accessed February 2019, https://dictionary.cambridge.org/us/dictionary/english/occult) and "any system claiming use or knowledge of secret or supernatural powers or agencies." ("Occult," Dictionary. com, accessed February 2019, https://www.dictionary.com/browse/occult)

Does it Really Matter?

Some may wonder, "Does it really matter *how* Joseph Smith translated the *Book of Mormon?* What difference does it make if he used the Urim and Thummim or a seer stone?" Upon closer inspection, however, the implications have a far greater impact than we might realize.

If we accept that Joseph Smith dictated the *Book of Mormon* using a dark occultic seer stone he presumably found from an alleged career in treasure digging, scrying, and magic, this means the *Book of Mormon* was revealed through an occultic instrument and not by revelation and instruments provided by God. No true Christian can accept as God's word, a book which came from this "bitter fountain."[11] The very foundations of our faith crumble.

Additionally, if we accept that Joseph Smith dictated the *Book of Mormon* from words magically appearing on a seer stone, even a stone that was not occultic, Joseph Smith's character and integrity are shattered and our history is not viable. Critics antagonistic to the Church use this logic:

- If Joseph Smith never used the plates, why did the Lord burden generations of Nephite prophets with the painstaking recording and preservation of their history? Why was Moroni doomed to spend years on the run, hunted by the Lamanites, while he finished his father's abridgment and hid the record from those who were seeking to destroy it? Why was Joseph Smith warned by Moroni that he would be "cut off"[12] if he lost the plates, if he never used them? Was the Lord just wasting everyone's time?

- If Joseph Smith never used the plates, relying instead on words that appeared on a stone, to what degree does the *Book of Mormon* text we read today correspond with the original Nephite plates, if there is any correlation at all? Is the *Book of Mormon* even an historical text? Why not simply an inspired parable with heart-warming

---

11　See Moroni 7:10-12. "Wherefore, a man being evil cannot do that which is good; neither will he give a good gift. For behold, a bitter fountain cannot bring forth good water; neither can a good fountain bring forth bitter water; wherefore, a man being a servant of the devil cannot follow Christ; and if he follow Christ he cannot be a servant of the devil. Wherefore, all things which are good cometh of God; and that which is evil cometh of the devil; for the devil is an enemy unto God, and fighteth against him continually, and inviteth and enticeth to sin, and to do that which is evil continually."

12　Joseph Smith—History 1:59.

lessons "for our day"? How can we know the book's validity, the book's authenticity, and the book's truth, if this is our foundation?

- The "seer stone in a hat" narrative[13] contradicts the testimonies of Joseph Smith and Oliver Cowdery in every respect. Critics point out that Joseph and Oliver were simply covering up the true occultic origins of Mormonism—they were lying. Why do Joseph and Oliver tell an entirely different story from their antagonists? Whom should we trust?

Joseph Smith and the Occult

Perhaps most disturbing to those we talk to is the new assertion that Joseph Smith was involved in "ritual magic." The prominent progressive promoters of the "seer stone in a hat" narrative, particularly those who are endeavoring to write a "new narrative" of Church History, hold to the position that Joseph Smith used peep stones to search for buried treasure and lost objects, and then later used at least one of those stones to dictate the *Book of Mormon* that we read today. Richard L. Bushman seems foremost in leading the charge in this new direction. He stands as the chief evangelist for promoting a new "Joseph Smith." The new "Joseph Smith" uses the occult as a stepping stone to becoming a seer for Jehovah:

❙❙ . . . [Joseph Smith was a] boy who **gazed into stones and saw treasure** [that] grew up to become a translator who looked in a stone and saw words.[14]

Bushman has stressed that years of folk magic and treasure seeking prepared the "prophet" for the translation. At the same time, Bushman ironically stresses that Joseph Smith had to "purge" the preparation:

❙❙ It may have taken four years [after Moroni appeared on September 21, 1823] for Joseph to purge himself of his **treasure-seeking greed**. Joseph Jr. never repudiated the stones or denied their

---

13 This volume will address seer stone use during the translation process. A later volume in this book series will address all known statements on Joseph Smith's possession and use of seer stones. In this later volume, we will explain why peep stones are not seer stones and why Joseph Smith's seer stones were distinctly different from occultic stones. In our history, there are statements made by Brigham Young, Wilford Woodruff, and others who better understood the use of stones by seers. Again, we will further discuss these interesting statements in a later volume.

14 Richard L. Bushman, *Joseph Smith: Rough Stone Rolling* (New York: Alfred A. Knopf, 2005), 73; emphasis added.

power to find treasure. Remnants of the **magical culture stayed with him to the end. . . .**

Magic had served its purpose in his life. In a sense, it was a **preparatory gospel.**[15]

Can grievous errors in life truly be preparation? Can dabbling in Satanism lead to good? For the progressives, the answer seems to be "yes." For traditionalists, the answer has always been "no, never." This is the major point of contention.

The new narrative's "Joseph Smith" is a man who has serious character flaws. The prophet is "greedy," self-centered and superstitious; a mere stone-gazer. In the progressive worldview, the "preparatory gospel" is confused with soothsaying, necromancy, sorcery, alchemy, conjuring, divination, enchantment, mysticism, and magic.[16] For traditionalists, this is an insurmountable obstacle. In the modernist viewpoint, there is no devil. In the worldview of academia, spiritualism (communication with dark spirits) and magic are simply unknowns.

Progressive historian Steven E. Snow echoes the "new narrative" and promotes this new occultic "Joseph Smith" in these words:

> **//** By 1825, young Joseph had a reputation in Manchester and Palmyra for his activities as a **treasure seer,** or someone who used a seer stone to locate **gold** or other **valuable objects** buried in the earth.[17]

---

15   Ibid, 51-54; emphasis added.

16   Bushman states that "magic" was Joseph Smith's "preparatory gospel." The Lord in the revelations explains that the Aaronic Priesthood holds the key to and authority over the "preparatory gospel." "And the lesser priesthood continued, which priesthood holdeth the key of the ministering of angels and the preparatory gospel;" (Doctrine and Covenants 84:26).

17   Steven E. Snow, "Joseph Smith in Harmony," *Ensign*, September 2015, 52; emphasis added. The footnotes used in the original article cite disreputable sources including *Mormonism Unvailed* (1834) and *Tiffany's Monthly*. Mormonism Unvailed was the first significant published opposition to the Prophet Joseph Smith and the Restoration. It included material gathered by D. P. Hurlbut, who was excommunicated from the Church in 1833 for immoral conduct. See an extensive review of *Mormonism Unvailed* in chapters 9-12. *Tiffany's Monthly* was a 19th-century periodical published by Joel Tiffany. Joel Tiffany was an evangelist and advocate of Spiritualism, an occultic movement originating in New York in the 1840s.

For those concerned how this occultic "Joseph Smith" could make its way into Church publications, President Ezra Taft Benson offered this advice, "Sometimes from behind the pulpit, in our classrooms, in our Council meetings and in our church publications we hear, read or witness things that do not square with the truth. . . . Now do not let this serve as an excuse for your own wrong-doing. The

Contrast Steven E. Snow's approach with that of President Gordon B. Hinckley. President Hinckley noted:

❚❚ ... the fact that there were superstitions among the people in the days of Joseph Smith is no evidence whatever that the Church came of such superstition.[18]

President Joseph F. Smith also weighed in on this divisive and pivotal discussion:

❚❚ No man or woman who enjoys the Spirit of God and the influence and power of the holy Priesthood can believe in these superstitious notions, and those who do, will lose, indeed have lost, the influence of the Spirit of God and of the Priesthood, and are become subject to the witchery of Satan . . . These peepstone-men and women are inspired by the devil . . . [19]

The progressive new narrative promotes the viewpoint that leaders of the past, including Gordon B. Hinckley and Joseph F. Smith, were either dishonest with our history or misinformed.

Brant A. Gardner is another popular Latter-day Saint researcher and promoter of the "new narrative" and the new "Joseph Smith." Traditionally, "weak things" in the Church have been the humble and meek who listen to the promptings of the Spirit of God and do the Lord's work without worldly accolades. Brant Gardner changes all of this:

❚❚ Joseph couldn't learn to read the text on the plates—there was no Nephite dictionary available. What God used to effect the transformation was yet another weak thing. God used the **folk beliefs** of the rural population . . .

Lord is letting the wheat and the tares mature before he fully purges the Church. He is also testing you to see if you will be misled. The devil is trying to deceive the very elect." Ezra Taft Benson, "Our Immediate Responsibility" (BYU Devotional, Provo, October 25, 1996), https://speeches.byu.edu/talks/ezra-taft-benson_immediate-responsibility.

18 Gordon B. Hinckley, "Lord, Increase Our Faith," The Church of Jesus Christ of Latter-day Saints, accessed December 2016, https://www.lds.org/general-confer-ence/1987/10/lord-increase-our-faith?lang=eng; emphasis added.

19 Improvement Era 5 (September 1902): 897, https://archive.org/details/im-provementera0511unse/page/896; emphasis added.

Joseph was only one of several seers in that region. As a local seer, he was consulted to find things that were lost or to see into the future. . . .

It was Joseph's belief that he could see the unseeable that the Lord used as the fulcrum to **leverage the village seer into a translator** and then into a prophet of God.[20]

For Gardner, "weak things" are superstitions, involvement in magical rituals and fortune telling, the use of peep stones, and other occultic activities traditionally considered anti-Christian. Gardner claims that in 1828-29, Joseph Smith used the same occultic "skills" he used as the "village seer" to dictate the *Book of Mormon*. Gardner continues:

> **❙❙** The meaning on the plates was certainly hidden and lost. Joseph could not translate as the scholars did. However, with God's help, he would do so using the instrument and **methods he had successfully used before.** This time he wasn't finding a lost object, but rather a lost meaning.[21]

Is Gardner, almost unbelievably, hypothesizing that God helped Joseph Smith use folk magic—occultic, "Satanic"—methods, practices, and skills to bring forth the *Book of Mormon?* More than that, does Gardner also believe "God" helped the prophet do this?

The *Book of Mormon* itself teaches that a bitter fountain cannot bring forth pure water and a pure fountain cannot bring forth bitter water.[22] If Joseph Smith's origins were a bitter fountain, does it not follow that the work he produced would also be bitter? On the other hand, if the Prophet Joseph Smith, his family, and ancestry were noble, honorable, and faithful, would it not also follow that the works he produced—the *Book of Mormon,* the *Doctrine and Covenants,* the *Pearl of Great Price,* the *Joseph Smith Translation,* the original temple ceremonies, and the Prophet's other teachings, also be good? Does this not suggest that we are involved in a struggle for the very heart of our faith? Because of such disinformation, is it any wonder that many thousands of Latter-day Saints, including a majority of the youth, are currently struggling with their own personal crisis of faith?

---

20   Brant A. Gardner, "Translating the Book of Mormon," in *A Reason for Faith: Navigating LDS Doctrine & Church History* (Provo: Religious Studies Center, Brigham Young University, 2016), 22-23; emphasis added.

21   Ibid, 23; emphasis added.

22   Moroni 7:11.

2

Has the Church Been Deceptive?

For almost two hundred years, The Church of Jesus Christ of Latter-day Saints has promoted the narrative that Joseph Smith translated the *Book of Mormon* using the ancient Nephite plates and a Nephite artifact known as the Urim and Thummim. This narrative has been promoted in our artwork, manuals, Church publications, histories, and so forth.

One Latter-day Saint artist conducted a study wherein he and a research assistant analyzed the first 43 years of *Ensign* magazines from 1971 to 2014.[1] Their research documented overwhelming support for the traditional narrative, not the seer stone narrative, in our religious art.

- From 1971 to 2014, 17 images depicted the translation. The most popular image was Del Parson's "Joseph Smith Translating the Book of Mormon."

- Every painting portrayed the use of the plates.

- Eleven of the 17 images depicted Joseph Smith's finger on the plates, usually in a studious pose showing the Prophet putting serious intellectual effort into the translation of the *Book of Mormon*.

- One painting gave an artist's interpretation of the Urim and Thummim, but not one of the 17 images portray a seer stone, or a stone in a hat. The "seer stone in a hat" narrative was not to be found.

---

1   Anthony Sweat, "By the Gift and Power of Art," in *From Darkness Unto Light: Joseph Smith's Translation and Publication of the Book of Mormon* (Provo: Religious Studies Center, Brigham Young University, 2015), 229-243.

Critics have accused the Church of being "dishonest" and "deceptive" because the Church has taught that Joseph Smith translated the *Book of Mormon* using actual plates and the "Nephite interpreters," also known as the Urim and Thummim, not a dark colored seer stone. For example, a recent essay published by "Mormon Stories" podcast, hosted by former member John Dehlin, states:

> // For generations, the LDS Church has promoted the inspiring story of Joseph Smith translating ancient text while diligently scrutinizing a stack of gold plates before him. . . . First-hand participants consistently reported seeing Joseph bury his face in his hat while telling the story. The golden plates were never present in the room during translation, much less on the table as described in Church sponsored art. In our humble experience, the Church has been dishonest in its dealings, relying upon elaborate **deception, indirect language and altered narratives to mask inconvenient facts.**[2]

If John Dehlin is correct and Joseph Smith did translate the *Book of Mormon* using a seer stone in a hat, we must concede that yes, the Church has been "dishonest in its dealings." But has it?

Critics are not the only individuals accusing the Church of being deceptive. Historian Richard L. Bushman believes the traditional artwork depicting the translation of the Nephite plates, promoted by The Church of Jesus Christ of Latter-day Saints, is deceptive and needs to be changed:

> // . . . we still have pictures on our Ward bulletin boards of Joseph Smith with the Gold Plates in front of him. That has become an **irksome point** and I think it is something the church should pay attention to. Because anyone who studies the history knows that is *not* what happened. There is *no* church historian who says that is what happened and yet it is being propagated by the church and it feeds into the notion that the church is trying to **cover up embarrassing episodes** and is sort of **prettifying its own history.**[3]

---

2   "Translation Process," Mormon Stories, accessed January 2018, https://www.mormonstories.org/truth-claims/the-books/the-book-of-mormon/book-of-mormon-authorship-translation-timeline/.

3   "FAIR Podcast, Episode 3: Richard L. Bushman P.1.," FairMormon, October 12, 2010, accessed April 2018, https://www.fairmormon.org/blog/2010/10/12/

Has the Church been trying to "cover up embarrassing episodes"? Have we "prettified" our own history? The progressive new narrative would lead us to believe that all informed individuals conclude that the Nephite plates were not used while translating the *Book of Mormon*. Latter-day Saint progressives claim that no church historian would agree with the artwork produced by the Church for years. Is the new narrative correct?

"No Authentic Statement"

One of the most prominent Church historians in our history, President Joseph Fielding Smith, thoroughly studied the seer stone hypothesis and concluded that the narrative is hearsay and has no authentic historical support:

❝ While the statement has been made by some writers that the Prophet Joseph Smith used a seer stone part of the time in his translating of the record, and information points to the fact that he did have in his possession such a stone, yet there is **no authentic statement** in the history of the Church which states that the use of such a stone was made in that translation. The information is all **hearsay**, and personally, I do not believe that this stone was used for this purpose.[4]

Was President Joseph Fielding Smith qualified to make such a statement? President Smith worked as a Church historian for 69 years and served as the "Church Historian and Recorder" for 49 years. He was sustained as the President of the Quorum of the Twelve Apostles for nearly 20 years, and in 1970, he succeeded David O. McKay as the 10th President of the Church.

Joseph Fielding Smith's decades of service in the Church were complemented by his own family heritage. He was the grandson of President Hyrum Smith and the son and personal secretary of President Joseph F. Smith. Born one year prior to the death of President Brigham Young, Joseph Fielding Smith knew Presidents John Taylor, Wilford Woodruff, Lorenzo Snow, Joseph F. Smith, Heber J. Grant, George

---

fair-podcast-episode-3-richard-l-bushman-p-1; emphasis added.

4   Joseph Fielding Smith, *Doctrines of Salvation*, comp. Bruce R. McConkie, vol. 3 (Salt Lake City: Bookcraft, 1999), 225-226; emphasis added.

Albert Smith, David O. McKay, Harold B. Lee, Spencer W. Kimball, Ezra Taft Benson, Howard W. Hunter, Gordon B. Hinckley, Thomas S. Monson, and Russell M. Nelson. In other words, Joseph Fielding Smith personally knew every President of the Church, except Joseph Smith and Brigham Young. He not only studied Church history, he *lived* it. He spent hours, days, months, and years working directly with many of its key players. Moreover, President Smith studied the lives and teachings of Joseph Smith and Brigham Young, perhaps more than any other man in this dispensation.

Furthermore, he worked as the personal secretary to his father (President Joseph F. Smith) for many years. Joseph F. Smith knew his father, President and Patriarch Hyrum Smith, and his uncle, the Prophet Joseph Smith. President Joseph F. Smith also served in the First Presidency with Brigham Young, John Taylor, Wilford Woodruff, and Lorenzo Snow. There is no one since the 19th century who approaches Joseph Fielding Smith's firsthand knowledge of the events of Church history.

If there ever was a Church historian who grappled with difficult issues and believed in telling the real, bare truth, it was Joseph Fielding Smith. Joseph Fielding Smith authored nearly two dozen books, addressing everything from the Mountain Meadows Massacre, to polygamy, to science and Darwinian Evolution, to *Book of Mormon* geography, to the Signs of the Times, to blood atonement, and the personal writings of the Prophet Joseph Smith.[5] When it came to the translation of the *Book of Mormon*, President Smith acknowledged to members and non-members alike, that Joseph Smith did possess a seer stone or seer stones. This fact was not concealed or hidden. However, claims that this seer stone was used in the translation are "hearsay," according to historian and President Joseph Fielding Smith.

Outdated Research or New Interpretation?

There is a growing trend to throw Joseph Fielding Smith, and specifically his evaluation of the seer stone hypothesis, under the bus, claiming his historical research is outdated. Since President Joseph Fielding Smith

5   See works including *Blood Atonement and the Origin of Plural Marriage, Essentials in Church History, Origin of the Reorganized Church and the Question of Succession, The Life of Joseph F. Smith, Answers to Gospel Questions, Church History and Modern Revelation, Teachings of the Prophet Joseph Smith* and *Doctrines of Salvation.*

passed away in 1972, many progressive historians promote the idea that because of the *Joseph Smith Papers* project and other research, new information on the translation process is now available.

What are these newly discovered sources that presumably invalidate President Joseph Fielding Smith's conclusions, while shedding new light on the translation of the *Book of Mormon*? Have Church materials and counsel from past First Presidencies been misguided or deceptive? Or could it be that President Smith's conclusions regarding the seer stone hypothesis, based on historical evidence at his disposal, are even more pertinent today?

As of the date of this printing, we are not aware of a single new source that has been discovered during the last several decades which materially challenges our understanding of how the translation took place. If there are no new sources, why are progressive historians calling for a "new narrative"? Is the debate over the so-called "new" sources, or rather, a new *interpretation* of existing sources?

How to Approach the *Book of Mormon* Translation

There are two primary schools of thought when it comes to the translation of the *Book of Mormon*, and all other positions seem to fall somewhere in between.

On the one hand, there are those who believe that Joseph Smith was *not* a prophet, and that he may or may not have been honest. Therefore, to determine how the translation occurred, we should analyze the data available about each individual who was present ("eyewitnesses") during the translation process to determine who is telling the truth, who is inconsistent, and so forth. From this evaluation, one might reconstruct a reasonable representation of what took place. Adherents of this viewpoint, including acclaimed author Dan Vogel, or those who believe Joseph Smith was a "pious fraud," conclude that since Joseph Smith and Oliver Cowdery's accounts of the translation contradict what they consider the "eyewitness" accounts from David Whitmer, Emma Smith, and Martin Harris, non-believing historians assume that Joseph Smith was not straightforward, or worse, he was deliberately deceptive. The dissidents argue that the revelations in the *Doctrine and Covenants*, the *Book of Mormon* itself, and the writings of Joseph Smith hold very little, if any weight, and that we should stick with the so-called "eyewitness" accounts. If we were evaluating nearly any other case, we might agree with Vogel and the other critics: this would be a logical and impartial way to deal with the subject.[6]

The implications of the non-believer model are (1) the "spectacles" or "Urim and Thummim" never existed or were fabricated, but Joseph tossed them aside in favor of his treasure-digging seer stone.[7] (2) There were no Nephite plates, since, as David Whitmer said, Joseph never used them to translate.[8] (3) The credibility of David Whitmer and Martin Harris is questionable due to frequent inconsistencies with their respective stories[9], which forces researchers to evaluate alternative accounts, all of which are hostile toward the Prophet Joseph Smith. For the critics, Joseph Smith was not a "prophet." Therefore, his antagonists were and are merely exposing a fraud.

However, there is a better way to approach a discussion of the translation of the *Book of the Mormon*. We, the authors of this book, know that the Prophet Joseph Smith was an inspired witness of Jesus Christ. We know that he "lived great, and he died great in the eyes of God and his people."[10] We know that the revelations given through the Prophet Joseph Smith contain the words of the Lord to His people in the Last Days. This book was written to and for those who share this same belief and desire to better understand how the translation of the *Book of Mormon* took place.

Acknowledging the prophetic calling of Joseph Smith changes a few fundamental factors when determining who is, and who is not, an "eyewitness" to the translation of the *Book of Mormon*. When Moroni was preparing the boy prophet to receive the plates, he gave Joseph a strict charge:

---

6   To those who hold to Joseph Smith as a true Prophet of God and believe they have knowledge of this through revelation, Joseph Smith's statements regarding the translation are the final word. Believing Latter-day Saints view Joseph Smith's revelations as received from God. This means that the Prophet's statements on the translation outweigh all other statements for believers. For nonbelievers, Joseph's statements hold less weight.

7   For example, "Joseph Smith's Magic Spectacles - Dan Vogel," YouTube video, posted by "Dan Vogel," June 2, 2014, https://www.youtube.com/watch?v=ksnbSh51itg.

8   David Whitmer, "Mormonism," *Kansas City Journal*, June 5, 1881.

9   See chapter "David Whitmer vs. David Whitmer."

10   Doctrine and Covenants 135:3.

> "... he [Moroni] told me [Joseph Smith], that when I got those plates of which he had spoken ... I should **not show them** to any person; neither the breastplate with the Urim and Thummim; only to those to whom I should be commanded to show them; if I did I should be **destroyed.**
>
> ... the same heavenly messenger delivered them up to me [September 22, 1827] with this charge: that I should be responsible for them; that if I should let them go **carelessly**, or through any **neglect** of mine, I should be **cut off**...[11]

Joseph had scarcely obtained the record before he was showered with bribes to see the plates. Others tried more violent means, but each time the Prophet was able to successfully repel their attacks and protect the plates.

When we examine the testimony of the Lord and the Prophet Joseph Smith (see chapters "Witness #1 - The Lord," "Witness #2 - Joseph Smith: Translation Instruments," and "Witness #2 - Joseph Smith: Translator or Reader?"), we see clear proof that according to their firsthand accounts, the plates, the Nephite engravings, and the Urim and Thummim were present and used. In fact, the plates were present and used during the *entire* translation. Since no one saw the plates other than Joseph Smith, and perhaps Oliver Cowdery[12] (at least until the arrangement of formal viewings to the Three Witnesses and Eight Witnesses), the only genuine "eyewitnesses" to the translation were the Prophet Joseph, possibly Oliver Cowdery, and those assisting from the other side, including the Lord, Moroni, and others.[13] Again, for any contemporary in our day who believes or knows that Joseph Smith was an honest, righteous man, the revelations and the words in

---

11 Joseph Smith History, circa June 1839–circa 1841, draft 2, 6-8, The Joseph Smith Papers; emphasis added.

12 *Doctrine and Covenants* 9:5. It appears that Oliver Cowdery did "begin to translate." "And, behold, it is because that you did not continue as you commenced, when you began to translate, that I have taken away this privilege from you." Oliver Cowdery was also shown a vision of the plates before he met the Prophet Joseph Smith. See chapter "Witness #6 - Oliver Cowdery."

13 In the "Wentworth Letter," Joseph Smith spoke of "many visits from the angels of God" that assisted in preparing him to receive the Nephite plates. A number of the early Brethren reported that Alma, Nephi, Mormon, Moroni, the Nephite Twelve Apostles (including the Three Nephites), and "others of the ancient Prophets who formerly lived on this Continent" all visited and taught Joseph Smith repeatedly. See chapter "Witness #2 - Joseph Smith: Translator or Reader?"

the *Book of Mormon* are accurate and from God. As we shall see, the scriptures are clear that Joseph Smith translated using the Urim and Thummim and not a seer stone or peep stone. Conversely, if we do not believe that Joseph Smith was honest in describing the translation process, why would we take seriously the *Book of Mormon* as scripture? If we do not believe that Joseph Smith was honest, can we maintain our faith in the Restoration? Or better, why would we?

With these considerations, how does one approach the translation accounts of David Whitmer? Emma Hale Smith Bidamon? Martin Harris and newspapers antagonistic toward The Church of Jesus Christ of Latter-Day Saints? In this book series, we apply a series of simple questions to their testimonies to determine if their recollections are based on fact . . . or fiction.

How did Joseph Smith translate the *Book of Mormon*? Where does the evidence lead? To answer this question, we will respond to the progressive seer stone plaintiff who has placed the translation of the *Book of Mormon* on trial. We will review the accounts given concerning the translation of the *Book of Mormon* and discover the truth–fact vs. fiction. As the charge has been laid, we will play the role of a defendant, and you will play the role of jury and judge. So, if it please the court, allow us to offer our defense by calling our first witness.

3

WITNESS #1 – THE LORD

The first witness in our defense and preeminent eyewitness of the translation is the Son of God. Therefore, we petition the Lord Jesus Christ, respectfully asking if He would like to take the stand.

In doing so, we present an unimpeachable testimony, for this witness is not only under oath, but He "cannot lie."[1] He is continuously under oath and "cannot deny [His] word."[2] His comments include the definite clarification that "[Joseph Smith] has translated the book, even that part which I have commanded him, and as your Lord and your God liveth it is true."[3] He has also affirmed the translation process stating that the Prophet translated "by the means of the Urim and Thummim."[4]

As we begin our interrogatory, let the record show that the Lord never referred to, or even hinted that a seer stone or "stone in a hat" was used to translate the *Book of Mormon*. Instead, the Lord testifies in revelation that the entire *Book of Mormon* was translated by means of the Urim and Thummim. While some imagine that the Nephite plates were covered or even hidden during translation, the revelations clearly state that the *Book of Mormon* text we read today was translated into English using tangible engravings on literal, physical plates, as opposed to plates buried in a field, sitting under a bed, or hidden under a napkin. The plates and Urim and Thummim were present and essential to the translation process.

As some of the revelations in the *Doctrine and Covenants* were revised by the Prophet Joseph Smith, this chapter will refer to the

1   Doctrine and Covenants 62:6.

2   Doctrine and Covenants 39:16.

3   Doctrine and Covenants 17:6.

4   Doctrine and Covenants 10:1.

text from the 1844 edition of the *Doctrine and Covenants*, including references which will allow readers to find the verses in the current edition of the *Doctrine and Covenants*, published by The Church of Jesus Christ of Latter-day Saints. Joseph Smith approved the text for the 1844 edition of the *Doctrine and Covenants* and as we shall see throughout this chapter, the Lord and Joseph Smith used the term "Urim and Thummim" to refer to the instrument used during the translation in these revelations.

To begin our examination of our first witness' testimony, we ask the following questions.

Did Joseph Smith Translate the Entire *Book of Mormon* Using the Nephite Urim and Thummim? Or Only a Part?

After Joseph lost the *Book of Lehi* (or the 116 pages) in 1828, the Lord gave a revelation to the Prophet wherein he explained that the *Book of Lehi* had been translated by means of the Urim and Thummim. After the 116 pages were lost, the gift and power to translate was taken from the Prophet, but was eventually restored with the Lord's definitive command to the Prophet Joseph that he continue translating the remainder of the *Book of Mormon* "as [he had] begun," with the Urim and Thummim:

> Now, behold I say unto you, that because you delivered up those writings which you had power given unto you to translate, **by the means of the Urim and Thummim**, into the hands of a wicked man [Martin Harris], you have lost them; and you also lost your gift at the same time, and your mind became darkened; nevertheless, it [the power to translate by means of the Urim and Thummim] is now restored unto you again, therefore see that you are faithful and continue on unto the finishing of the remainder of the **work of translation as you have begun** . . . [5]

Some have speculated, based on claims made by Emma Smith, David Whitmer, and others, that after the 116 pages vanished, Joseph Smith lost the Urim and Thummim and never regained it. But if we examine our witness' testimony, the Lord's testimony, we understand that the

---

5   Doctrine and Covenants 36:1, 1844 ed. [D&C 10:1-3], 240-241, The Joseph Smith Papers; emphasis added.

Lord "restored" the gift and commanded the Prophet to continue translating the remainder of the *Book of Mormon* as "he had begun."[6] Why would the Lord have restored this special instrument, the Urim and Thummim, if Joseph Smith was going to set it aside and use his seer stone instead? Why was Joseph Smith not able to continue translating, after the Urim and Thummim and the plates were taken away, if he was "translating" by simply reading words that appeared on his seer stone? For those who argue that the Prophet did not use the Urim and Thummim or the plates, why were they returned to him? Did the Lord and His angels just have extra time on their hands, or did they believe Joseph Smith needed some toys to play with in the evening?

In all seriousness, for faithful Latter-day Saints there is no doubt that the Urim and Thummim and the plates played an essential part in the translation process, and without them, no translation could have occurred.

Was the Urim and Thummim Used by Joseph Smith His Personal Seer Stone? Or Was it a Jaredite Artifact that Passed Through Nephite Hands to Joseph Smith?

Eight to nine months following Joseph Smith's recovery of the Nephite plates and Jaredite–Nephite Urim and Thummim, the Lord prepared the three witnesses to view the ancient plates and other artifacts. The Lord clarified that the Urim and Thummim used by the Prophet to translate the *Book of Mormon*, was the same Urim and Thummim given to the Brother of Jared:

❝ Behold I say unto you, that you must rely upon my word, which if you do, with full purpose of heart, you shall have a view of the plates, and also of the breastplate, the sword of Laban, the **Urim**

---

6   Joseph Smith's history, later published in the *Times and Seasons in 1842*, testified that the angel returned the Urim and Thummim to him after the 116 pages were lost: ". . . I [Joseph Smith] was walking out a little distance when behold the former heavenly messenger appeared and handed to me the Urim and Thummim again . . . After I had obtained the revelation [*Doctrine and Covenants* 3], both the plates and the Urim and Thummim were taken from me again; but in a few days they were returned to me." Joseph Smith History, circa June 1839–circa 1841, draft 2, 10-11, The Joseph Smith Papers.

In her personal history, Lucy Mack Smith also described the event when the plates and the Urim and Thummim were restored to her son, the Prophet Joseph Smith, after they had been taken following the loss of the 116 pages. Her account will be reviewed in the next chapter.

and Thummim, which were given to the brother of Jared upon the mount, when he talked with the Lord face to face . . . and [Joseph Smith] has translated the book, even that part which I have commanded him, and as your Lord and your God liveth it is true.[7]

This ancient tool, the Urim and Thummim, was specifically prepared and preserved *with* the plates as a means whereby Joseph Smith could translate the record into English.

> *Note*: Moroni, Joseph Smith, and other witnesses described the Jaredite—Nephite Urim and Thummim as two (not one), transparent (not opaque), stones, set in the rim of a bow and fastened to a breastplate.[8]

Did the Lord Command the Three Witnesses to Bear Testimony of the Urim and Thummim?

We often think of the Three Witnesses as testimony bearers of the plates, but how often do we think of them as testimony bearers of the Urim and Thummim? In the original revelation, the Lord commanded the Three Witnesses to bear witness of the Urim and Thummim *along with* the plates:

❛❛ And after that you have obtained faith, and have seen them with your eyes, you shall **testify of them**, by the power of God; and this you shall do that my servant Joseph Smith, jr. may not be destroyed, that I may bring about my righteous purposes unto the children of men, in this work.[9]

Were the witnesses shown a seer stone? No! The witnesses were shown and commanded to testify of the Urim and Thummim, the same Urim and Thummim given to the Brother of Jared. The Prophet would

---

7   Doctrine and Covenants 42:1-2, 1844 ed. [D&C 17:1, 6], 254-255, The Joseph Smith Papers; emphasis added.

8   See later chapters in this volume, including "Witness #2 - Joseph Smith: Translation Instruments" and "Witnesses #3-5 - Ancient Prophets."

9   Doctrine and Covenants 42:2, 1844 ed. [D&C 17:3-4], 254-255, The Joseph Smith Papers; emphasis added.

later describe the Urim and Thummim as two transparent stones set in the rim of a bow fastened to a breastplate.[10] Why would the Lord have shown the witnesses the Urim and Thummim and commanded them to bear testimony of it, if this particular artifact was never used? Conversely, since the Lord never showed the witnesses the seer stone and never commanded the witnesses to bear testimony of the seer stone, why should we believe the seer stone was used to translate the *Book of Mormon*?

Each artifact revealed to the Three Witnesses was connected to the Nephite legacy and the *Book of Mormon* record. The plates, whereon the record was transcribed, the breastplate and Urim and Thummim, which were the revelatory tools Joseph used to translate, the sword of Laban, which was brought to the promised land by Nephi and preserved by his descendants; each Nephite artifact bore its own testimony to this sacred message, crying from the dust. The Three Witnesses were commanded to bear testimony of each one of these artifacts individually, including the Urim and Thummim. If a seer stone had been the means whereby the record had been translated, that seer stone should have been present rather than the Urim and Thummim, but it was not.

For those who believe that the *Book of Mormon* is not historical, that it never actually happened, that there never really was a "Nephi" or a "Laban" or a "Moroni,"[11] the Lord's revelations establish each of these. There actually was a Laban that carried the "sword of Laban"; there really was a breastplate and a Urim and Thummim handled and used by the "brother of Jared" and "Mosiah" and "Moroni"; there really was a Liahona that directed and informed Lehi and Nephi both in the wilderness and on an actual ship that carried Lehi's family to a literal promised land. The Lord in His revelation testifies that the *Book of Mormon* is true and that the *Book of Mormon* is historical.

The Lord testified that the Prophet Joseph Smith faithfully translated the *Book of Mormon* and "as your Lord and your God liveth" the translation is "true." He commanded the witnesses to bear testimony of the objects directly involved in the translation: the plates, the breastplate, and the Urim and Thummim.

---

10   Joseph Smith, "Church History," *Times and Seasons* 3, (March 1, 1842): 707.

11   See discussion on historicity of the Book of Mormon in chapter "Witness #2 - Joseph Smith: Book of Mormon Historicity."

Under oath, the Lord affirms that if His testimony is false, if Joseph used a seer stone and not the Urim and Thummim, if the *Book of Mormon* is simply a 19th century text, if the *Book of Mormon* is riddled with cultural errors (as many modernist scholars would have us believe), He will cease to be God. As the Lord lives, His testimony and the *Book of Mormon* record are true.

Translate the Engravings

Both the Prophet Joseph Smith and the Lord Jesus Christ referred to the coming forth of the *Book of Mormon* as a "translation,"–a term coined and used purposefully by the Lord Himself.[12] In the revelations known to have been received during the translation process, the Lord used the term "translation" to describe the coming forth of the *Book of Mormon* at least *30 times*. A few examples include:

- "... you have a gift to **translate** the plates; ... when thou hast **translated** a few more pages ... then thou mayest **translate** again...."[13]

- "... writings which you had power given unto you to **translate** by the means of the Urim and Thummim ... the work of **translation** ... means provided to enable you to **translate** ... in asking to **translate** it over again ... you shall not **translate** again those words which have gone forth out of your hands ... show it not unto the world until you have accomplished the work of **translation**... **translate** the engravings which are on the plates of Nephi ... until you come to that which you have **translated** ... it is wisdom in me that you should **translate** this first part of the engravings of Nephi."[14]

- "I grant unto you a gift, if you desire of me, to **translate**, even as my servant Joseph."[15]

---

12   A discussion of the translation of the Bible (JST), the Book of Abraham, as well as other records contrasted with non-translated records, such as most of the *Doctrine and Covenants*, will be discussed in a later volume confirming again that the Lord's use of the term "translation" was intentional.

13   Doctrine and Covenants 5:4, 30; emphasis added.

14   Doctrine and Covenants 10:1-45; emphasis added.

15   Doctrine and Covenants 6:25; emphasis added.

- "assist in bringing to light those things of which has been spoken—yea, the **translation** of my work . . . my word which shall come forth among the children of men, or that which is now **translating**."[16]

- "[Oliver Cowdery] you did not **translate** . . . I will give unto you power that you may assist to **translate** . . . not expedient that you should **translate** at this present time. . . when you began to **translate** . . . you could have **translated**; nevertheless, it is not expedient that you should **translate** now."[17]

The chapter, "Witness #2 - Joseph Smith: Translator or Reader?" will further document historical accounts and evidence that the translation of the *Book of Mormon* was a genuine, mechanical translation performed by a man who, though he was "unlearned"[18] in the precepts of the world, accomplished the incredible feat through the gift and power of God.

In the *Doctrine and Covenants,* Section 10 (Section 36 in the 1844 edition), the Lord does not instruct the Prophet to *read* words that appear on a stone, but commands specifically that the Prophet *translate* the *engravings* that are on plates:

▌▌ . . . because the account which is **engraven upon the plates** of Nephi, is more particular concerning the things, which in my wisdom I would bring to the knowledge of the people in this account: therefore, you shall **translate the engravings** which are on the plates of Nephi, down even till you come to the reign of king Benjamin. . . .[19]

Clearly, Joseph Smith was using the engravings upon the plates. He had them in front of him, he thumbed through the leaves, and he felt the etchings made many hundreds of years ago by ancient Nephite prophets. The Lord commanded Joseph Smith to open the plates, to identify the leaves containing the engravings of Nephi, and then to

---

16   Doctrine and Covenants 11:19, 22; emphasis added.

17   Doctrine and Covenants 9:1-10; emphasis added.

18   Isaiah 29:11-12 (KJV used throughout this work unless otherwise specified); 2 Nephi 27:19; Doctrine and Covenants 35:13.

19   Doctrine and Covenants 36:9, 1844 ed. [D&C 10:40-41], 244, The Joseph Smith Papers; emphasis added.

translate those engravings, character by character, until he came to the reign of King Benjamin:

// Behold there are many things **engraven on the plates of Nephi**, which do throw greater views upon my gospel: therefore, it is wisdom in me, that you should translate this **first part of the engravings** of Nephi, and send forth in this work.[20]

This entire experience creates a problem for those who believe that the *Book of Mormon* was translated, or rather, "read," using a "seer stone in a hat." Why would the Lord command Joseph Smith to work down through the plates, if the Prophet merely looked at a seer stone to read words that appeared mysteriously? How would Joseph Smith know anything about the "plates of Nephi" if he was not intimately familiar with those plates?

Note that the Lord uses the term "engravings" or "engraven" in this one revelation five times. In another revelation given to Oliver Cowdery in 1829, the Lord again refers to the translation of "engravings" when He promises Oliver that he will receive "a knowledge concerning the engravings of the old records, which are ancient."[21] This further establishes that the Lord identifies through revelation the following:

1. There are actual plates.

2. Those plates are engraven with an ancient American language, the language of the Nephites.

3. The *Book of Mormon* text we read today comes from those plates and the engravings on them.

The Lord is clear that the translation process of the *Book of Mormon* used an ancient Nephite and Jaredite tool, known as the Urim and Thummim, as well as literal, tangible plates from which ancient engravings were translated into English. The seer stone hypothesis finds no support in the revelations and testimony of the Lord Jesus Christ.

---

20   Ibid, 245; emphasis added.
21   Doctrine and Covenants 8:1.

4

WITNESS #2 – JOSEPH SMITH: TRANSLATION INSTRUMENTS

The Prophet Joseph Smith is the only mortal man who can be confidently described as an "eyewitness" of the translation of the *Book of Mormon*. Why? Because he was the only man who successfully translated and therefore understood the process. He may have also been the only mortal to have used the plates in the latter days, therefore, we submit Joseph Smith Jr., revelator, translator, and prophet-restorer of The Church of Jesus Christ of Latter-day Saints, as our second defense witness. We will divide his defense into three categories, comprising this and the following two chapters.

Did the Prophet Joseph Smith Comment on the Translation of the *Book of Mormon*?

Joseph Smith testified unequivocally that he translated the *Book of Mormon* using the Nephite interpreters, also known as the Urim and Thummim. Given Joseph Smith's firsthand knowledge of and experience with the translation of the *Book of Mormon*, one would suppose that faithful Latter-day Saint researchers and authors would treat the Prophet Joseph Smith's words as authoritative, placing them in a pre-eminent position within their works. We have at least 13 documented statements, directly from the Prophet Joseph Smith, in which he discusses the translation.[1] In addition to this compilation, we have second-hand statements written down by those who heard Joseph Smith speak of his experiences. Surprisingly, several modern

---

1   "Translation of the Book of Mormon," Latter-day Answers, https://ldsanswers. org/translation.

progressive historians put forth the charge that the Prophet Joseph Smith "said very little" or "never gave any details." For example, Roger Nicholson comments:

❝❝ As it turns out, he [Joseph Smith] said **very little** about the actual translation method used to produce the Book of Mormon, except to note that it was performed "by the gift and power of God."[2]

Was the only detail Joseph Smith ever gave regarding the translation that the work was performed "by the gift and power of God"? The FAIR Blog on *LDS Living* alleges similarly:

❝❝ How did Joseph Smith translate the Book of Mormon? Joseph **didn't share many details** of the translation process other than the fact that he received the translation by the gift and power of God.[3]

Avowed detractors of the Prophet Joseph Smith and the Restored Gospel of Jesus Christ mimic the same claim, as if there was a coordinated attempt to discredit the Prophet Joseph Smith and erase his testimony from history. "MormonThink" also commented:

❝❝ When Joseph was asked how exactly he translated the Book of Mormon, he **never gave any details,** he only said that he did it by the "gift and power of God."[4]

Coincidentally, the same historians who claim that Joseph Smith "didn't share any details" are also those who claim that Joseph Smith translated the *Book of Mormon* using a seer stone in a hat. However, we shall endeavor to demonstrate throughout this work that Joseph Smith *did* speak on the translation, and that his statements contradict

---

2   Roger Nicholson, "The Spectacles, the Stone, the Hat, and the Book: A Twenty-first Century Believer's View of the Book of Mormon Translation," *Interpreter: A Journal of Latter-day Saint Faith and Scholarship* 5 (2013): 125, accessed January 2019, https://www.mormoninterpreter.com/the-spectacles-the-stone-the-hat-and-the-book-a-twenty-first-century-believers-view-of-the-book-of-mormon-translation/; emphasis added.

3   FAIR Blog, "How Did Joseph Smith Translate the Book of Mormon?" LDS Living, June 14, 2016, accessed March 2019, http://www.ldsliving.com/How-did-Joseph-Smith-translate-the-Book-of-Mormon-/s/72921; emphasis added.

4   "Translation of the Book of Mormon," MormonThink, accessed February 2019, http://www.mormonthink.com/transbomweb.htm; emphasis added.

plainly the seer stone hypothesis in every respect. Is our history being rewritten by eliminating inconvenient statements from Joseph Smith? *FAIRMormon* again dogmatically declares that Joseph Smith gave only one detail regarding translation, that it was performed "by the gift and power of God":

/ / How exactly did Joseph Smith translate the gold plates? Joseph Smith **only stated** that he translated the *Book of Mormon* by the "gift and power of God." ... Joseph Smith himself never recorded the precise physical details of the method of translation ... the translation of the *Book of Mormon* was carried out "by the gift and power of God." These are the **only words** that Joseph Smith himself used to describe the translation process.[5]

Could it be that these historians never studied the statements made by the Prophet Joseph Smith regarding the translation? Such a case seems inconceivable, but perhaps that is the reality. How else does such an egregious historical inaccuracy get perpetuated? In our experience, historians too often quote each other, establishing a tautological frame of reference wherein their inaccurate claims rely on an internal, self-supporting web of unreliable statements, and they fail to do their own original research. Contrary to the claims of these progressive authors, an analysis of Joseph Smith's written testimonies provides the following data points:

1. Joseph Smith used ancient, physical, Nephite plates to translate the *Book of Mormon*. He did not leave them covered or hiding underneath his bed or elsewhere during translation.

2. Joseph Smith translated using the Urim and Thummim and not a seer stone. The Urim and Thummim and the seer stone are two *different* artifacts.

3. Joseph Smith *temporarily* lost the Urim and Thummim in 1828 after the 116 pages (*Book of Lehi*) were stolen, but the plates and the Urim and Thummim were returned after a period of sorrow and contrition.

---

5   "Question: How Exactly Did Joseph Smith Translate the Gold Plates?" FAIR Mormon, accessed August 2018, https://www.fairmormon.org/answers/Book_of_Mormon/Translation/The_interpreters,_seer_stone,_hat_and_the_%22gift_and_power_of_God%22#Question:_How_exactly_did_Joseph_Smith_translate_the_gold_plates.3F; emphasis added.

4. Moroni and other Nephite prophets once lived. They are legitimate historical figures and the *Book of Mormon* is an historical record. The Jaredite, Nephite, and Lamanite civilizations once existed and the descendants from these nations are still alive today.

5. Joseph Smith "translated," in the true sense of the word, the Nephite plates to produce the *Book of Mormon* we read today.

6. Many "false reports" were spread in Joseph Smith's day regarding the translation of the *Book of Mormon*. These false reports, antagonistic to the clear statements made by the Prophet Joseph Smith, still circulate today and are now heavily incorporated into the progressive "new narrative."

In this chapter, we will discuss the Prophet Joseph Smith's testimony regarding the translation instruments he used.

Did Joseph Smith Use the Nephite Plates to Translate the *Book of Mormon?*

In 1839, Joseph Smith explained that he did not compose the title page of the *Book of Mormon*. Instead, the title page was of ancient origin and was taken from the last leaf of the Nephite plates:

❝ ... the Title Page of the Book of Mormon is a literal translation, taken from the very **last leaf**, on the **left hand side** of the collection or book of plates, which contained the record which has been translated; the language of the whole running **same as all Hebrew writing** in general; and that, said Title Page is not by any means a modern composition either of mine or of any other man's who has lived or does live in this generation. . . . the Title Page of the English Version of the Book of Mormon . . . is a **genuine and literal translation** of the Title Page of the Original Book of Mormon, as recorded on the plates.[6]

One wonders how Joseph Smith knew the title page was on the last leaf, if he never used the plates, as the "new narrative" asserts, or how he knew that *all* of the writing ran the "same as all Hebrew writing

---

6   Joseph Smith History, circa June 1839–circa 1841, draft 2, 34, The Joseph Smith Papers; emphasis added.

in general." This means Joseph Smith saw, and more importantly, he understood the writing pattern on every leaf of the plates. Since the Prophet understood the writing pattern on every leaf, he would have had to understand every character, every engraving upon the plates, otherwise how would he know which direction to read them?

Additionally, Joseph Smith declared that the title page is a "genuine and literal translation . . . as recorded on the plates." From Joseph's declaration, we learn that the text of the title page did not come from a seer stone. For those who know or believe that Joseph Smith spoke the truth as a man of integrity, the title page is a literal English translation of the characters engraven upon the metal plates.

In chapter 5, "Witness #2 - Joseph Smith: Translator or Reader?," we provide additional evidence that the translation process involved the plates directly. First-hand accounts establish that they were not covered with a cloth, hidden under the Prophet's bed, or buried in a field during translation. Joseph Smith spent at least three months studying hieroglyphics (possibly a type of reformed Egyptian "alphabet"?) taken from the plates before he began translating the record.[8] Years later in Kirtland, there are documents that indicate the early Brethren were studying Nephite characters and their English translation.[9] Joseph Smith clarified in an 1843 letter that, "there was no Greek or Latin upon the plates,"[10] demonstrating his awareness of the Nephite hieroglyphics and at the very least, a cursory familiarity with Greek and Latin. Joseph Smith spoke of translating "hieroglyphics" to James Arlington Bennett in 1843[11] and reportedly showed some of the Nephite characters to George Moore in Nauvoo.[12]

The Prophet described the physical appearance of the Nephite plates in what is known today as the "Wentworth Letter." John Wentworth,

7   Lucy Mack Smith, History, 1845, 117, The Joseph Smith Papers.

8   Joseph Smith History, volume A-1, September 1827–February 1828, 9, Joseph Smith Papers.

9   Characters Copied by Oliver Cowdery, circa 1835–1836, The Joseph Smith Papers. See also Writings and Characters Copied by Frederick G. Williams, circa 1830, The Joseph Smith Papers.

10   Joseph Smith History, volume D-1, 20 May 1843, 1554, The Joseph Smith Papers.

11   Joseph Smith to James Arlington Bennet, 13 November 1843, 1a, The Joseph Smith Papers.

12   Donald Q. Cannon, "Reverend George Moore Comments on Nauvoo, the Mormons, and Joseph Smith," *Western Illinois Regional Studies* 5 (1978): 10-11.

editor and proprietor of the *Chicago Democrat*, requested that the Prophet Joseph Smith write an account of the origin of The Church of Jesus Christ of Latter-day Saints in 1842. Joseph Smith agreed to share his history with a strict stipulation that Wentworth "publish the account entire, ungarnished, and without misrepresentation"[13]:

// These [Nephite] records were engraven on plates which had the appearance of gold: each plate was six inches wide and eight inches long, and not quite so thick as common tin. They were filled with engravings in Egyptian characters and bound together in a volume as the leaves of a book, with three rings running through the whole. The volume was something over six inches in thickness, part of which was sealed. The characters on the unsealed part were **small and beautifully engraved**. The whole book exhibited **many marks of antiquity** in its construction, and much skill in the art of engraving.[14]

Did Joseph Smith Translate Using the Urim and Thummim, or a Dark Seer Stone?

Joseph Smith must have been asked repeatedly regarding the details of his experiences. In 1838, Joseph Smith wrote in his journal, "in the afternoon I answered the questions which were frequently asked me while on my last Journey . . . ." Surely, one of the most frequent questions was, "How and where did you obtain the book of Mormon?" Joseph responded on May 8, 1838:

// Moroni, the person who deposited the plates from whence the Book of Mormon was translated, in a hill in Manchester, Ontario County, New York, being dead, and raised again therefrom appeared unto me, and told me where they were and gave me directions how to obtain them. I obtained them [the plates] and the **Urim and Thummim** with them, **by the means of which I translated** the plates and thus came the Book of Mormon.[15]

Now the plaintiff—the progressive historians who propound the "seer stone in a hat" narrative—may attempt to construe Joseph Smith's

---

13   Joseph Smith, "Church History," *Times and Seasons* 3, (March 1, 1842): 706.

14   Ibid, 707; emphasis added.

15   Joseph Smith History, vol. B-1, 8 May 1838, 794, The Joseph Smith Papers; emphasis added. See also *Elders' Journal* 1 (July 1838): 42-43; emphasis added.

use of the phrase "Urim and Thummim" as vague and undefined. They might ask, "Joseph Smith used the term 'Urim and Thummim' rather ambiguously. Could the 'Urim and Thummim' not simply be a dark seer stone?"

To answer this charge, we will again turn to the testimony of the Prophet Joseph Smith in his own words. We read, that in addition to the description of the plates, the *Wentworth Letter* included the Prophet's description of the Urim and Thummim as two transparent stones, set in the rim of a bow:

> ▮▮ With the records was found a curious instrument which the ancients called "Urim and Thummim," which consisted of **two transparent stones** set in the rim of a **bow** fastened to a **breastplate.** Through the medium of the **Urim and Thummim** I translated the record by the gift, and power of God.[16]

An early historian described the *Wentworth Letter* as "one of the choicest documents in our church literature."[17] In this letter, Joseph Smith provided an official, accurate account of the translation of the *Book of Mormon* and gave a clear, unambiguous description of the Urim and Thummim; what it is and what it is not. The Prophet described the Urim and Thummim as a set of two transparent stones, not a single, dark, chocolate-colored stone. The two stones were set in the rim of a bow, fastened to a breastplate. Throughout the letter, there is, unsurprisingly, no mention of a seer stone or a "stone in a hat." The Prophet also specified that "through the medium of the Urim and Thummim [he] translated."

In 1835, Joseph Curtis related that Joseph Smith and the Prophet's parents visited him in Michigan. During the course of conversation Joseph Smith shared some of his experiences, including the First Vision and the coming forth of the *Book of Mormon*. Curtis remembered:

> ▮▮ ... [Joseph Smith] saw an angel with a view of the hill cumorah & the plates of gold had certain instructions got the plates & by the **assistance of the Urim & Thumim** [*sic*] **translated** them by the gift & power of God also stated he [had] done nothing more

---

16   Joseph Smith, "Church History," *Times and Seasons* 3, (March 1, 1842): 707; emphasis added.

17   *History of the Church*, vol. 4 (Salt Lake City: Deseret Book, 1950), 541.

than he was commanded to do & for this his name was cast out
as evil for this he was persecuted . . . [18]

In the Curtis account, Joseph Smith reiterates that he translated the
plates with "the assistance of the Urim and Thummim" and that he
had been intensely persecuted and "cast out as evil" for no more than
obeying the voice of the Lord. Such has been the pattern throughout
history for all of God's true and holy prophets.[19]

In another 1835 conversation, recorded in his personal journal,
Joseph Smith related the experience he had with Moroni on the night
of September 21, 1823. From the very beginning, Moroni made it
clear to the Prophet that the translation was to take place through
the means of the Urim and Thummim, and that God would give him
the power to do so using this sacred instrument:

❝ . . . he [Moroni] told me of a sacred record which was written
on plates of gold, I saw in the vision the place where they were
deposited, he said the indians, were the literal descendants of
Abraham . . . the Urim and Thumim [*sic*], was **hid up with the
record**, and that God would give me power to translate it, with
the **assistance of this instrument** . . . [20]

Today, very few believers dispute that the translation occurred by
the "gift and power of God," but they question the means. However,
the incident in the Prophet Joseph Smith's personal journal recounting
Moroni's visit, is one of many records that clarify that the means *was*
the Urim and Thummim. Why is there dispute over the means, but
agreement on the "gift and power of God?" Is it an attempt to keep
the translation vague, to introduce an agenda?

---

18   Curtis, Joseph 1818-1883. Joseph Curtis reminiscences and diary, p. 6,
https://catalog.lds.org/assets/24463061-0287-4460-8a45-62d078b75991/0/11
(accessed: February, 2019); emphasis added.

19   See Matthew 5:10-12. "Blessed are they which are persecuted for righteousness' sake: for theirs is the kingdom of heaven. Blessed are ye, when men shall revile
you, and persecute you, and shall say all manner of evil against you falsely, for my
sake. Rejoice, and be exceeding glad: for great is your reward in heaven: for so persecuted they the prophets which were before you."

20   Joseph Smith conversation with Robert Matthews, Joseph Smith Journal,
"Sketch Book for the use of Joseph Smith, jr.," 9–11 November 1835, 24-25, The
Joseph Smith Papers; emphasis added.

Did Joseph Smith Lose the Urim and Thummim Permanently After the 116 pages Were Lost?

After becoming bitter against Joseph Smith and antagonistic toward the Church, David Whitmer repeatedly spread the false rumor that after the 116 pages were lost, the Lord never allowed Joseph Smith to regain the plates or the Urim and Thummim. Instead, he claimed Joseph used a seer stone to dictate the *Book of Mormon* we read today. He also claimed several priesthood offices were not inspired[21] and that Joseph Smith was a fallen prophet who received false revelations from the devil.[22] In the chapter, "David Whitmer: Friend or Foe?," we will uncover David Whitmer's true motive; he wanted to convince the world that although Joseph Smith *began* as a true prophet, he faltered almost immediately and soon thereafter, led the Church and his followers into darkness and apostasy. His venom, along with the vitriol of other antagonists, including William E. McLellin, spawned the narrative for those hostile to the true followers:

// The "Interpreters" were **taken** from Joseph after he allowed Martin Harris to carry away the 116 pages of Ms [manuscript?] of the Book of Mormon as a punishment, but he was allowed to go on and translate by the use of a **"Seers stone"** which he had, and which he placed in a hat into which he buried his face . . .[23]

The **plates**, however, were **not returned** . . .[24]

[The Lord] took from the prophet the **urim and thummum** [*sic*] and otherwise expressed his condemnation. . . . [the Prophet] was presented with a strange oval-shaped, chocolate-colored stone about the size of an egg, only more flat . . . With this stone all of the present Book of Mormon was translated.[25]

---

21   David Whitmer, *An Address to All Believers in Christ by a Witness to the Divine Authenticity of The Book of Mormon* (Richmond, 1887), 62.

22   Ibid 31, 38.

23   Zenas H. Gurley, "Questions Asked of David Whitmer," holograph, 1, 3, 4, Gurley Collection, Church History Library; emphasis added.

24   "The Book of Mormon," *Chicago Tribune*, December 17, 1885, 3; emphasis added. Quoted in *Kansas City Daily Journal*, June 5, 1881.

25   *Omaha Herald*, October 17, 1886. See also *Chicago Inter Ocean*, October 17, 1886; and *Saints' Herald* 33 (November 13, 1886): 707; emphasis added.

As we established in the previous chapter, "Witness #1 - The Lord," the Urim and Thummim, and the plates were returned to the Prophet Joseph Smith (following the loss of the 116 pages).[26] Joseph Smith's history, later published in the *Times and Seasons* in 1842, testified that the angel returned the Urim and Thummim to him after the 116 pages were lost:

❞ ... I was walking out a little distance when behold the former heavenly messenger appeared and handed to me the **Urim and Thummim** again ...

After I had obtained the revelation *[Doctrine and Covenants* 3], both the plates and the Urim and Thummim were taken from me again; but in a few days they were **returned** to me ...[27]

Lucy Mack Smith's personal history details the restoration of the Urim and Thummim to the Prophet Joseph Smith, along with the celebration and joy that followed. Chapter 27 of her 1845 manuscript begins, "Urim and Thummim is taken from Joseph— he receives them again"[28]

Mother Smith recalled that sometime after the tragic loss of the 116 pages, she and her husband set out to visit Joseph and Emma in Harmony, Pennsylvania. Before they arrived at their home, they found Joseph coming to meet them, apparently having been apprised of their coming by divine revelation:

❞ When he met us his countenance wore so pleasant an aspect, that I was convinced he had something agreeable to communicate, in relation to the work in which he was engaged. And when I entered his house the first thing that attracted my attention was a red morocco trunk, that set on Emma's bureau; which trunk Joseph shortly informed me, contained the **Urim and Thummim** and the **plates.**[29]

---

26   Doctrine and Covenants 10.

27   Joseph Smith History, volume A-1, April–July 1828, 10-11, Joseph Smith Papers; emphasis added.

28   Lucy Mack Smith, History, 1845, 135, The Joseph Smith Papers; emphasis added.

29   Ibid, 135-136; emphasis added.

That night, Joseph shared with his parents that when the angel appeared to reclaim the Urim and Thummim and the plates after Joseph had lost the 116 pages, the angel left Joseph with a promise, "If you are very humble and penitent, it may be you will receive them again." The Prophet then related:

> **//** ... I [Joseph Smith] had the joy and satisfaction of again receiving the **Urim and Thummim**; and have commenced **translating** again, and Emma writes for me; but the angel said that the Lord would send me a scribe, and I trust his promise will be verified. The angel also seemed pleased with me, when he gave me back the Urim and Thummim; and he told me that the Lord loved me, for my **faithfulness** and **humility**.[30]

Joseph Smith recorded his firsthand recollection of the promise made to him, that if he was humble and penitent, he would again receive both the plates and the Urim and Thummim. According to his personal history, the Lord promised him:

> **//** ... remember God is merciful: therefore repent of that which thou hast done, which is contrary to the commandment which I gave you, and thou art still chosen and art again called to the work ... thou has lost thy privileges for a **season** ...
>
> Nevertheless my work shall go forth ... and for this very purpose are these **plates preserved** which contain these records, that the promises of the Lord might be fulfilled, which he made to his people ... [31]

David Whitmer was aware of the promise that Joseph would regain the Urim and Thummim and the plates. As one of the Three Witnesses, he certainly understood that the Urim and Thummim was not only returned, but also that Joseph used it for the remainder of the translation. What motive was behind David Whitmer's later insistence that Joseph never regained the Urim and Thummim and the plates when the historical record is clear that the artifacts *were*, in fact, returned?

One of David Whitmer's chief complaints against the Prophet was a revelation Joseph was given on the day the Church was organized.

---

30   Ibid, 138; emphasis added.

31   Joseph Smith History, circa June 1839–circa 1841, draft 2, 10-11, The Joseph Smith Papers; emphasis added.

This revelation commanded the Church in this dispensation to "give heed unto *all* his [Joseph Smith's] words and commandments." As Whitmer had major disagreements with the Prophet, he needed to create a new narrative wherein he argued the Prophet Joseph Smith had been out of harmony with the Lord even from before the organization of the Church. Therefore, in Whitmer's new history, Joseph failed to reconcile himself with the Lord. He falsely claimed that Joseph never regained the Urim and Thummim or the plates because of pride and disobedience, resorting instead to peering at a dark seer stone in a hat to read the *Book of Mormon*. Whitmer's tale that Joseph read the *Book of Mormon* through a stone was convenient because it meant he did not have to be righteous and necessarily in tune with God to read; presumably he only needed a "gift."[32] In a sense, the seer stone represented an icon symbolizing Joseph's alleged disobedience and pride.

However, Joseph Smith clarified that he *did* regain the plates and the Urim and Thummim. His mother recorded that the Lord "loved [him] for [his] faithfulness and humility."[33]

In summation, there is no evidence from the Prophet's testimony that a seer stone was ever used in the translation of the *Book of Mormon*. The record shows that Joseph Smith, the translator, employed the use of an ancient Jaredite–Nephite interpreter that consisted of two transparent stones set in the rim of a bow, and that through these stones, he viewed and interpreted the ancient Nephite characters engraven on plates with the appearance of gold. The record also shows that subsequent to the removal of the plates and interpreters due to Joseph's loss of the 116-page manuscript, the Lord did return the translation instruments with a command to continue the translation.

---

32   David Whitmer, *An Address to All Believers in Christ by a Witness to the Divine Authenticity of The Book of Mormon* (Richmond, 1887), 37.

33   Lucy Mack Smith, History, 1845, 138, The Joseph Smith Papers.

5

WITNESS #2 – JOSEPH SMITH: TRANSLATOR OR READER?

When the Lord coined the use of the term "translation" to describe the coming forth of the *Book of Mormon*,[1] this term was thereafter used by Joseph Smith, Oliver Cowdery, Lucy Mack Smith, and all other official histories of the early Church. Joseph Smith testified of the coming forth of the *Book of Mormon* as a "translation," sometimes using the phrase, "work of translation," inferring that there was a translator. Was Joseph a Translator or a Reader? This is the substance of our next examination.

Some progressive historians insist the term "translation" does not accurately describe the work Joseph Smith completed:

❝ Joseph **couldn't learn** to **read** the text on the **plates**—there was no Nephite dictionary available. . . .

The meaning on the plates was certainly hidden and lost. Joseph could not translate as the scholars did.[2]

Richard L. Bushman likewise asserts that the coming forth of the *Book of Mormon* was more of a "reading," than it was a genuine "translation," but admits that this picture is "weird":

---

1   See examples in Doctrine and Covenants 3:12, 5:4, 30 and other uses of the term "translate" or "translation" in the revelations.

2   Brant A. Gardner, "Translating the Book of Mormon," in *A Reason for Faith: Navigating LDS Doctrine & Church History*, ed. Laura H. Hales (Provo, UT: Religious Studies Center, Brigham Young University, 2016), 22-23; emphasis added.

❛❛ I am not sure we need a lot of pictures in our chapels of Joseph looking into his hat, but we certainly should tell our children that is how it worked. . . . It's weird. It's a **weird picture.** It implies it's like darkening a room when we show slides. It implies that there is an image appearing in that stone and the light would make it more difficult to see that image. So, that implies a translation that's a **reading** and so gives us a little clue about the whole translation process. It also raises the strange question, "**What in the world are the plates for?** Why do we need them on the table if they are just wrapped up into a cloth while he looks into a seer stone?"[3]

Indeed. Why would we need the plates with the seer stone hypothesis? Another example can be found in the introduction to Volume 3 of the *Joseph Smith Papers Revelations and Translations* series:

❛❛ Joseph Smith's translation of the plates was not the scholarly **process normally associated with that word.** Rather than drawing upon familiarity with a foreign or ancient language, Smith declared that he translated "by the gift and power of God."[4]

The substance of the argument here is that the Prophet did not know the Nephite language, therefore, according to the researchers, the *Book of Mormon* "translation" was not a translation.

The Lord Himself coined the use of the term "translation" when referring to the coming forth of the *Book of Mormon*. However, since "translation" does not support the seer stone hypothesis, progressive scholars argue that the term is not precise or accurate. Did Joseph Smith bring forth the *Book of Mormon* simply by reading English words that appeared on a seer stone or did he *translate* ancient Nephite characters into English? Apparently scholars see a discrepancy between a genuine translation and a translation done by the "gift and power of God."

In this chapter we endeavor to share credible evidence revealing that the translation of the *Book of Mormon* was both a genuine translation

---

3   Richard L. Bushman, "FAIR Podcast, Episode 3: Richard L. Bushman P.1," *FairMormon (podcast)* October 12, 2010, accessed October 2017, https://www. fairmormon.org/blog/2010/10/12/fair-podcast-episode-3-richard-l-bushman-p-1; emphasis added.

4   "Introduction to Revelations and Translations: Volume 3," The Joseph Smith Papers, accessed July 2018, https://www.josephsmithpapers.org/intro/introduc-tion-to-revelations-and-translations-volume-3; emphasis added.

and a "marvelous work and a wonder" performed by the "gift and power of God."

Term "Translate"

We cannot, perhaps, reiterate enough that the Lord coined the use of the term "translate" to describe the coming forth of the *Book of Mormon*. It did not come from the scholars, it did not come from the historians, neither did it come from speculative members in the 19th century. The designation "translation" appears at least 30 times in the revelations Joseph is known to have received during the translation process. Why did the Lord use the term "translation" repeatedly if He did not mean "translation"? He could have used any word; He could have used any set of words. Should we question the Lord's choice of words in the revelations?

According to Webster's 1828 dictionary, one of the definitions of "translate" means: "To interpret; to render into another language; to express the sense of one language in the words of another."[5]

Per this definition, the Lord tasked the Prophet Joseph Smith to take the literal record, written in the Nephite language, and transition that record into a manuscript written in English. The Prophet was required to convert each Nephite character into terms that 19th century English-speaking people could read and understand.

Any individual who has studied a foreign language or attempted to translate words from his or her native tongue into a secondary language has some awareness of the factors necessary to complete a translation properly. One word in English may require a long string of words to convey the same meaning in another language and vice versa. The quality of the translation depends on the skill and proficiency of the translator. When it comes to the language of the *Book of Mormon*, one must ask, did the words we read today magically appear on a seer stone, or did Joseph Smith use the gift given to him from God, to exercise the power of translation to dictate the language and choose the specific verbiage recorded in the book we study today?

On July 13, 1862, President Brigham Young taught that words of scripture are given to men in a way that "suits" their "circumstances

---

5   Noah Webster, *An American Dictionary of the English Language*; emphasis added.

and capacities" and that the *Book of Mormon* would be different if it were written today:

II Should the Lord Almighty send an angel to rewrite the Bible, it would in many places be very different from what it now is. And I will even venture to say that if the Book of Mormon were now to be rewritten, in many instances it would materially **differ** from the present **translation**. According as people are willing to receive the things of God, so the heavens send forth their blessings. If the people are stiffnecked, the Lord can tell them but little.[6]

While there is little to argue that Joseph Smith was capable of choosing the words without revelation or without experiencing the gift of tongues, that is not to say that he "turned off his brain" during the translation process. The words Joseph Smith chose for the *Book of Mormon*, while studying the Nephite characters, came from the Prophet *and* from revelation he received from the Lord. If he was in tune with the Spirit of the Lord, the words are inspired. Conversely, if he did not receive revelation from the Lord, the words are strictly his own. This understanding has serious implications for us in how we view the *Book of Mormon*. Is the book "correct"; is it doctrinally true? Can we trust the record, or in other words, did Joseph Smith give an accurate translation or should we be cautious about considering it the revealed "word of God"?

How does Joseph Smith's personal character affect the purity of the *Book of Mormon*? If Joseph Smith dabbled in the occult, one might argue that his magical background skewed his choice of words in the *Book of Mormon*. If Joseph Smith spent his early life digging for treasure, how might a presumptuous greed for easy money and superstitious belief in treasure digging rituals and spells transform his understanding of the *Book of Mormon* and influence his choice of words and terms? Detractors have attacked the Prophet for racism early, and even later in his life. If he struggled with early racism, does this mean that politically incorrect passages from the *Book of Mormon* are actually uninspired and need to be changed?

How one views the Prophet Joseph Smith, particularly in regard to his personal character, influences greatly the respect one has for the

---

6   Brigham Young, "The Kingdom of God," in *Journal of Discourses*, vol. 9 (Liverpool, 1862), 311; emphasis added.

manuscript he produced, the *Book of Mormon*. At the end of the day, his personal spiritual aptitude influenced his choice of language in the *Book of Mormon*. Because he was a man of honor and integrity, his character positively impacted the *Book of Mormon*. If he had been a man of wickedness, the *Book of Mormon* would, instead, be questionable. Was the fountain—the Prophet Joseph Smith—from which the *Book of Mormon* came bitter or pure?[7]

When the Lord called Oliver Cowdery, David Whitmer, and Martin Harris as witnesses of the plates, the Urim and Thummim, and other Nephite artifacts, He added His witness that the translation produced by the Prophet Joseph Smith was *true*:

// And he [Joseph Smith] has **translated** the book, even that part which I have commanded him, and **as your Lord and your God liveth it is true.**[8]

Here we see the Lord willing to stake His own existence on the translation produced by the Prophet Joseph Smith. We have heard repeatedly Joseph Smith's statement that the *Book of Mormon* is the "most correct of any book on earth":

// Joseph Said the Book of Mormon was the **most correct** of any Book on Earth & the **key stone** of our religion & a man would get **nearer to God** by abiding by its precepts than **any other Book.**[9]

The reason the *Book of Mormon* stands as the "most correct" of any book is because the writers of the *Book of Mormon*, (Mormon, Moroni, Ether, and Nephi) were holy men, some of the greatest who ever lived. Additionally, the translator, the Prophet Joseph Smith, was the greatest, most holy prophet, ever to live excepting the Son of God.[10]

---

7   Moroni 7:11.

8   Doctrine and Covenants 17:6; emphasis added.

9   Wilford Woodruff's Journal, November 28, 1841; Church History Library, https://catalog.churchofjesuschrist.org/assets?id=28b53d73-2ba2-418b-8ef7-dafcc935bee3&crate=0&index=120.

10   "Latter-day Prophets Testify of the Prophet Joseph Smith's Greatness," Latter-day Answers, January 30, 2017, accessed February 2019, http://ldsanswers.org/latter-day-prophets-testify-prophet-joseph-smiths-greatness/.

Familiarity with Nephite Culture

When translating ancient documents, a knowledge of the history, culture, and day-to-day practices of the ancient people who recorded them is absolutely essential. Terms that are anachronistic must be recognized and familiar to the translator so that he or she can select an accurate contemporary term to take its place. Understanding the political environment, the structure of the society, the attitudes and philosophies of the ancient peoples is essential as the translator endeavors to "translate" an ancient world with an archaic culture into the language and culture of his or her present day. The *Book of Mormon* poses an even greater challenge as the Nephite civilization alone spans approximately 1000 years of history, and the Jaredite civilization preceding them could be nearly double that time; at least two distinct civilizations, cultures, and histories—their rise and their fall.

It would not have been possible for the Prophet to perform this feat without assistance from the Lord. The *Book of Mormon* truly was produced by the gift and power of God. However, the Lord never delivers anything to His children without effort, faith, diligence, and labor on their part, because He knows how much more His children will value it when they do so. The Lord *allowed* and *required* Joseph to do everything he could, before intervening to help with the rest.

The Lord provided numerous opportunities for Joseph to familiarize himself with Nephite culture and history, even before he obtained the plates. Lucy Mack Smith remembered:

 … **Joseph continued to receive instructions from the Lord**; and we, to get the children together every evening for the purpose of listening while he imparted the same to the family. I presume we presented an aspect as singular, as any family that ever lived upon the face of the Earth: all seated in a circle, father, mother, sons, and daughters, and giving the most profound attention to a boy, eighteen years of age, who had never read the Bible through in his life; for he was much less inclined to the perusals of books then [*sic*] any of the rest of our children, but far more given to meditation and deep study.[11]

---

11   Lucy Mack Smith, History, 1845, 86-87, The Joseph Smith Papers; emphasis added.

Joseph Smith prepared himself for four years in order to obtain the plates. That preparation included training and tutoring by angelic prophets sent by the Lord to perform the translation of the ancient record. What did the Lord teach him? According to Lucy Mack Smith, Joseph was extensively educated regarding the Nephite culture. He became familiar with their fashion, their travel, their religion, their history, their geography, and many other aspects of Nephite society:

▌▌ During our evening conversations, Joseph would occasionally give us some of the most amusing recitals that could be imagined: he would **describe** the ancient inhabitants of **this continent** [North America]; their **dress, mode of travelling**, and the **animals** upon which they rode; their **cities**, and their **buildings**, with every particular; he would describe their **mode of warfare**, as also their **religious worship**. This he would do with as much ease, seemingly, as if he had **spent his whole life with them.**[12]

Why was it important for Joseph Smith to understand Jaredite "dress" and Nephite fashion? Why was he shown ancient architecture and history? What did Nephite travel have to do with the translation of the *Book of Mormon*? Why was Joseph Smith's familiarity with Jaredite and Nephite history, which his mother described, "as if he had spent his whole life with them," needed to perform the translation of the *Book of Mormon*?

When Joseph Smith wrote to John Wentworth, editor and proprietor of the *Chicago Democrat*, the Prophet explained that he was also taught by angelic instructors about the ancient legal systems and history of "this country [the United States of America]":

▌▌ I was also informed concerning the aboriginal inhabitants of **this country**, and shown who they were, and from whence they came; a brief sketch of their **origin, progress, civilization, laws, governments**, of their righteousness and iniquity, and the blessings of God being finally withdrawn from them as a people was made known unto me . . . [13]

---

12   Ibid, 87; emphasis added.

13   Joseph Smith History, vol. C-1, 1 March 1842, 1282, The Joseph Smith Papers; emphasis added.

Angelic Nephite Tutors

On October 9, 1843, Joseph Smith preached at the funeral of James Adams, a probate judge for Hancock County, and a member of the Church. During the sermon, the Prophet commented that gaining knowledge through reading amounts to very little, when compared to learning by "gazing into heaven":

◢◢ ... could we read and comprehend all that has been writtn [*sic*] from the days of Adam on the relation of man to God & angels. in a future state. we should know **very little** about it. could you **gaze in heaven 5 minute**. you would **know more**— than you would by [reading] all that ever was writtn [*sic*] on the subject.[14]

If gazing into heaven for "five minutes" imparts more knowledge than you could ever read on the subject, what did Joseph Smith achieve by gazing into heaven for hours, by pondering great visions of Nephite, Lamanite, and Jaredite cultures? Joseph Smith's personal acquaintances revealed that he was visited and taught by a number of Nephite prophets in addition to Moroni. John Taylor described Joseph Smith's angelic tutors as including Mormon, Moroni, Nephi, and other Nephite prophets:

◢◢ And when Joseph Smith was raised up as a Prophet of God, **Mormon, Moroni, Nephi** and others of the **ancient Prophets** who formerly lived on **this Continent**, and Peter and John and others who lived on the Asiatic Continent, came to him and communicated to him certain principles pertaining to the Gospel of the Son of God.[15]

On another occasion, John Taylor again referred to these angelic ministrants, mentioning additional visitors including Abraham, Isaac, Jacob, Noah, Adam, Seth, Enoch, "and the **apostles** that lived on **this [North American] continent**," adding that the Prophet "seemed to be as familiar with these people as we are one with another."[16] This

14   Joseph Smith, Discourse, 9 October 1843, as Reported by Willard Richards, p. 121, The Joseph Smith Papers; emphasis added.

15   John Taylor, "Man, the Offspring of God, Etc.," in *Journal of Discourses*, vol. 17 (Liverpool, 1875), 374; emphasis added. Discourse given on April 8, 1875.

16   John Taylor, "Effects of the Preaching of the Gospel," in *Journal of Discourses*,

informs us that he experienced more than just visions of these men, but that he interacted with each of them, and by so doing, understood their personalities, their habits and culture, and knew the prophets as if he had lived with them in their day. In 1879, President Taylor reiterated to the Saints, the angelic ministrations of ancient Nephite prophets to Joseph Smith, adding that Nephi "had an interest in the welfare of the people" and that:

⫽ ... who more likely than **Mormon** and **Nephi,** and some of those prophets who had ministered to the people upon this continent, under the influence of the same Gospel, to operate again as its representatives?[17]

Clearly, Joseph Smith did not begin the process of translation as an ignorant neophyte. While he was "unlearned" in the precepts and philosophies of men, he was well-versed in divine doctrine, true history, and spiritual gifts. John Taylor's brother commented, "He seemed to be **just as familiar** with the Spirit World, and as **well acquainted** with the other side, as he was here."[18]

Orson Pratt also taught that Joseph Smith received visits from Nephi, Moroni, and "the three Nephites."[19] George Q. Cannon expressed similar views.[20] What did Nephi teach Joseph Smith? When the

---

vol. 21 (Liverpool, 1881), 9; emphasis added. Discourse given on April 13, 1879. "The principles which he had, placed him in communication with the Lord, and not only with the Lord, but with the ancient apostles and prophets; such men, for instance, as Abraham, Isaac, Jacob, Noah, Adam, Seth, Enoch, and Jesus and the Father, and the apostles that lived on this continent as well as those who lived on the Asiatic continent. He seemed to be as familiar with these people as we are one with another."

17   John Taylor, "How a Knowledge of God Is Obtained, Etc.," in *Journal of Discourses,* vol. 21 (Liverpool, 1881), 163; emphasis added. Discourse given on December 7, 1879.

18   William Taylor, "Joseph Smith, the Prophet," *Young Woman's Journal* 17 (December 1906): 548; emphasis added.

19   Orson Pratt to John Christensen, 11 March 1876, Orson Pratt Letterbook, LDS Church Archives, Salt Lake City, Utah. "The prophet often received visits from Nephi, Moroni, Peter, James, John (the beloved), John (the Baptist), Elijah, Moses, the three Nephites, etc. etc."

20   George Q. Cannon, "The Right and Authority of President Brigham Young," in *Journal of Discourses,* vol. 13 (Liverpool, 1871), 47. Discourse given on December 5, 1869. "If you will read the history of the Church from the beginning, you will find that Joseph was visited by various angelic beings ... Moroni, who held the keys of the record of the stick of Ephraim, visited Joseph; he had doubtless, also, visits

three Nephites visited, what was the subject of their conversation or rather, conversations? How did the Nephite disciples and the prophet-historian Mormon prepare the Prophet Joseph Smith to translate the record of his people?

Instead of reading about the Nephites, Joseph Smith talked *with* the Nephites. He saw their day in vision and conversed for unknown periods of time with their greatest leaders. When Joseph Smith carried the ancient record to his home for the first time, he was already as familiar with the Nephite culture "as if he had spent his whole life with them."[21] He knew their customs, their dress, their mode of travel, their animals, their cities, their buildings, their military prowess, their religious worship, their governments, their laws, and their history. As Moroni placed the record into his pupil's hands, Joseph Smith was now prepared to take the next step: he was about to study the Nephite language; about to translate their history into his own native tongue.

Studying the Characters

With a thorough understanding of Nephite culture and history, Joseph Smith prepared to begin his study of the Nephite characters. Documents from early Church history reveal that the Nephite language itself carried a high value and was studied, even after the *Book of Mormon* translation was finished.

Present scholarship indicates that Oliver Cowdery inscribed a document with Nephite characters, possibly between 1835 and 1836 in Kirtland, Ohio.[22] Available for viewing on the Joseph Smith Paper's website, the document displays two phrases from the book of Jacob (in the *Book of Mormon*) written in English, with the same line translated into the Hebrew language. Following these lines, Oliver wrote in English, "The Book of Mormon" and the phrase, "the interpreters of languages," and directly below each are what appear to be Nephite characters. Oliver recorded on the paper, "Written & kept for profit & learning— By Oliver."

Scholars believe this document was penned at the same time Joseph Smith convened the School of the Prophets (or School of the Elders)

from Nephi and it may be from Alma and others . . ."

21   Lucy Mack Smith, History, 1845, 87, The Joseph Smith Papers.

22   Characters Copied by Oliver Cowdery, circa 1835–1836, The Joseph Smith Papers.

in Kirtland, Ohio, in 1833. The Lord directed the Prophet Joseph Smith to establish a school wherein men could be educated and trained as missionaries. The school included lessons in penmanship, history, literature, politics, arithmetic, English, and the Hebrew language.

A similar manuscript, in the handwriting of Frederick G. Williams (a member of the First Presidency), includes the same ancient characters preceded again by, "The Book of Mormon" and, "the interpreters of languages."[23] Williams' copy includes the title, "Characters on the Book of Mormon."

From these documents, it appears that the Prophet Joseph tutored some early leaders in the Nephite language, leaving us to wonder, "Were there classes organized to study the Nephite language in the early days of the Church?" At the very least, it appears that the Nephite language was valued and that fragments were preserved and studied. Moreover, for Joseph Smith to instruct his learners in this language he had to have known it.

Joseph's study of the Nephite language probably began with the translation of the *Book of Mormon* in 1827. Joseph Smith narrated a firsthand account of the coming forth of the *Book of Mormon* in 1839, in which he explained that after receiving the plates and relocating to live with Emma's parents in Harmony, Pennsylvania, he spent three months copying and translating "characters":

❝ ... immediately after my arrival there [Harmony, Pennsylvania] I commenced **copying** the **characters** of the plates. I copied [*sic*] a **considerable number** of them and by means of the Urim and Thummin [*sic*] I **translated** some of them which I did between the time I arrived at the house of my wife's father in the month of December, and the February following.[24]

How did Joseph Smith spend the three months before the appearance of Martin Harris, his first scribe? Studying and translating characters.

Estimates suggest that Joseph and Oliver spent from about 57 to 85 days translating the *Book of Mormon* and transcribing it into the

---

23   Writings and Characters Copied by Frederick G. Williams, circa 1830, The Joseph Smith Papers.

24   Joseph Smith History, circa June 1839–circa 1841, draft 2, 9, Joseph Smith Papers; emphasis added.

text we read today.[25] However, he spent the first three months, *before* translating with Martin Harris or Oliver Cowdery, with the plates alone, investing time by studying the ancient characters. Why did the Prophet Joseph spend more time studying the characters than he spent translating and dictating the *Book of Mormon* to his principal scribe, Oliver Cowdery?

We know that Joseph Smith spent at least three months devoted to studying the characters, but he likely spent significant time on other occasions becoming familiar with the Nephite language. The Prophet received the plates and the Urim and Thummim from their sacred caretaker on September 22, 1827 and returned them after finishing the translation, which seems to have occurred between late June and early July, 1829. There was a brief interlude where the plates and the Urim and Thummim were withheld after the loss of the 116 pages. Oliver did not arrive to assume his role as scribe for Joseph until April 1829. Almost all of the *Book of Mormon* text we have today was written after his arrival. This identifies another significant block of time between 1827-1829, during which time Joseph had possession of the plates. While we do not know for certain, it appears that the Prophet had ample time to devote to learning the language before performing the final translation.

What were the "characters" that Joseph Smith translated during those first three months in Harmony, Pennsylvania, before Martin Harris arrived? Joseph Smith's mother, Lucy Mack Smith, recorded in her personal history, that the characters Joseph Smith studied consisted of "the alphabet: which characters were called reformed Egyptian":

> *❞* ...Joseph began to make arrangements to accomplish the translation of the Record; And the first step which he was instructed to take in regard to this matter, was, to take a Fac-Simile of the **characters** composing the **alphabet**: which characters were called **reformed Egyptian** ...
>
> It was agreed, that, when Joseph had had a sufficient time to transcribe the **Egyptian Alphabet**, after arriving at his fatherinlaw's

---

25   Trent Toone, "BYU Professor's Lecture Examines the Timeline of Joseph Smith's Translation of the Book of Mormon," Deseret News, November 11, 2017, accessed January 2018, https://www.deseretnews.com/article/865692589/BYU-professor-calculates-how-long-it-took-Joseph-Smith-to-translate-the-Book-of-Mormon.html.

[*sic*], Martin Harris should follow him: and that he (Martin) should take this Alphabet to the East, and call on his way on all the professed linguists in order to give them an opportunity to display their talents in giving a translation of the same.[26]

Lucy Mack Smith seemed to indicate that the plates contained an alphabet of sorts, perhaps a "Rosetta Stone" beginning, that allowed Joseph Smith to study and become familiar with the Nephite language. Did Mormon and/or Moroni include a helpful guide with the plates as another tool to assist Joseph Smith in the translation? At this point, we do not know.

We do know that after transcribing this alphabet and translating the characters, Joseph Smith sent Martin Harris to New York City to allow the learned of the age to try and match the translation completed by the Prophet's effort and by the "gift and power of God." Perhaps this was done for Martin Harris' sake, or perhaps it was for our sake. Certainly it was done to fulfill Isaiah's words written many centuries before.[27] In one sense, this can be compared to Moses' experience while he was in the court of Pharaoh. When Aaron threw down his staff, the Pharaoh's magicians threw down their own staffs to become serpents. In the end, Aaron's serpent "swallowed up"[28] the serpents of the "learned" of Moses' day. We see this lesson reenacted in Joseph Smith's day when Joseph translated ancient characters and then sent them back East with Martin Harris in an epic display or juxtaposition of power and knowledge between God and the learning of the world. In the end, the translation by the gift and power of God swallowed up the learning of the world with the triumphant publishing of the *Book of Mormon* and the reestablishment of the gospel on Earth. The great and spacious building, in this case, fell "and the fall thereof was exceedingly great."[29]

In 1843, Joseph Smith demonstrated his intimate understanding of the Nephite language when he explained, in a letter, that contrary to popular rumor suggesting that the name "Mormon" was derived from

---

26   Lucy Mack Smith, History, 1845, 117, 122, The Joseph Smith Papers; emphasis added.

27   Isaiah 29; 2 Nephi 27.

28   Exodus 7:12.

29   1 Nephi 11:36.

the Greek word "mormo," there were "no Greek or Latin" characters on the plates:

// Through the medium of your paper, I wish to correct an error among men that profess to be learned, liberal and wise; and I do it the more cheerfully, because I hope sober-thinking and sound-reasoning people will sooner listen to the voice of truth, than be led astray by the vain pretentions [sic] of the self-wise. The error I speak of, is the definition of the word "MORMON." It has been stated that this word was derived from the Greek word *mormo*. This is not the case. There was **no Greek or Latin upon the plates** from which I, through the grace of God, translated the Book of Mormon.[30]

How did the Prophet know that there was "no Greek or Latin upon the plates" if he never *used* the plates or if he was not familiar with the Nephite characters, as well as at least a cursory familiarity with Greek and Latin? Progressives are dogmatic in believing that the Prophet never learned the Nephite language. On the contrary, throughout his life, Joseph Smith repeatedly described "translating the characters" and studying the "writing engraven upon the plates."

After dispelling the false "mormo" rumor, the Prophet gave a "literal" definition of the word "Mormon":

// I may safely say that the word Mormon stands independent of the learning and wisdom of this generation.— Before I give a definition, however, to the word, let me say that the Bible in its widest sense means <u>good</u>; for the Savior says according to the gospel of John "I am the <u>good</u> shepherd"; and it will not be beyond the common use of terms to say that <u>good</u> is among the most important in use, and though known by various names in different languages, still its meaning is the same, and is ever in opposition to <u>bad</u>. We say from the Saxon, <u>good</u>; the Dane, <u>God</u>; the Goth, <u>goda</u>; the German <u>gut</u>; the Dutch, <u>goed</u>; the Latin, <u>bonus</u>; the Greek, <u>kalos</u>; the Hebrew, <u>tob</u>; and the **Egyptian, mon**. Hence, with the addition of **more**, or the **contraction**,

---

30   Joseph Smith History, vol. D-1, 20 May 1843, 1554, The Joseph Smith Papers. See also, Joseph Smith to Editor of the *Times and Seasons*, "Correspondence," Times and Seasons 4, (May 15, 1843): 194; emphasis added.

mor, we have the word <u>mormon</u>; which means literally **more good**. Yours. Joseph Smith.[31]

What is the Prophet doing here, if not translating? When the Reverend George Moore visited with the Prophet in Nauvoo, he reported that Joseph Smith displayed some of the hieroglyphics he found on the plates.[32] In a letter to James Arlington Bennett in 1843, the Prophet specifically described translating "hieroglyphics":

❡❡ ... truth is a matter of fact; and the fact is, that by the power of God I **translated** the Book of Mormon from **hieroglyphics**; the knowledge of which was lost to the world; in which wonderful event I stood alone, an unlearned youth, to combat the worldly wisdom, and multiplied ignorance of eighteen centuries, with a new revelation; which (if they would receive the everlasting gospel,) would open the eyes of more than eight hundred millions of people, and make "plain the old paths" ... [33]

The Lord also mentioned the hieroglyphics on the plates, referring to them as "engravings." Through revelation, the Lord specifically commanded Joseph Smith to "translate the engravings"[34] and He promised Oliver that, if faithful, he would receive "a knowledge concerning the engravings of old records."[35] If Joseph Smith was merely reading from a seer stone, why would the Lord single out the "engravings" as the object of Joseph's attention? In the context of a divinely inspired translation, however, the Lord's reference to "engravings" and "translation" not only makes perfect sense, but it reminds us that the Lord Himself placed special emphasis on the plates and the characters engraved thereon.

Skeptics balk at the idea that a simple, unlearned farm boy could master such a language and then translate. However, Joseph Smith

---

31   Ibid, 1555; emphasis added (underlines in original).

32   Donald Q. Cannon, "Reverend George Moore Comments on Nauvoo, the Mormons, and Joseph Smith," *Western Illinois Regional Studies* 5 (1978): 10-11.

33   Joseph Smith History, vol. E-1, 14 November 1843, 1775, The Joseph Smith Papers. Originally printed in Joseph Smith, "REPLY. Nauvoo, Illinois, Nov. 13, 1843," *Times and Seasons* 4 (November 1, 1843): 373; emphasis added.

34   Doctrine and Covenants 10:41.

35   Doctrine and Covenants 8:1.

learned firsthand that, with the Lord's help, all things are possible for those that believe.[36]

A few decades ago, when one of the authors was learning Korean in the Provo Missionary Training Center (MTC), and again later as a teacher in the MTC, personnel from the United States military would visit, studying our methods. The military was interested in the approach taken at our facility, as they had a difficult time understanding how a 19-year-old could enter with no language background and leave 6-8 weeks later with basic speaking and writing skills. Even the MTC instructors, at that time, were young, undergraduate (unlearned) students attending BYU. This anecdote demonstrates, to a very small degree, the power that can be harnessed in approaching an undertaking with faith and prayer in the Lord's way. In a profoundly more inspired way, Joseph Smith was able to learn and translate Reformed Egyptian at a rate seemingly impossible by worldly learning and worldly standards alone.

We see this pattern repeated in other places throughout scripture and history. We see Nephi building a boat, and the Brother of Jared building barges. We read of Noah building an ark, and Brigham Young settling the barren and hostile Rocky Mountains and nearly every western state. There are countless instances where seemingly impossible feats were accomplished because of the application of the "gift and power of God," and never without great effort by those involved.

Also, in every case where the Lord was directing, whether with Joseph Smith, Nephi, the Brother of Jared, Noah or Brigham Young, the student acquired the skills by joining in partnership *with* the Lord. In other words, when the task was completed the student had mastered the skill. With the "seer stone in a hat" hypothesis, the "reader" never learns the Nephite language or any skill for that matter. For those who understand this principle of Heaven, this fact alone proves, beyond doubt, that the seer stone hypothesis is false.

How Did Joseph Smith Translate the Characters?

In Joseph Smith's own official history, now included in the standard works, the Prophet explained *how* he translated the *Book of Mormon*:

---

36   Matthew 19:26, Mark 10:27.

❙❙ At length the time arrived for obtaining the **plates**, the **Urim and Thummim**, and the **breastplate**.

... by the wisdom of God, they remained safe in my hands, until I had accomplished **by them** what was required at my hand.[37]

"By them" are the keywords here: by the plates; by the Jaredite–Nephite Urim and Thummim and the breastplate. The Prophet emphasized repeatedly that he translated literal characters on literal plates using the Urim and Thummim:

❙❙ I obtained [the plates], and the Urim and Thummim with them; by the **means** of which, I **translated** the plates; and thus came the book of Mormon.[38] (1838)

I copyed [*sic*] a considerable number of [characters] and by **means** of the **Urim and Thummin** I **translated** some of them.[39] (1839)

Through the **medium** of the **Urim and Thummim** I **translated** the record by the gift, and power of God.[40] (1842)

How did the Urim and Thummim operate? Joseph Smith's answer to this intriguing question was never recorded fully, and possibly never addressed at all. We do know that it required mental effort and study before approaching the Lord for a confirmation of truth. We discuss these requirements in the chapter, "'Study it Out in Your Mind' vs. a Free Gift" later in this book series.

During an important Church conference in 1831, Joseph Smith's brother, Hyrum, asked Joseph to relate further details regarding how the *Book of Mormon* was translated. Joseph Smith responded that "*all the particulars*" were not for the world to know:

---

37   Joseph Smith—History 1:59-60; emphasis added.

38   "Joseph Smith Jr. Editor Far West, MO. July, 1838," *Elders' Journal* 1 (July 1838): 43; emphasis added.

39   Joseph Smith History, circa June 1839–circa 1841, draft 2, 9, The Joseph Smith Papers; emphasis added.

40   Joseph Smith, "Church History," *Times and Seasons* 3, (March 1, 1842): 707; emphasis added.

❚❚ Brother Hyrum Smith said that he thought best that the information of the coming forth of the book of Mormon be related by Joseph himself to the Elders present that all might know for themselves. Brother Joseph Smith Jr. said that it was not intended to tell the world **all the particulars** of the coming forth of the book of Mormon, & also said that it was **not expedient** for him to relate these things &c.[41]

We find it curious that many disaffected members of the Church long after the Prophet's death, such as David Whitmer and Martin Harris (after their respective descent into apostasy), felt suddenly eager to provide details—details about a translation process they never experienced personally. Joseph Smith was the only man who had successfully *translated* the Nephite record. With Oliver as the only possible exception, even those serving as Joseph's scribes were never permitted to see the plates or the Urim and Thummim at work, therefore, they neither witnessed nor experienced the *Book of Mormon* translation. Thus, they were not "eyewitnesses."

Some historians construe the Prophet's comment that "it was not intended to tell the world all the particulars of the coming forth of the book of Mormon" to mean that we don't know *anything* about the *Book of Mormon* translation from Joseph Smith. This, however, is not the case. Throughout his life, Joseph Smith explained that he translated the *Book of Mormon* using the Nephite plates and the Nephite Urim and Thummim; he described studying the characters and becoming familiar with the writing and the layout. However, additional intricate details regarding how the Urim and Thummim operated, or other particulars concerning his visions and revelations, were not for the world to know. The world and the worldly, or in other words, the "learned" are not capable of understanding.

We know that the Jaredite–Nephite Urim and Thummim was specifically prepared and preserved for the purpose of translating languages, but details regarding the "how" have remained largely hidden. Such understanding requires commentary from a "seer," and Joseph Smith, the great Seer of this dispensation, declined to comment when asked for additional details. As no one in this generation understands

---

41   Minute Book 2, 25 October 1831, 13, The Joseph Smith Papers; emphasis added.

seership as Joseph Smith did,[42] we will all have to wait for further details, until we have greater faith. We await greater righteousness and humility as a people, before the Lord can reveal more on this subject.

42   In an interview with David Ransom on November 9, 1997, President Gordon B. Hinckley explained, ". . . we have a great body of revelation, the vast majority of which came from the prophet Joseph Smith. We don't need much revelation. We need to pay more attention to the revelation we've already received. Now, if a problem should arise on which we don't have an answer, we pray about it, we may fast about it, and it comes . . . we don't need a lot of continuing revelation. We have a great, basic reservoir of revelation." Gordon B. Hinckley, "Sunday Interview -- Musings of the Main Mormon," interview by Don Lattin, SFGATE, April 13, 1997, accessed December 2018, https://www.sfgate.com/news/article/SUNDAY-INTERVIEW-Musings-of-the-Main-Mormon-2846138.php.

During a Christmas devotional on December 7, 2003, he again reiterated, "I look to [Joseph Smith]. I love him. I seek to follow him. I read his words, and they become the standards to be observed in guiding this great Church as it moves forward in fulfilling its eternal destiny." Gordon B. Hinckley, *First Presidency Christmas Devotional*, 7 December 2003, The Church of Jesus Christ of Latter-day Saints.

Elder Bruce R. McConkie taught, "Every dispensation head is a revealer of Christ for his day; every prophet is a witness of Christ; and every other prophet or apostle who comes is a reflection and an echo and an exponent of the dispensation head. All such come to echo to the world and to expound and unfold what God has revealed through the man who was appointed to give his eternal word to the world for that era. Such is the dispensation concept. . . . [Joseph Smith] was as near perfection as mortals can get without being translated. He was a man of such spiritual stature that he reflected the image of the Lord Jesus to the people. His voice was the voice of the Lord. . . . The test of discipleship is how totally and completely and fully we believe the word that was revealed through Joseph Smith, and how effectively we echo or proclaim that word to the world. . . . Joseph Smith had, as no other man in our dispensation, the ability to be in tune with the Comforter and to speak forth things that were the mind and voice of the Lord, including things that are not in the standard works. . . . Those things that have come through the revelations and sermons of others of the brethren who have lived since Joseph Smith, as for instance, the vision of the redemption of the dead that President Joseph F. Smith received, or what any inspired person in the Church says, these things are a reflection, an explanation, an amplification of what originated with the Prophet Joseph Smith. . . . Joseph Smith has given the word, and we echo the message . . ." Bruce R. McConkie, "This Generation Shall Have My Word through You" (Sperry Symposium, Brigham Young University, January 27, 1979), https://www.lds.org/study/ensign/1980/06/this-generation-shall-have-my-word-through-you?lang=eng.

Brigham Young commented, "A person was mentioned to-day who did not believe that Brigham Young was a Prophet, Seer, and Revelator. I wish to ask every member of this whole community, if they ever heard him profess to be a Prophet, Seer, and Revelator, as Joseph Smith was? He [Brigham Young] professed to be an Apostle of Jesus Christ, called and sent of God to save Israel." Brigham Young, "The Lord at the Head of His Kingdom," in *Journal of Discourses*, vol. 6 (London, 1859), 319.

Referring to President Young's statement, John Taylor remarked, "Brigham Young in saying that He did not profess to be a prophet seer & Revelator as Joseph Smith was, was speaking of men being born Natural Prophets & seers." Diary of Wilford Woodruff, Feb 11, 1861.

Joseph Smith: Seer and Translator

On the day the Church was organized, the Lord gave a revelation wherein He designated Joseph Smith a "translator," revealing, "Behold there Shall a Record be kept among you & in it thou shalt be called a seer & Translater [*sic*] & Prophet."[43] For all those who believe the revelations are given by God, the Lord spoke literally and accurately when He called Joseph Smith a "translator." If, as the "seer stone in a hat" petitioner would postulate, the Prophet only read words appearing on a seer stone, why was he given the honorary title, "translator"?

We previously established that Joseph Smith did indeed perform a "translation" of the Nephite records into the English language. Through revelation and the gift of tongues, *he* chose the verbiage or wording we read in the *Book of Mormon* today; he was tutored in Nephite culture and history (allowing him to be thoroughly familiar with the civilization from which the Nephite plates were written); he studied the Nephite characters and used the divine Jaredite—Nephite instrument known as the Urim and Thummim to produce a work he would later describe as the "most correct Book."

The testimony given by our witness in this chapter demonstrates that while we cannot describe the coming forth of the *Book of Mormon* as a "secular" translation, disregarding the term "translation" entirely is also inaccurate. Correctly stated, we can call the *Book of Mormon* translation a divinely inspired *translation,* requiring study, effort, and work with ancient languages. No doubt the gift of tongues, the interpretation of tongues, and revelation illuminated the Prophet's mind as he endeavored to express in English, (a language he was hardly proficient with himself) concepts, ideas, and principles recorded and preserved by both Nephite and Jaredite prophets for hundreds, even thousands of years.

---

43   Revelation, 6 April 1830 [D&C 21], in Revelation Book 1, 28, The Joseph Smith Papers.

6

WITNESS #2 – JOSEPH SMITH: BOOK OF MORMON HISTORICITY

Throughout his life, Joseph Smith made it clear that the *Book of Mormon* was an ancient record and that the events detailed therein are historical facts, not literary fiction or even historical fiction. In addition to identifying the *Book of Mormon* as the "history of ancient America" and the "record of the forefathers of our western Tribes of Indians,"[1] Joseph Smith related on numerous occasions that he had spoken and visited with Moroni, a prophet and one of the last of the ancient Nephites.[2] On another occasion, he identified a skeleton in southern Illinois as the remains of a "white Lamanite who fought with the people of Onedagus for freedom."[3] He called Oliver Cowdery, Parley P. Pratt, and others on a mission to the "borders of the Lamanites [Missouri],"[4] to "preach [the Lord's] gospel" "unto the Lamanites."[5]

---

1   Joseph Smith to N. E. Sexton [N. C. Saxton], Joseph Smith History, volume A-1, 4 January 1833, 261, Joseph Smith Papers.

2   Joseph Smith, *Elders' Journal* 1 (July 1838): 42-43. "Question 4th. How, and where did you obtain the book of Mormon? Answer. Moroni, the person who deposited the plates, from whence the book of Mormon was translated, in a hill in Manchester, Ontario County New York, being dead; and raised again therefrom; appeared unto me [Joseph Smith], and told me where they were; and gave me directions how to obtain them." See also, Revelation, circa August 1835 [D&C 27], in Doctrine and Covenants, 1835 ed., 180, The Joseph Smith Papers. ". . . I [Jesus Christ] will drink of the fruit of the vine with you on the earth, and with Moroni, whom I have sent unto you to reveal the book of Mormon . . . "

3   Hancock, Levi Ward 1803-1882. Levi W. Hancock autobiography, p. 150, https://catalog.lds.org/assets/83e294f2-1197-4d99-884f-3855fa17c3d2/0/149 (accessed: February, 2019).

4   Joseph Smith History, circa June 1839–circa 1841, draft 2, 54, The Joseph Smith Papers. Also *History of the Church*, vol. 1, 120.

5   Doctrine and Covenants 28:8.

According to Oliver Huntington, Joseph Smith prophesied in Nauvoo that the Saints would "go into the Rocky Mountains, right into the midst of the Lamanites."[6]

Joseph Smith also identified geographical locations as former Nephite landmarks. He confirmed in 1838 that the hill known to the Nephites as Cumorah (known to the Jaredites as Ramah[7]) was the same hill we call "Hill Cumorah" in Manchester, New York.[8] He named a place near Adam-Ondi-Ahman, "Tower Hill . . . in consequence of the remains of an old Nephite altar or tower that stood there"[9] and through revelation, appointed a town just west of Nauvoo, in Iowa, with the name "Zarahemla."[10] Joseph Smith recognized and acknowledged the historical authenticity of the *Book of Mormon*.

Book of Mormon Historicity & the Seer Stone Hypothesis

Many people remain unaware of a growing school of thought among contemporary Latter-day Saint historians and authors who suggest that the *Book of Mormon* is not historical. Contrary to the testimony of the Prophet Joseph Smith and others, some modernists believe that the *Book of Mormon* narrative is mere allegory. They speculate that Mormon, Moroni, Nephi, Captain Moroni, and other *Book of Mormon* prophets never lived physically; that they are nothing more than figures or figments of Joseph Smith's imagination. They view the narrative in the *Book of Mormon* as just a well-meaning parable.

Challenging the historicity of the *Book of Mormon* is a natural consequence of the seer stone hypothesis. Many are asking, "If Joseph Smith never used the plates, relying solely on words that appeared on a stone, to what degree does the *Book of Mormon* text we read today

---

6   Oliver B. Huntington, "Prophecy," *Young Woman's Journal* 2, no. 7 (April 1891): 315.

7   Ether 15:11

8   Joseph Smith, Editorial, *Elders' Journal* 1 (July 1838): 42-43.

9   Joseph Smith History, vol. B-1, 19 May 1838, 797, The Joseph Smith Papers. Also in *History of the Church*, vol. 3, 34-35.

10   Revelation, circa early March 1841 [D&C 125:3], *Book of the Law of the Lord*, 16, The Joseph Smith Papers. "Let them build up a city unto my name upon the land opposite to the city of Nauvoo and let the name of Zarahemla be named upon it."

relate to the text engraven on the original Nephite plates, if there is any correlation at all?"

In 2018, Richard Bushman described the confusion that has arisen because the seer stone narrative challenges and obscures the origin of the *Book of Mormon* text:

> ❛❛ The plates perplex even believers. Latter-day Saints themselves **cannot agree on how the writings engraved on the gold surfaces, relate to Joseph Smith's oral dictation** to his secretaries. ... Later descriptions have him [Joseph Smith] looking at one of his seer stones in a hat with the plates wrapped in a cloth on the table. The plates themselves were not even visible to him. During parts of the translation, the plates were not even present—Smith claimed they were hidden away to keep them safe.[11]

Bushman makes a logical point. If the plates were not even present, we have **no** assurance that the *Book of Mormon* text came *from* the plates. From his viewpoint, no one knows whether the words, "I Nephi, having been born of goodly parents"[12] were actually inscribed on the plates or if they were ever stated by Nephi in the first place. If the verse didn't come from the plates and it came from a seer stone, from where was the seer stone pulling the words and *how*? Bushman continues:

> ❛❛ Was the dictation, then, really **coming from the plates** like a computer sending information to a wireless printer or like a cell phone using Google Translate? Or was the seer stone delivering **something else**? What was it Smith saw, or believed he saw, or at least told others that he saw? Accounts of believing Latter-day Saints do not agree.[13]

Among the ranks of seer stone proponents, Bushman recognizes three groups: those who believe Joseph Smith saw words, those who believe Joseph *thought* he saw words (in other words, he experienced a

---

11   Richard L. Bushman, "The Gold Plates as Foundational Text," in *Foundational Texts of Mormonism* (New York: Oxford University Press, 2013), 15; emphasis added.

12   1 Nephi 1:1.

13   Richard L. Bushman, "The Gold Plates as Foundational Text," in *Foundational Texts of Mormonism* (New York: Oxford University Press, 2013), 15-16; emphasis added.

psychological phenomenon wherein he imagined that he saw words) and those who believe he only claimed to see words but never actually did. For the progressives, the Prophet's motives are difficult to determine. Bushman comments on the confusion:

> ❙❙ The entire process of translation has been the subject of debate among Mormon scholars. Even those who believe the text came by the inspiration of God, as Joseph Smith said, **differ on the relationship between inscribed plates and translated text.**[14]

"Seer stone in a hat" proponents have downgraded the coming forth of the *Book of Mormon* from a translation of ancient plates, to a magical, esoteric experience that remains mysterious; its nebulous origin opening the door to skeptics refuting the authenticity of the book. In this myopic view and with no firm foundation or support to defend it, the words in the *Book of Mormon* didn't come from plates, so why would anyone accept the book as historical? If it is a magical literary text that came from a seer stone, it may or may not be an ancient record, and with that, the keystone of our religion begins to topple. Bushman's argument continues to undermine the sanctity of the record:

> ❙❙ Was it word-for-word, an exact conveyance of meaning from 'reformed Egyptian' to English; or did Smith get **impressions of meaning** that he couched in his own language? Some have suggested that he injected **commentary of his own** to expand the translation, thus introducing **nineteenth-century content.** Other Mormon scholars offer evidence from the translation manuscripts that the translation was tightly controlled, implying that the resulting English text closely conformed to the words Smith saw in the seer stone.[15]

Bushman further argues that "Latter-day Saints themselves cannot agree," listing a number of possible theories seer stone adherents must evaluate when hypothesizing on the origin of the *Book of Mormon* text.

First, did the seer stone "generate" text that was an **exact** translation of the characters on the plates? If this is true, who performed the

---

14   Ibid, 16; emphasis added.
15   Ibid, 15-16; emphasis added.

translation? Who chose the words? The Lord? Angels? A force in the universe? If the words came from a treasure-digging seer stone, originally used for occultic purposes, were the words tampered with by the adversary?

Second, did the seer stone "generate" text that gave Joseph an "impression of meaning" or a vague idea that he put into his own words? Some scholars take this position further, suggesting that Joseph Smith began inserting his own ideas into the text--ideas unrelated to engravings on the plates (presumably because he never used the plates). What portions of the *Book of Mormon* came from Nephi vs. Mormon vs. the seer stone vs. Joseph Smith's own ideas? Suddenly, we have a melting pot of sources and ideas such that the *Book of Mormon* is no longer an historical text abridged by Mormon, but rather it is literature that may, or by inference, may not be "based on a true story." Or at best, a literary work fraught with uninspired opinions inserted by the Prophet as a "product of his own time." In other words, discussing the historicity of the *Book of Mormon* is moot because we do not know how to discern between the ancient and 19th century passages. Therefore, if a portion of the *Book of Mormon* seems controversial, we are not bound to accept it as the "revealed word of God" because we do not know the true origin of the book.

Third, did the seer stone "generate" words that were repeated by Joseph Smith to his scribe with perfect exactness? From time to time, a number of textual changes have been made throughout the *Book of Mormon;* some by accident, others deliberately. For example, in the 1830 edition of the *Book of Mormon*, 1 Nephi 20:1 reads:

❒❒ Hearken and hear this, O house of Jacob, which are called by the name of Israel, and are come forth out of the waters of Judah, which swear by the name of the Lord . . .[16]

In the 1840 edition of the *Book of Mormon*, Joseph Smith added a phrase so that it now reads, "come forth out of the waters of Judah, **or out of the waters of baptism,** which swear by the name of the Lord . ..." If the original text of the *Book of Mormon* was dictated exactly as it appeared on a seer stone, why did Joseph Smith alter the wording?

---

16   Book of Mormon, 1830 ed., 52 [1 Nephi 20:1], The Joseph Smith Papers.

Another instance includes several changes made by Joseph Smith to the 1837 edition, where he added, "son of" to references for God. For example, 1 Nephi 11:21 reads in the *original* manuscript written by Joseph's scribe, Oliver Cowdery:

> ❧❧ & the angel said unto me behold the lam [*sic*] of god yea even **the eternal father** knowest thou the meaning of the tree which thy father saw[17]

The 1837 edition was altered to read:

> ❧❧ And the angel said unto me, behold the Lamb of God, yea, even **the Son of the Eternal Father!** Knowest thou the meaning of the tree which thy father saw?[18]

We will discuss the textual changes to the *Book of Mormon* in depth in a later volume in this series.

In summary, if the seer stone narrative is believed or taken to be credible, we have no solid case to support the historicity of the *Book of Mormon*. Instead, there is what Bushman calls an "interpretive gap," making it impossible to decipher to any degree the relationship between characters engraven on the plates and the manuscript Joseph and Oliver delivered to E. B. Grandin, the first publisher of the *Book of Mormon*:

> ❧❧ The space between the wrapped plates sitting on the table and Joseph nearby looking into a stone in a hat symbolizes the **interpretive gap** where various explanations of translation have been inserted even by those who accept the premise of the plates' existence.[19]

For Bushman and the other "seer stone in a hat" advocates, the fact that the plates were not directly used opens a quagmire of interpretive uncertainty. There is no way in the progressive perspective to know the

---

17   Printer's Manuscript of the Book of Mormon, circa August 1829–circa January 1830, 17, The Joseph Smith Papers; emphasis added.

18   Book of Mormon, 1837 ed., 25-28 [1 Nephi 11:21], The Joseph Smith Papers; emphasis added.

19   Richard L. Bushman, "The Gold Plates as Foundational Text," in *Foundational Texts of Mormonism* (New York: Oxford University Press, 2018), 16; emphasis added.

degree to which the text on the plates corresponds with the English translation, a complication proven by the multitude of scholarly disagreement on the matter. Bushman continues:

// What then can be said about the relationship of the current edition of the *Book of Mormon* to its original text on the gold plates? The subject is so fraught there is **no agreement** at any level.[20]

Have we reached a time in the history of the Restoration where the narrative accepted generally as mainstream has reached a level of confusion such that even with all of our "learning" and study we cannot reliably answer the question of the origin of the Book of Mormon text? We are left to wonder, did any of it come from ancient Nephite prophets or was it merely a form of historical fiction created by Joseph Smith?

The editor of a recent popular book, comprised of essays by progressive scholars who promote the "new narrative," summed up our situation in these words:

// Let people know, we don't have definitive answers. We had a really hard time finding a title for this book. . . . but one thing that every single author was insistent on was that the **words "truth" and "answers" did not appear in the title**, because these chapters are open ended. They're meant to summarize the best scholarship.[21]

When ancient prophets looked down upon our day, they saw a world, and even the covenant people, in a state of "ever learning, and never able to come to the knowledge of the truth."[22] Scholarship without revelation can only lead to confusion and turmoil in the hearts and minds of believers.

Should we accept the *Book of Mormon* as an historical text? Why not simply an inspired parable with heart-warming lessons "for our

---

20   Ibid, 16; emphasis added.

21   Benchmark Books, "Laura Hales & Contributors (A Reason for Faith)--Benchmark Books, 5/11/16," YouTube, 1:01:59, May 18, 2016, https://www.youtube.com/watch?v=zlVGqk5hjlI; emphasis added.

22   2 Timothy 3:7.

day?" How can we know the book's validity, the book's authenticity, or the book's truth?

Challenging the historicity of the *Book of Mormon* has become increasingly popular among scholars within the Church. Author and historian, Gregory A. Prince, called for those who still believe in the historicity of the *Book of Mormon* to "grow up" during a 2013 address:

> ❛❛ ... there are many who are willing to die on the hill of ancient historicity. To them I say, '**grow up!**' [laughter] **Science has already informed greatly on the issue of historicity** and will continue to inform many great and important things. Relax and don't throw the baby out with the bathwater.[23]

Has science truly proven the Book of Mormon to be nonhistorical? Is it true that the provenance and historicity of the *Book of Mormon* are not important, as Prince suggests?

Provenance is the chronology of the ownership, custody, or location of an historical object. It is "the place of origin"[24] or "the history of ownership of a valued object or work of art or literature."[25]

According to the traditional narrative, the provenance of the *Book of Mormon* consists of metal plates which were constructed and engraven by Mormon and Moroni (4th and 5th century AD), who sourced a large portion of their material from other records (Jaredite and Nephite). The historicity of the Nephite records begins with Nephi (~600 BC), though portions of his text came from the Brass Plates which date back even further. The plates from which Mormon and Moroni drew their material were handed down and added to from generation to generation, through men such as Mosiah, Alma the Younger, Helaman, Ammoron, and finally, to the historian, Mormon, and his son Moroni. Fulfilling his role as caretaker, Moroni buried the final abridgment in the Hill Cumorah. Secondhand accounts from early brethren who worked with Joseph Smith tell of a cave in or near Cumorah filled

---

23   Greg Prince, "Pillars of My Faith" speech, Sunstone Symposium, August 2, 2013; emphasis added.

24   "PROVENANCE | Definition in the Cambridge English Dictionary.," Cambridge Dictionary, accessed February 2019, https://dictionary.cambridge.org/us/dictionary/english/occult.

25   "Definition of Provenance," Merriam-Webster, accessed March 2019, https://www.merriam-webster.com/dictionary/provenance.

with wagonloads of other plates.[26] These likely included Mormon's source material for the *Book of Mormon*. Joseph Smith was led to the hill by revelation in 1823, accompanied by Moroni. Joseph Smith later obtained the ancient plates and translated them into English. This summarizes the "traditional narrative" of the provenance of the *Book of Mormon*.

Although Prince admits that the *Book of Mormon* has converted many to a "better place of living," he believes its origin, or provenance, does not matter. It does not matter whether there ever was a Nephi, a Mormon, a Captain Moroni, or an Alma. To him, it does not matter whether there ever was a "Nephite" nation. Instead, Prince insinuates that science has debunked the idea that the history of the *Book of Mormon* actually happened. For those who are willing to "die on the hill of ancient historicity," for those who take pictures with their family on the Hill Cumorah in New York, saying, "Moroni once stood here," for those who devote their life to *Book of Mormon* archaeology, for those who imagine that they are a descendant of Lehi or Nephi, for those who believe that physical Nephite angels appeared to Joseph Smith, this scholar has two words for you, "Grow up!"

In Prince's worldview, there never was a Nephi, a Mormon, a Helaman; or at best, only portions of the *Book of Mormon* are accurate, but it is impossible to determine what is original history and what portions are "loosely based on a true story." "Relax!" Prince advises, "Don't throw the baby out with the bathwater . . ." In other words, don't entirely throw your faith away in the goodness of the book, even if the book isn't "true" in the sense we have always taught. Don't worry that it never really happened.

The position taken by scholars such as Greg Prince is gaining a following among many members of the Church. When Jana Riess

---

26   Brigham Young, "Trying to Be Saints," in *Journal of Discourses*, vol. 19 (Liverpool, 1873), 38. Discourse given on June 17, 1877. According the President Brigham Young, "Oliver says that when Joseph and Oliver went there, the hill opened, and they walked into a cave, in which there was a large and spacious room. . . . They laid the plates on a table; it was a large table that stood in the room. Under this table there was a pile of plates as much as two feet high, and there were altogether in this room more plates than probably many wagon loads; they were piled up in the corners and along the walls."

Find additional historical accounts on the *Joseph Smith Foundation* website. "Hill Cumorah Cave," Joseph Smith Foundation Wiki, https://josephsmithfoundation.org/hill-cumorah-cave/.

conducted her *Next Mormons Survey* in 2016, she recorded that over half (51%) of "non-Utah Mormons" renounce the historicity of the *Book of Mormon* and almost a third (31%) of "Utah Mormons" disagree that the *Book of Mormon* is a "literal, historical account."[27] The seer stone narrative serves to bolster the modernist attack on the historicity of the *Book of Mormon*. Ideas have consequences.

Does the historicity and provenance of the *Book of Mormon* matter? If the *Book of Mormon* is not historical, Joseph Smith initiated perhaps the greatest hoax in modern history. If this is the case, Joseph Smith's adherents have perpetuated a grand lie.

According to the testimony of Joseph Smith, presented in this "trial," he repeatedly claimed to have spoken face to face with Moroni, an ancient Nephite warrior and historian. He asserted that the Nephite plates were "records of the ancient prophets that had existed on this continent [the North American continent]."[28] During the Zion's Camp march from Ohio to Missouri, the Prophet stood on a mound in southern Illinois and told his followers that the skeletal remains they had discovered were once a "white Lamanite" named "Zelph" who "was a warrior and chieftain under the great prophet Onandagus who was known from the Hill Cumorah or eastern sea to the Rocky Mountains."[29] Joseph Smith led his followers to believe that the Book of Mormon was literal, American history and that he, the Prophet, was fluent in this ancient culture.

"History of Ancient America"

In the "Wentworth Letter" (published in the 1842 *Times and Seasons*), Joseph Smith provided an overview of the *Book of Mormon*, revealing that he considered it the "history of ancient America," that the Lord physically appeared "upon this continent [North America]," and that

---

27   Jana Riess, "10 Ways Utah Mormons Are a Breed Apart," Religion News Service, January 11, 2019, accessed February 2019, https://janariess.religionnews.com/2019/01/11/10-ways-utah-mormons-are-a-breed-apart/. Also, Jana Riess, "Commentary: 10 Ways Utah Latter-day Saints Are Different than Other U.S. Latter-day Saints," *The Salt Lake Tribune*, January 15, 2019, accessed February 2019, https://www.sltrib.com/religion/2019/01/11/commentary-ways-utah/.

28   Joseph Smith, "Church History," *Times and Seasons* 3, (March 1, 1842): 707.

29   Joseph Smith History, volume A-1, 30 May–3 June 1834, 483, Joseph Smith Papers.

the "America in ancient times has been inhabited by two distinct races of people":

❯❯ In this important and interesting book the **history of ancient America** is unfolded, from its first settlement by a colony that came from the tower of Babel, at the confusion of languages to the beginning of the fifth century of the Christian era. We are informed by these records that America in ancient times has been **inhabited by two distinct races of people.** The first were called Jaredites and came directly from the tower of Babel. The second race came directly from the city of Jerusalem, about six hundred years before Christ. They were principally Israelites, of the descendants of Joseph. The Jaredites were destroyed about the time that the Israelites came from Jerusalem, who succeeded them in the inheritance of the country. The principal nation of the second race fell in battle towards the close of the fourth century. The remnant are the **Indians that now inhabit this country** [United States of America].[30]

Joseph Smith's description clearly denotes that the *Book of Mormon* is not a book of parables or folklore, but the history of two races—one that settled America after the tower of Babel and another group of Israelites who fled the area of Jerusalem before its destruction by King Nebuchadnezzar. The history concludes toward the "close of the fourth century." Joseph Smith continues by describing the appearance of the Son of God to the Nephites "upon this continent [North America]." Joseph Smith is identifying geographical markers, historical timelines, and even ancient artifacts as originating from actual societies and cultures that once inhabited this continent:

❯❯ This book also tells us that our Saviour made his appearance upon **this continent** [North America] after his resurrection, that he planted the gospel here in all its fulness, and richness, and power, and blessing; that they had apostles, prophets, pastors, teachers and evangelists; the same order, the same priesthood, the same ordinances, gifts, powers, and blessing, as was enjoyed on the eastern continent, that the people were cut off in consequence of

---

30   Joseph Smith History, vol. C-1, 1 March 1842, 1282, The Joseph Smith Papers; emphasis added.

their transgressions, that the last of their prophets who existed among them was commanded to write an abridgement of their prophesies [*sic*], history &c., and to hide it up in the earth, and that it should come forth and be united with the bible for the accomplishment of the purposes of God in the last days.[31]

Joseph Smith's account documents that he understood where some of the Latter-day Lamanites, a small portion of Lehi's seed, were located. He explained that "the people were cut off in consequence of their transgressions" and the "remnant are the Indians that now inhabit this country [United States of America]."

The Prophet also declared that he was familiar with the "origin," "laws" and "governments" of the "aboriginal inhabitants of this country [the United States of America]":

// I was also informed [by Moroni] concerning the aboriginal inhabitants of **this country**, and shown who they were, and from whence they came; a brief sketch of their **origin, progress, civilization, laws, governments**, of their righteousness and iniquity, and the blessings of God being finally withdrawn from them as a people was made known unto me: I was also told where there was deposited some plates on which were engraven an abridgement of the records of the ancient prophets that had existed on **this continent**. The angel appeared to me three times the same night and unfolded the same things. After having received many visits from the angels of God unfolding the majesty, and glory of the events that should transpire in the last days, on the morning of the 22nd of September A.D. 1827, the angel of the Lord delivered the records into my hands.[32]

In 1833, Joseph Smith also wrote a letter to Noah C. Saxton, a newspaper editor, explaining that:

// The Book of Mormon is a record of the **forefathers of our western Tribes of Indians**, having been found through the ministration

---

31   Joseph Smith, "Church History," *Times and Seasons* 3, (March 1, 1842): 707-708; emphasis added.

32   Joseph Smith History, vol. C-1, 1 March 1842, 1282, The Joseph Smith Papers; emphasis added.

of an holy Angel **translated** into our own Language by the gift and power of God . . .[33]

In the chapter, "Witness #2 - Joseph Smith: Translator or Reader?," we discovered that a number of the early Brethren reported that Nephi,[34] Mormon,[35] Moroni,[36] the Nephite Twelve Apostles[37] (including the Three Nephites),[38] and "others of the ancient Prophets who formerly lived on this Continent"[39] all visited and taught Joseph Smith repeatedly. If none of these events are historical, Joseph Smith was a pathological liar. If the *Book of Mormon* is not historical, the Prophet Joseph Smith bore false testimony and perjured himself, not once or twice, but repeatedly and even constantly throughout his life.

Did these prophets once walk the earth as mortal men, or are they only the protagonists of a 19th century text, mere fragments of an inspired or uninspired allegory? For every individual who values honesty and integrity, this is the deal breaker.

---

33   Joseph Smith to N. E. Sexton [N. C. Saxton], Joseph Smith History, volume A-1, 4 January 1833, 261, Joseph Smith Papers; emphasis added.

34   John Taylor, "Man, the Offspring of God, Etc.," in *Journal of Discourses*, vol. 17 (Liverpool, 1875), 374. Discourse given on April 8, 1875.

35   Ibid.

36   Ibid.

37   John Taylor, "Effects of the Preaching of the Gospel," in *Journal of Discourses*, vol. 21 (Liverpool, 1881), 94.

38   Orson Pratt to John Christensen, 11 Mar. 1876, Archives of The Church of Jesus Christ of Latter-day Saints, Salt Lake City.

39   John Taylor, "Man, the Offspring of God, Etc.," in *Journal of Discourses*, vol. 17 (Liverpool, 1875), 374. Discourse given on April 8, 1875.

7

WITNESSES #3-5: ANCIENT PROPHETS

In addition to the Lord Jesus Christ and the Prophet Joseph Smith, those perhaps most familiar with the translation process were the ancient prophets who saw our day and bore testimony to the coming forth of the *Book of Mormon*. Continuing our trial, we call to the stand the following witnesses: Moroni, the Brother of Jared (Mahonri Moriancumer), and Mosiah, respectively.

Moroni

Historian, warrior, and angelic mentor of the Prophet Joseph Smith, Moroni was the last steward of the ancient Nephite artifacts under scrutiny in our trial. He described the appearance and purpose of the Urim and Thummim when he visited the Prophet Joseph Smith on September 21, 1823:

> *"* ... [Moroni said] that there were **two stones** in silver bows—and these **stones**, fastened to a **breastplate**, constituted what is called the **Urim and Thummim**— deposited **with the plates**; and the possession and the use of these stones were what constituted "seers" in ancient or former times; and that God had prepared them for the purpose of translating the book.[1]

Critics of the Restoration do not consider the description Moroni delivered on September 21 as a valid testimony because his words come to us through the Prophet Joseph Smith. Since some believe that Joseph Smith invented the story of Moroni and his "spectacles," they

---

1   Joseph Smith—History 1:35; emphasis added.

dismiss Moroni's witness as an invention of the Prophet. However, if one accepts Joseph Smith as a prophet and views him as a man of integrity, which is the view of this publication, Moroni's testimony provides a compelling and definitive witness as to the appearance, authenticity, and use of the Urim and Thummim.

Moroni's description reveals a few important details, including the assertion that God "prepared" the Urim and Thummim for the "purpose" of "translating" the Nephite plates. In light of this, it is clear that unless Joseph Smith chose to disregard rebelliously the will of the Lord by tossing aside the Urim and Thummim in favor of a seer stone, then he must have translated the Nephite plates, as the true witnesses agree, with the interpreters.

Furthermore, some historians suggest that the term "Urim and Thummim" and "seer stone" are interchangeable. Moroni's description, however, dispels all doubt on this question. The translation instrument Moroni and Joseph Smith referred to as the Urim and Thummim consisted of two stones, not one, and they both described the stones as transparent—not opaque or dark—set in the rim of a bow.

Finally, the Urim and Thummim, the instrument Joseph Smith used to translate, was found *with* the plates where Moroni had deposited them. There is no evidence that any of Joseph Smith's seer stones were ever found with the plates in the stone box in Cumorah, leaving no doubt that the Urim and Thummim described by Moroni and any of the seer stones the Prophet may have had were *different* objects entirely.

As Moroni finished his abridgment of the Jaredite records and added them to his father Mormon's compilation, Moroni recognized that the ancient American language written by the Nephites would be lost. "[N]one other people knoweth our language," he observed. To resolve this obstacle, the Lord provided a solution, the same solution he had provided for the prophet Mahonri Moriancumer many centuries previously—he "prepared means for the interpretation thereof"[2]:

// Wherefore the Lord hath commanded me to write them [the things which the brother of Jared saw]; and I have written them. And he commanded me that I should seal them up; and he also hath commanded that I should **seal up the interpretation** thereof;

2   Mormon 9:34.

wherefore I have **sealed up the interpreters**, according to the commandment of the Lord.[3]

Mormon was commanded by the Lord to "seal up" the interpretation, the key to deciphering the language engraven on the Nephite plates. A millennia and a half later, Moroni returned to the earth (as a resurrected being) to deliver the plates and the interpreters (Urim and Thummim) into the hands of the Prophet Joseph Smith.

For those who claim that Joseph Smith used a "seer stone in a hat" to "translate," Ether 4:5 presents a puzzling dilemma. Moroni testifies that the contents of the plates would forever remain a mystery unless a man could access the "interpretation thereof." The "interpretation," Moroni clarified, was not a seer stone but the "interpreters," the "two transparent stones set in the rim of a bow fastened to a breast plate,"[4] the Urim and Thummim buried in Cumorah *with* the plates. No other tool could be substituted. A seer stone wouldn't work. A magic mirror wouldn't work. A Harvard dictionary wouldn't work.

The Urim and Thummim/"interpreters" was far more than a helpful tool, a curious novelty Joseph Smith could fiddle with while translating the plates. The Urim and Thummim was *the* "interpretation," the key to unlocking the lost Nephite language. According to Moroni, without the interpreters, the plates and other Nephite artifacts were essentially useless.

Was Moroni qualified to make this claim? Not only did Moroni finish the *Book of Mormon* abridgment and fulfill the Lord's command to "seal up the interpreters," he was also endowed with "the keys of the record of the stick of Ephraim [Book of Mormon]."[5] Moroni held and still holds the authority over the *Book of Mormon*, hence the translation was done under his authority and supervision. Orson Hyde taught that Moroni is the "guardian angel of these United States," that he gave "deep impressions," "dreams," and "visions" to Columbus, that he "was in the camp with Washington" and will yet fulfill important missions in saving the Constitution of the United States.[6] According

---

3   Ether 4:5; emphasis added.

4   Joseph Smith, "Church History," *Times and Seasons* 3 (March 1, 1842): 707.

5   Doctrine and Covenants 27:5.

6   Orson Hyde, "Celebration of the Fourth of July," in *Journal of Discourses*, vol. 6 (Liverpool, 1859), 368. Discourse given on July 4, 1854.

to Orson Hyde, Moroni not only holds the key over the record that came forth out of the Hill Cumorah in New York but he also holds sacred keys dealing with the destiny of America (United States). Moroni holds the keys of the "stick of Ephraim"; he sealed up the record and the "interpretation"; he tutored Joseph Smith and his involvement continues in this last dispensation. The reader should take note that we have yet to receive a large portion of the Brother of Jared's vision and the writings of Moroni. One day, in the future, we are promised those writings will be made available (as soon as we have sufficient faith and righteousness) to faithful Saints.[7]

The Brother of Jared

Our next ancient prophetic witness is the Brother of Jared, whose name the Prophet Joseph Smith reportedly identified as "Mahonri Moriancumer."[8] When President Joseph Fielding Smith determined that the "seer stone narrative" was hearsay, he appealed to the testimony of the Brother of Jared:

---

7   Bruce R. McConkie, "The Doctrinal Restoration," in *The Joseph Smith Translation: The Restoration of Plain and Precious Truths*, ed. Monte S. Nyman and Robert L. Millet (Provo: Religious Studies Center, Brigham Young University, 1985). Elder Bruce R. McConkie commented, "I am clear in my mind that the sealed portion of the Book of Mormon will not come forth until the Millennium. The same is undoubtedly true of the fulness of the Bible, though some additions could well be made before that time. . . . The perfected Bible of the future will surely include all that was on the brass plates of Laban. . . . Someday the Lord will raise up a prophet, who will also be a seer and a translator, to whom he will give the brass plates that they may be translated for the benefit and blessing of those in all nations. Would God that the work might commence at least in our day though in fact we have no such hope. Why should the Lord give us what is on the brass plates or in the sealed portion of the Book of Mormon when we do not even treasure up and live by what he has already given us."

8   George Reynolds, "The Jaredites," *Juvenile Instructor* 27, no. 9 (1 May 1892): 282. See account from George Reynolds, "While residing in Kirtland Elder Reynolds Cahoon had a son born to him. One day when President Joseph Smith was passing his door, he called the Prophet in and asked him to bless and name the baby. Joseph did so and gave the boy the name of Mahonri Moriancumer. When he had finished the blessing he laid the child on the bed, and turning to Elder Cahoon he said, 'The name I have given your son is the name of the brother of Jared; the Lord has just shown [or revealed] it to me.' Elder William F. Cahoon who was standing near heard the Prophet make this statement to his father; and this was the first time the name of the brother of Jared was known in the Church in this dispensation."

❙❙ ... there is **no authentic statement** in the history of the Church which states that the use of such a stone [seer stone] was made in that translation. The information is all **hearsay**, and personally, I do not believe that this stone was used for this purpose. The **reason** I give for this conclusion is found in the **statement of the Lord to the Brother of Jared** as recorded in Ether 3:22–24.[9]

Ether 3:22-24 records the promises of the Lord to the Brother of Jared. His records were of such great import, that the Lord required him to seal them and show them "to no man."[10] Mahonri Moriancumer and his people likely spoke a form of the Adamic language.[11] Since the Jaredite tongue would eventually be lost, the Son of God promised that the two stones He had prepared would allow future generations to understand the Brother of Jared's writings. Here again we read of *two* stones, not one seer stone:

❙❙ And behold, when ye shall come unto me, ye shall write them and shall seal them up, that no one can interpret them; for ye shall write them in a language that they cannot be read. And behold, these **two stones** will I give unto thee, and ye shall **seal them up also *with*** the things which ye shall write. For behold, the language which ye shall write I have confounded; wherefore I will cause in my own due time that **these stones** shall **magnify** to the eyes of men these **things which ye shall write.**[12]

---

9   Joseph Fielding Smith, *Doctrines of Salvation*, vol. 3 (Salt Lake City: Bookcraft, 1956)226; emphasis added.

10   Ether 3:21.

11   See Ether 1; also Bruce R. McConkie, *Mormon Doctrine* (Bookcraft, 1966), 15; Joseph Fielding Smith, *The Way to Perfection* (Deseret Book, 1978), 69. "Jaredites Retained the Adamic Language: It is stated in the Book of Ether that Jared and his brother made the request of the Lord that their language be not changed at the time of the confusion of tongues at the Tower of Babel. Their request was granted, and they carried with them the speech of their fathers, the Adamic language, which was powerful even in its written form, so that the things Mahonri wrote "were mighty even ... unto the overpowering of man to read them." That was the kind of language Adam had and this was the language with which Enoch was able to accomplish his mighty work. This being true, is there any wonder then that puny man, in his endeavor to search out the beginnings of things is baffled when he discovers what he is pleased to call primitive mankind, or, the most ancient peoples of which history records, a language rich in metaphor and in complex combinations?"

12   Ether 3:22-24; emphasis added.

Mahonri Moriancumer sealed up together his records and the "two stones," Urim and Thummim, the Lord had prepared for the express purpose of revealing the lost language. Generations later, King Mosiah used these two transparent stones to translate a portion of the Jaredite record, which gave his people "much knowledge."[13] Many generations later, the last prophet of the Nephite civilization, Moroni, sealed up these "two stones" with his records. They continued to represent the key necessary to unlocking the interpretation and translation. Centuries later, the Prophet Joseph Smith used these same "two stones" to translate the Nephite record; the stones passed down through many hands from the Brother of Jared, to Mosiah (and many other Nephite prophets), to Moroni, and then to the Prophet Joseph Smith. The Lord works in repeating patterns and as we can see, His pattern has remained consistent through generations of prophets and throughout time.

Mosiah and the Urim and Thummim

Joseph Smith was not the first prophet-seer to use the Jaredite Urim and Thummim. Mosiah 28 records that King Mosiah translated Jaredite gold plates, found by a group of wandering Nephites in a land of "ruins." The engravings on these plates were unknown to the Nephites, but Mosiah translated them by the aid of "two stones."[14] In 2013, the *Joseph Smith Foundation* released the *Book of Mormon* based "For Our Day" model which proposes that Mormon saw the Latter-days—our day—in vision, and purposely abridged Nephite history to include stories and narratives that parallel the Latter-day signs of the times, nearly always in chronological order.[15] This suggests that we can read the *Book of Mormon* as a prophetic history of the Latter-days by matching each *Book of Mormon* passage with its corresponding Latter-day event(s).

---

13   Mosiah 28:18.

14   Mosiah 28:13.

15   To learn more about the "For Our Day" model, see the documentary films, *For Our Day: Covenant on the Land* (2013) and *For Our Day: Divinely Sanctioned Governments* (2013). You may also be interested in poster models available through the *Joseph Smith Foundation*. These models overlay the *Book of Mormon* history with Latter-day prophetic history, organizing the matching events. Learn more at: www.JosephSmithFoundation.org.

Book of Mormon Prophetic Parallels Timeline

Art by Joseph F. Brickey, www.JosephBrickey.com
For copies visit: www.JosephSmithFoundation.org/store

Mosiah 8 contains the account of King Mosiah translating gold plates by the gift and power of God. These plates contained the history of the Jaredites, a people who formerly inhabited this land, America, but were destroyed when they ripened in iniquity. The focus of this message was a warning to the inhabitants that would follow.

Joseph Smith similarly translated a record of scripture, engraven on plates "hav[ing] the appearance of gold,"[16] which contained the warning of a fallen people, the Nephites, who formerly inhabited this land, America, after the Jaredites had fallen. Like the Jaredites, they were destroyed because of their wickedness. Their record—both Jaredite and Nephite—became a warning to the Latter-day inhabitants of this promised land of America.

Mosiah translated the Jaredite gold plates using the Urim and Thummim, just as Joseph Smith translated the Nephite "gold" plates using the same special instrument, the Urim and Thummim.

The Lord has always foretold future events and calamities to his covenant people, Israel, through prophecy.[17] The Nephites were given the Jaredite gold plates as a witness and warning to them. They rejected this counsel and their abridged history was left to us as a foreshadowing of our own history.

Mormon specifically highlights the acquisition, translation, and usage of the Jaredite history by the Nephites, including how they refused to heed Ether's warning. Mormon then applies the same warning to us, declaring that the prophecies contained in the *Book of Mormon* apply to us, in our day. In other words, the translation of the Jaredite record is a foreshadowing or a type of the translation of the *Book of Mormon*.

A close analysis of the account of Mosiah's translation of the Jaredite plates of gold using the Urim and Thummim, reveals many specific details, which further discredit the "new" seer stone narrative.

The record states that Nephite explorers found the Jaredite plates "in a land among many waters."[18] Approximately 120 B.C., King Limhi had sent a band of men to find Zarahemla and to secure relief for his enslaved people. The exploratory group did not succeed in their quest to find Zarahemla, but they did find the ruins of a large society—the Jaredite civilization.

---

16   Joseph Smith, "Church History," *Times and Seasons* 3 (March 1, 1842): 707.

17   1 Nephi 20:1-3; Isaiah 48:1-3.

18   Mosiah 8:8.

Where were these men, geographically? Where did the Jaredite civilization end? Moroni identified the hill where the last surviving Jaredite armies made their final stand as "... the hill Ramah ... [which] was that same hill where my father Mormon did hide up the records unto the Lord, which were sacred."[19] In other words, the Jaredite civilization ended in the Great Lakes region of the United States of America, as did the Nephite civilization.

Joseph Smith identified that "same hill" as the Hill Cumorah in Manchester, New York.[20] Oliver Cowdery seconded the Prophet's geographical identification of the Hill Ramah and the Hill Cumorah in a letter to W. W. Phelps in July 1835.[21] Joseph Fielding Smith clarified that Oliver's letter was "written at the Prophet [Joseph Smith's] request and under his personal supervision."[22] Heber C. Kimball's son also remembered, "Heber C. Kimball said it was revealed to him that the last great destruction of the wicked would be on the lakes near the Hill Cumorah."[23] The Jaredite civilization foreshadowed the Nephite civilization which in turn foreshadows our civilization.

Returning to the account of Limhi's men who had been searching for Zarahemla when they discovered the ruins of the Jaredite civilization:

> *❞* ... they were lost in the wilderness for the space of many days ... having discovered a land which was **covered with bones of men**, and of beasts, and was also covered with **ruins of buildings** of every kind, having discovered a land which had been peopled with a people who were as numerous as the hosts of Israel.[24]

---

19   Ether 15:11.

20   Joseph Smith History, volume B-1, 8 May 1838, 794, The Joseph Smith Papers. "Moroni, the person who deposited the plates, (from whence the Book of Mormon was translated,) in a hill in Manchester, Ontario County, New York ... " Published in *Elders' Journal* 1 (July 1838): 42-43.

21   Joseph Smith History, 1834–1836, 87, The Joseph Smith Papers. "... he [Mormon] deposited ... all the records in this same hill, Cumorah ... This hill, by the Jaredites, was called Ramah ... in full view from the top of this same hill ... may be seen where once sunk to nought the pride and strength of two mighty nations ..."

22   Joseph Fielding Smith, *Doctrines of Salvation*, vol. 3 (Salt Lake City: Bookcraft, 1956), 236.

23   N. B. Lundwall, *Inspired Prophetic Warnings to All Inhabitants of the Earth* (Salt Lake City: N.B. Lundwall, 1970), 52.

24   Mosiah 8:8; emphasis added.

The early colonizers of the United States in the 19th century stumbled across similar "ruins" and "destructions," only this time they belonged predominantly to the Nephite civilization. Heber C. Kimball remarked:

// From the time Father Bosley located near Avon, [Livingston County, NY] he found and plowed up **axes** and **irons**, and had sufficient to make his mill irons, and had always **abundance of iron** on hand without purchasing. In the towns of Bloomfield, Victor, Manchester, and in the regions round about, there were hills upon the tops of which were **entrenchments** and **fortifications**, and in them were **human bones, axes, tomahawks, points of arrows, beads** and **pipes,** which were **frequently found**; and it was a **common occurrence** in the country to plow up axes, which I have done many times myself. I have visited the **fortifications** on the tops of those hills frequently, and the one near Bloomfield I have crossed hundreds of times . . . The hill Cumorah is a high hill for that country, and had the **appearance of a fortification or entrenchment around it.** In the State of New York, probably there are **hundreds** of these **fortifications** which are now visible, and I have seen them in many other parts of the United States.[25]

In the mid-1800s, E. G. Squire "documented over 200 hilltop fortifications in Western New York State dated from 200 B.C. to 400 A.D., the very region of the Hill Ramah where the Jaredites were destroyed (~200 B.C.) also known as the Hill Cumorah where the Nephites were destroyed (385 A.D.).[26]" Researchers have observed that the soil in the area of New York is ". . . rich in calcium and phosphate—indicative of decaying bones of armies that perished there . . ."[27]

Limhi's men also found "bones" and "ruins" indicative of a fallen populace, "who were as numerous as the hosts of Israel."[28] Among the ruins, they also discovered gold plates. When they returned to their king and shared their historic find with Limhi, they showed him the

---

25   Orson F. Whitney, *Life of Heber C. Kimball* (Salt Lake City, 1888), 40-41; emphasis added.

26   David R. Hocking and Rodney L. Meldrum, eds., *Annotated Edition of the Book of Mormon* (Digital Legend Press, 2018), 492.

27   Riley L. Dixon, *Just One Cumorah* (Bookcraft, 1958).

28   Mosiah 8:8.

plates, breastplates, and swords as a "testimony that the things they had said" were true:

▌▌ And for a testimony that the things that they had said are true they have brought twenty-four **plates** which are filled with engravings, and they are of pure **gold**. And behold, also, they have brought **breastplates**, which are large, and they are of brass and of copper, and are perfectly sound. And again, they have brought **swords**, the hilts thereof have perished, and the blades thereof were cankered with rust; and there is **no one** in the land that [was] able to **interpret** the **language** or the **engravings** that [were] on the plates.[29]

Notice that Limhi's men brought three items back with them as a witness of their account: gold plates, breastplates, and swords. By including these details in his abridgment, we might ask, "Was Mormon trying to remind us that among the items seen and testified of by the Three Witnesses were the gold plates, the breastplate, and the sword of Laban?" Is it merely coincidence that Limhi's men brought similar items as testimony of their discovery of the Jaredite record and the fall of the Jaredite civilization?

Limhi began searching for anyone who could translate the engravings on the plates his men had discovered. Eventually, he encountered a group of Nephite men from the very city Limhi's men had been searching for, Zarahemla. Limhi queried their leader, Ammon:

▌▌ Knowest thou of any one that can translate? For I am desirous that these **records** should be **translated** into our language; for, perhaps, they will give us a knowledge of a remnant of the people who have been destroyed, from whence these records came; or, perhaps, they will give us a knowledge of this very people who have been destroyed; and I am desirous to know the cause of their destruction.[30]

Ammon was an answer to prayer as he explained that he knew of a seer who could translate the plates—King Mosiah. How could Mosiah translate records engraven with a language that no one understood? Ammon explained:

29   Mosiah 8:9-11; emphasis added.
30   Mosiah 8:12; emphasis added.

❙❙ Now Ammon said unto him: I can assuredly tell thee, O king, of a man that can translate the records; for he has **wherewith that he can look**, and **translate all records** that are of ancient date; and it is a **gift from God**. And the things are called **interpreters**, and no man can look in them except he be commanded, lest he should look for that he ought not and he should perish. And whosoever is commanded to look in them, the same is called **seer**. And behold, the king of the people who are in the land of Zarahemla is the man that is commanded to do these things, and who has this **high gift** from God.[31]

From Ammon's conversation with Limhi, we learn some important points regarding divine translation. First, the Lord's servants who are seers, are given an instrument that is used to translate records. Second, no man can use this instrument unless they are commanded by the Lord. Third, this divine tool, consisting of two stones fastened in the rim of a bow, are called "interpreters." Fourth, the definition of a "seer" is a man who has been commanded by the Lord to use this divine instrument for translation:

❙❙ And the king [Limhi] said that a seer is greater than a prophet. And Ammon said that a **seer** is a **revelator** and a **prophet** also; and a **gift which is greater can no man have**, except he should possess the power of God, which no man can; yet a man may have great power given him from God.[32]

Notice that Ammon connects a "seer" with a man who is a revelator and a prophet, who uses the Urim and Thummim, or interpreters. In the chapter, "'Study it Out in Your Mind' vs. a Free Gift," later in this book series, we will discover that the Lord taught Joseph and Oliver the same principle, reiterating that being a seer requires work on the part of the revelator. True revelation from the Lord is not given without study and effort:

❙❙ But a seer can know of things which are **past**, and also of things which **are to come**, and by them shall all things be revealed, or, rather, shall **secret** things be made manifest, and **hidden** things

---

31   Mosiah 8:13-14; emphasis added.
32   Mosiah 8:15-16; emphasis added.

shall come to light, and things which are **not known** shall be made known by them, and also things shall be made known by them which otherwise could not be known. Thus God has provided a **means** that man, through faith, might work mighty miracles; therefore he becometh a great benefit to his fellow beings.[33]

Throughout the *Book of Mormon*, the Lord teaches that He prepares "means"[34] by which his work is performed. In the case of ancient records, Ammon explains that these "means" include divine "interpreters."

Why was all of this information incorporated into the *Book of Mormon*? The Lord has repeatedly taught us that nothing was included in this "most correct book"[35] that is not critical for our day.[36] Why would Mormon include all these parallels? Why the parallel of the interpreters? Why spend many verses discussing the Urim and Thummim, used by the Jaredites, hid up, and then used by the Nephites, if the subject is of no import and a seer stone was used rather than the interpreters? The very idea is ludicrous.

> *And now, when Ammon had made an end of speaking these words the king rejoiced exceedingly, and gave thanks to God, saying: Doubtless a great mystery is contained within these plates, and these interpreters were doubtless **prepared** for the purpose of unfolding all such mysteries to the children of men.*[37]

In a spirit of inspiration and thanksgiving, Limhi proclaims that the Lord prepared the "interpreters" so that men of faith could bring forward "mysteries" contained on ancient records. Alma teaches a similar principle to Helaman when he foretells that Joseph Smith/Gazelem will translate the Nephite record using the "interpreters," which "were prepared [so] that the word of God might be fulfilled."[38]

In our modernist world, many Latter-day Saints ask questions such as, "What does it mean to be a seer? What are seer stones used for? What

---

33   Mosiah 8:17-18; emphasis added.

34   Alma 37:7, 60:21; 1 Nephi 17:3.

35   Joseph Smith History, vol. C-1, 28 November 1841, 1255, The Joseph Smith Papers.

36   Jacob 1:2-4; 2 Nephi 5:28-33; 1 Nephi 19:5–6.

37   Mosiah 8:19; emphasis added.

38   Alma 37:24.

was the Urim and Thummim?" The answers, at least those answers we are ready to receive, have always been available in the scriptures. According to the *Book of Mormon*, seers are men of faith who are commanded by the Lord to translate ancient records, which unfold the mysteries of the Lord to the children of men. They use "interpreters" prepared for that very purpose. The Prophet Joseph Smith brought forward the *Book of Mormon*, a record prepared specifically for our day, which stands as the keystone of our religion, providing a key to our survival in these tumultuous days. This was done by using divine interpreters, as commanded by the Lord.

Returning to the account in the *Book of Mormon*, we learn what Mosiah's "interpreters" looked like. Was Mosiah using a dark seer stone?

After Limhi and his people were miraculously delivered from their enslavement to the Lamanites, they joined Mosiah's people in Zarahemla. With them came the Jaredite plates, which were given to Mosiah. The people begged their king to translate the records, feeling "desirous beyond measure to know concerning those people who had been destroyed." "And now he translated them by the means of those **two stones** which were fastened into the **two rims** of a **bow**."[39]

"Two stones fastened into the two rims of a bow"? This description matches the account of Joseph Smith's Urim and Thummim exactly. Remember that the Nephite prophet Moroni described the appearance of the Urim and Thummim when he visited the Prophet Joseph Smith on September 21, 1823:

> *❝* ... [Moroni said] that there were **two stones** in silver bows—and these **stones**, fastened to a **breastplate**, constituted what is called the **Urim and Thummim**— deposited **with the plates**; and the possession and the use of these stones were what constituted "seers" in ancient or former times; and that God had prepared them for the purpose of translating the book.[40]

President Joseph Fielding Smith also connected Mosiah's Urim and Thummim with the Urim and Thummim given to the Brother of Jared and the Urim and Thummim given to the Prophet Joseph Smith:

---

39   Mosiah 28:12-13; emphasis added.

40   Joseph Smith—History 1:35; emphasis added.

// JOSEPH SMITH RECEIVED JAREDITE URIM AND THUMMIM

The people of Limhi brought to Mosiah a record, "engraven on plates of ore," (Mosiah 21:27) which record **Mosiah translated**, by the aid of "**two stones** which were fastened into the two rims of a bow," and which gave an account of the Jaredites.... (Mosiah 28:11–19)

Joseph Smith received with the breastplate and the plates of the Book of Mormon, the Urim and Thummim, which were hid up by Moroni to come forth in the last days as a **means** by which the ancient record might be translated, which **Urim and Thummim** were given to the Brother of Jared.[41]

Returning to Mormon's account, of Mosiah translating the Jaredite plates of gold using the "interpreters," or Urim and Thummim, he defines the meaning of the term "seer":

// Now these things [the Urim and Thummim] were **prepared** from the **beginning**, and were **handed down** from generation to generation, for the **purpose** of **interpreting languages**; And they have been **kept** and **preserved** by the hand of the Lord, that he should discover to every creature who should possess the land the iniquities and abominations of his people; And whosoever has these things is called **seer**, after the manner of old times.[42]

What does it mean to be a seer? According to the Lord, the definition of a seer is not someone who uses rocks to see buried treasure or lost items. A seer is not a man or woman who engages in scrying or other magical activities. A seer is a righteous servant of the Lord who uses the "interpreters," identified as two stones fastened into the rims of a bow, to "interpret languages" and to translate ancient records; to reveal the rise and fall, the righteousness and the wickedness of the Lord's people throughout history.

When Joseph Smith sat down to translate the Nephite records, when he used the Urim and Thummim, he was continuing a faithful

---

41   Joseph Fielding Smith, *Doctrines of Salvation*, vol. 3 (Salt Lake City: Bookcraft, 1956), 224-225.

42   Mosiah 28:14-16; emphasis added.

legacy of righteous kings and prophets before him. Mosiah had used the interpreters to translate, and now the Prophet Joseph Smith would use the same instrument, which had been "kept and preserved" by the Lord, to translate the Nephite record:

// Now after Mosiah had finished **translating** these records, behold, it gave an account of the people who were destroyed, from the time that they were destroyed back to the building of the great tower, at the time the Lord confounded the language of the people and they were scattered abroad upon the face of all the earth, yea, and even from that time back until the creation of Adam.

Now this account did cause the people of Mosiah to mourn exceedingly, yea, they were filled with sorrow; nevertheless it gave them much **knowledge**, in the which they did rejoice.[43]

Mosiah's translation of the Jaredite gold plates, provided the people of Nephi with the same bittersweet "knowledge" that Joseph Smith's translation of the Nephite gold plates provides for us. The *Book of Mormon* is the keystone of our religion and as the Prophet Joseph Smith stated, "Take away the Book of Mormon and the revelations, and where is our religion? We have none."[44]

Approximately the same time Joseph Smith completed the translation of the *Book of Mormon*, the Lord declared in a revelation:

// ... in them [the *Book of Mormon* and revelations of Joseph Smith] are all things written concerning the **foundation of my church**, my gospel, and my rock. Wherefore, if you shall build up my church, upon the foundation of my gospel and my rock, the **gates of hell shall not prevail** against you.[45]

It isn't any wonder why the attacks against the *Book of Mormon* are greater now than ever before! No wonder so-called progressive historians and scholars have united to introduce a "new history" destined to destroy the credibility of the *Book of Mormon* and the

---

43   Mosiah 28:17-18; emphasis added.

44   Joseph Smith, Minute Book 1, 21 April 1834, 44, The Joseph Smith Papers; emphasis added.

45   Doctrine and Covenants 18:4-5; emphasis added.

Prophet Joseph Smith. No wonder we are being bombarded with a "new narrative." If the *Book of Mormon* goes down, the Gospel of Jesus Christ will also be lost. If the *Book of Mormon* is lost, the very foundation of our faith, the rock, the hope to survive, to stand against the "gates of hell," will crumble.

Joseph Fielding Smith's Analysis

After analyzing the revelations and the historical record, President Joseph Fielding Smith reasoned:

- since the Jaredite Urim and Thummim was the Nephite Urim and Thummim (they were one and the same) and

- since the Urim and Thummim was specifically prepared by the Lord for the purpose of translating the *Book of Mormon* and the Jaredite records, and

- since the Urim and Thummim was superior to any seer stone the Prophet may have possessed,

- therefore, it is natural to conclude the Prophet Joseph Smith used the Urim and Thummim to translate the *Book of Mormon*.

President Smith concluded:

❙❙ **These stones**, the **Urim and Thummim** which were given to the Brother of Jared, were preserved for this very **purpose** of **translating** the record, both of the Jaredites and the Nephites. Then again the Prophet was impressed by Moroni with the fact that these stones were given for that very purpose. It **hardly** seems **reasonable** to suppose that the Prophet would **substitute** something evidently **inferior** under these circumstances.[46]

Essentially, President Smith's case against the seer stone narrative is:

- There is no credible historical statement claiming Joseph Smith used a seer stone to translate the *Book of Mormon*. (President Joseph Fielding Smith's position will be further validated in this book series.)

---

46   Joseph Fielding Smith, *Doctrines of Salvation*, vol. 3 (Salt Lake City: Bookcraft, 1956), 226; emphasis added.

- The *Book of Mormon* clearly states that the Prophet Joseph would use the Nephite–Jaredite Urim and Thummim (a distinct instrument, different from Joseph's seer stone(s)).

- While Joseph Smith did possess seer stones, they were inferior to the Nephite Urim and Thummim interpreters. Why would Joseph Smith use a seer stone when he could use the Nephite Urim and Thummim? Why would you use a fork or chopsticks to eat a bowl of tomato soup if you have a spoon sitting there?

Summary of Testimony

All true eyewitnesses of the translation agree that the Urim and Thummim was used. Joseph Smith may very well have had a seer stone or seer stones, but that fact is independent of the translation process. The *Book of Mormon* was translated using the Jaredite and Nephite Urim and Thummim, which consisted of two transparent stones, "set in the rim of a bow fastened to a breast plate."[47]

---

47 Joseph Smith, "Church History," *Times and Seasons* 3 (March 1, 1842): 707.

8

WITNESS #6: OLIVER COWDERY

Of all Joseph Smith's acquaintances, Oliver Cowdery had the closest relationship to the Prophet during the translation period, evident in Cowdery's statement that he was the Prophet's scribe for "the intire [*sic*] book of mormon (save a few pages)."[1] As such, we submit Oliver Cowdery as the defense's next witness.

Meeting the Prophet Joseph Smith

Oliver Cowdery first became acquainted with the translation of the *Book of Mormon* after boarding with the Prophet's parents in Manchester, New York. Oliver taught school in the area and soon began to hear rumors of the "plates from all quarters."[2] He made earnest inquiry of Joseph's father, but Joseph Sr. and Lucy Mack were cautious, avoiding his questions until they were confident they could trust the young teacher. As they began to share, Oliver became strongly impressed that he should "have the privilege of writing for Joseph."[3] He informed Joseph Smith Sr. that he planned to visit the Prophet as soon as school was finished, but the next day Oliver changed his mind. He approached Joseph Smith Sr. with his resolve:

❝❝ The subject upon which we were yesterday conversing, seems working in my very bones, and I cannot for a moment get it out of my mind— finally, I have resolved on what I will do: Samuel [Joseph

1   Reuben Miller journals, 1848-1849; Journal, 1848, 15; Church History Library, https://catalog.lds.org/assets/22222322-f4fe-41e3-aa86-bfc54b94df92/0/14 (accessed: July, 2018).

2   Lucy Mack Smith, History, 1845, 140, The Joseph Smith Papers.

3   Ibid, 141.

Smith's brother], I understand, is going down to Pennsylvania to spend the spring with Joseph, and I shall make my arrangements to be ready to accompany him thither, by the time he recovers his health; for I have made it a subject of prayer, and I firmly believe that it is the **will of the Lord that I should go**— if there is a **work for me** to do in this thing I am determined to do it.[4]

Joseph Smith Sr. had encouraged Oliver, then a young man in his early twenties, to "seek for a testimony for himself." Oliver acted on this advice and subsequently experienced a miraculous vision wherein he was shown the plates, even before he had met the Prophet. As explained by Joseph Smith in his 1832 account of the First Vision:

> *❝* ... [the] Lord appeared unto a young man by the name of Oliver Cowdery and **shewed unto him the plates in a vision** and also the truth of the work and what the Lord was about to do through me his unworthy servant therefore he was desirous to come and write for me[5]

When spring arrived in 1829, Oliver Cowdery and Joseph Smith's brother, Samuel, set out for Harmony, Pennsylvania, in spite of freezing weather, impassable roads, and wind.[6] Their arrival could not have been more timely for the Prophet:

> *❝* ... we [Joseph and Emma Smith] had become reduced in property and my wives [*sic*] father was about to **turn me out of doors** & I had not where to go and I cried unto the Lord that he would provide for me to accomplish the work whereunto he had commanded me ...[7]

Joseph had been crying out to the Lord for three days before Oliver and Samuel arrived. In answer to his pleading, an angel of the Lord promised Joseph that the Lord was sending him a scribe:

---

4   Ibid, 141; emphasis added.

5   Joseph Smith History, in Letterbook 1, ca. 27 Nov. 1832–ca. 4 Aug. 1835, p. 6, The Joseph Smith Papers; emphasis added.

6   Lucy Mack Smith, History, 1845, 143, The Joseph Smith Papers.

7   Joseph Smith History, in Letterbook 1, ca. 27 Nov. 1832–ca. 4 Aug. 1835, p. 6, The Joseph Smith Papers.

❦❦ ... the same should be forth coming [*sic*] in a few days. Accordingly, when Mr. Cowdery told him [Joseph Smith] the business upon which he had come, Joseph was not at all surprized [*sic*].[8]

Translating With the Urim and Thummim

Joseph and Oliver began translating on April 7, 1829. Oliver later reflected on those early days:

❦❦ These were days never to be forgotten—to sit under the sound of a voice dictated by the *inspiration* of heaven, awakened the utmost gratitude of this bosom! Day after day I continued, uninterrupted, to write from his mouth, as he translated, with the *Urim* and *Thummim*, or, as the Nephites would have said, "Interpreters," the history, or record, called the "The book of Mormon."[9]

Oliver's description corroborates and supports the testimonies of the Lord, the ancient prophets, and the Prophet Joseph Smith in all respects. The coming forth of the *Book of Mormon* involved a "*translation*," a work that came to have special significance for Oliver as we shall see in the chapter, "'Study it Out in Your Mind' vs. a Free Gift," in a later volume of this book series. More than perhaps any other individual, Oliver learned that the term "translation" referred to a genuine, literal translation, a process firmly settled in his mind because of his own attempt to translate.[10]

Oliver describes Joseph Smith as using the Urim and Thummim to translate, equating the Urim and Thummim with the "Nephite interpreters," never mentioning a seer stone as part of the translation process. This affirms the testimonies of the ancient prophets, Mosiah, the Brother of Jared, and Moroni, who described the "interpreters" as having two stones,[11] and as the instrument Mosiah used to translate the Jaredite gold plates.[12]

---

8   Lucy Mack Smith, History, 1845, 144, The Joseph Smith Papers.

9   Oliver Cowdery, "Letter I," *Messenger and Advocate* 1 (October 1834): 14.

10   Doctrine and Covenants 8-9.

11   Mosiah 28:13; Ether 3:23-24, 28; Joseph Smith—History 1:35.

12   Mosaiah 28:13-16, 20.

There are other second- and third-hand accounts, based on statements allegedly from Oliver Cowdery, that share similar elements. These accounts mention Joseph translating a record "engraven on gold plates" using "two stones," also called "spectacles,"[13] or producing a "translation from the plates."[14] The one thing noticeably absent from these accounts is the notion that Joseph was reading from a seer stone.

Oliver Cowdery spoke of the Urim and Thummim as the "means" by which Joseph Smith translated the *Book of Mormon* in a letter to W. W. Phelps in 1835.[15] Oliver Cowdery wrote on the origin of the *Book of Mormon* and the rise of the Church. These letters contain historical nuggets for faithful readers of Church history. In "Letter VII," Cowdery declared that the Hill Cumorah, located in upstate New York, is the same geographical hill known to the Nephites as "Cumorah," and to the Jaredites as "Ramah." Brother Cowdery also attempted to dispel some of the derogatory rumors regarding Joseph Smith's character circulating throughout the community. In Letter IV, he recorded the words of Moroni to the Prophet Joseph Smith:

❝ He [Moroni] then proceeded and gave a general account of the promises made to the fathers, and also gave a history of the aborigines of this country [United States of America], and said they were literal descendants of Abraham. He represented them as once being an enlightened and intelligent people, possessing a correct knowledge of the gospel, and the plan of restoration and redemption. He said this history was written and deposited not far from that place, and that it was our brother's [Joseph Smith's] privilege, if obedient to the commandments of the Lord, to obtain, and **translate** the same by the **means of the Urim and Thummim**, which were deposited for that purpose with the record.[16]

Again, this description reminds us that the Urim and Thummim was specifically prepared and deposited to translate the *Book of Mormon*.

---

13   Josiah Jones, "History of the Mormonites," *Evangelist* 9 (June 1, 1841): 134.

14   Edward Stevenson, "The Three Witnesses to the Book of Mormon," *Millennial Star* 48 (July 5, 1886): 420; emphasis added.

15   Oliver Cowdery, "Letter IV," *Messenger and Advocate* 1 (February 1835): 80.

16   Ibid; emphasis added.

Mission to the Lamanites

Brother Cowdery's testimony, imparted throughout his life, includes two important elements relating to the origin, discovery, and translation of the *Book of Mormon*:

- The *Book of Mormon* is the literal, historical record of the ancient inhabitants of America. The hill they called Cumorah is the same geographic hill we recognize today as the "Hill Cumorah."[17] This same hill was also recognized by the Jaredites as the hill "Ramah."

- The *Book of Mormon* was translated by the gift and power of God using a method that very closely paralleled a genuine translation process. Joseph Smith used the ancient plates with their engraven characters to allow the Nephite prophets to speak "from the dust."

Oliver Cowdery bore testimony to both during what became known as the "mission to the Lamanites." Shortly after the 116 pages were lost, the Lord revealed to Joseph Smith that in spite of attempts to "frustrate" the work of God, the Lord would restore the "knowledge of a Savior" and the *Book of Mormon* to both the Latter-day Nephite and Lamanite remnants.[18]

Only six months after the Church was restored, Oliver Cowdery was called to take the Gospel to the Lamanites:

❝ And now, behold, I say unto you that you shall go unto the **Lamanites** *and preach my gospel unto them; and inasmuch as they receive thy teachings thou shalt cause my church to be established among them . . .*[19]

Shortly thereafter, Parley P. Pratt, Peter Whitmer Jr., and Ziba Peterson were called to accompany Oliver Cowdery:

---

17   Oliver Cowdery, "Letter VII," *Messenger and Advocate* 1 (July 1835): 158-159.

18   Doctrine and Covenants 3:17-18. ". . . the Nephites, and the Jacobites, and the Josephites, and the Zoramites, through the testimony of their fathers— And this testimony shall come to the knowledge of the Lamanites, and the Lemuelites, and the Ishmaelites . . ."

19   Doctrine and Covenants 28:8; emphasis added.

▎▎ And that which I have appointed unto him [Parley P. Pratt] is that he shall go with my servants, Oliver Cowdery and Peter Whitmer, Jun., into the wilderness **among the Lamanites.** And Ziba Peterson also shall go with them; and I myself will go with them and be in their midst; and I am their advocate with the Father, and nothing shall prevail against them.[20]

Oliver Cowdery signed a covenant before embarking on his mission, recording his commitment to "proclaim glad tidings of great joy unto [the Lamanites]."[21] Was the term "Lamanites" chosen by Oliver Cowdery or was it chosen by Joseph Smith? The revelations testify that it was the Lord who chose the term "Lamanites" when he referred to the tribes he intended these early missionaries to visit. Since these brethren were called to minister to the "Lamanites," to whom did they go and whom did they teach? According to Parley P. Pratt:

▎▎ ... [we] preached the gospel in its fullness, and distributed the **record of their forefathers** among three tribes, viz: the Catteraugus Indians, near Buffalo, N. Y., the Wyandots of Ohio, and the Delawares west of Missouri.[22]

While visiting with the Delaware, the missionaries approached the Indians by explaining that the *Book of Mormon* was a record of *their* ancestors and that they had been sent to deliver the translation of this ancient writing to their people:

---

20   Doctrine and Covenants 32:2-3; emphasis added.

21   Covenant of Oliver Cowdery and Others, 17 October 1830, The Joseph Smith Papers. Published in "Mormonism—Nos. VIII—IX," *The Ohio Star* 2 (December 8): 1831; emphasis added. "I, Oliver, being commanded by the Lord God, to go forth unto the Lamanites, to proclaim glad tidings of great joy unto them, by presenting unto them the fullness of the Gospel, of the only begotten Son of God; and also, to rear up a pillar as a witness where the temple of God shall be built, in the glorious New Jerusalem; and having certain brothers with me, who are called of God to assist me, whose names are Parley, and Peter and Ziba, do therefore most solemnly covenant with God that I will walk humbly before him, and do this business, and this glorious work according as he shall direct me by the Holy Ghost; ever praying for mine and their prosperity, and deliverance from bonds, from imprisonment, and whatsoever may befall us, with all patience and faith. Amen. [Signed] Oliver Cowdery."

22   Parley P. Pratt, *Autobiography of Parley P. Pratt* (Chicago: King & Law, 1888), 61.

❙❙ We immediately inquired for the residence of the principal Chief, and were soon introduced to an aged and venerable looking man .... He [the principal Chief] was at first unwilling to call his council; made several excuses, and finally refused; as he had ever been opposed to the introduction of missionaries among his tribe. We continued the conversation a little longer, till he at last began to understand the **nature of the Book.** He then **changed his mind**; became **suddenly interested**, and requested us to proceed no further with our conversation till he could call a council. He despatched a messenger, and in about an hour had some forty men collected around us in his lodge, who, after shaking us by the hand, were seated in silence; and in a grave and dignified manner awaited the announcement of what we had to offer.[23]

After the Delaware council gathered, Oliver Cowdery arose and introduced the *Book of Mormon* by giving a history of its translation.

❙❙ Thousands of moons ago, when the **red men's forefathers** dwelt in peace and possessed this whole land, the Great Spirit talked with them, and revealed His law and His will, and much knowledge to their wise men and prophets. This they **wrote in a Book**; together with their **history**, and the things which should befall their children in the latter days. This Book was written on plates of gold, and **handed down from father to son** for many ages and generations....

This Book, which contained these things, was hid in the earth by Moroni, in a hill called by him, Cumorah, which hill is now in the State of New York, near the village of Palmyra, in Ontario County.

In that neighborhood there lived a young man named Joseph Smith, who prayed to the Great Spirit much, in order that he might know the truth; and the Great Spirit sent an angel to him, and told him where this Book was hid by Moroni; and commanded him to go and get it. He accordingly went to the place, and dug in the earth, and found the Book written on golden plates.[24]

---

23   Ibid, 56-57; emphasis added.
24   Ibid, 58-59; emphasis added.

Oliver Cowdery clearly knew that the *Book of Mormon* record we read today was taken from literal plates, which contained the historical account of the ancient inhabitants of North America. He knew that the descendants of Lehi still lived and he told the Native American Delaware council that he had assisted Joseph in the translation of the record of *their* forefathers. There he stood, having traveled hundreds of miles to restore this history to a portion of Lehi's descendants, termed by the Lord, "Lamanites."

Oliver Cowdery described the coming forth of the *Book of Mormon* to the Delaware council in these terms:

// But it [the Nephite plates] was **written in the language of the forefathers of the red man**; therefor [*sic*] this young man, being a pale face, could not understand it; but the angel told him and showed him, and **gave him knowledge of the language**, and how to interpret the Book.[25]

The Nephite plates were engraven with an authentic "language of the forefathers of the red man," an ancient North American language. To read the *Book of Mormon* record, the Prophet Joseph Smith had to find a way to take these ancient characters and translate them into English. Since he "could not understand" the language, Oliver testified that the angel "gave him knowledge of the language" and "how to interpret the Book." Clearly, we can see that Joseph was not reading from a seer stone, but was translating metal plates with literal ancient characters:

// So he **interpreted** it into the **language of the pale faces**, and wrote it on paper, and caused it to be printed, and published thousands of copies of it among them; and then sent us to the red men to bring some copies of it to them, and to tell them this news. So we have now come from him, and here is a copy of the Book, which we now present to our red friend, the chief of the Delawares, and which we hope he will cause to be read and known among his tribe; it will do them good.[26]

Oliver Cowdery's approach to teaching the Lamanite tribes in Missouri was to appeal to the historicity of the *Book of Mormon*. This

25 Ibid, 59; emphasis added.
26 Ibid; emphasis added.

record was not a heart-warming fable read from a seer stone—it was an actual ancient record, which had been translated by one of the "pale faces." Since the Nephite language had been lost, how did Joseph Smith translate? Oliver Cowdery states that the angel, Moroni, "gave him knowledge of the language." He didn't give him a seer stone. He taught him the language. This was done through a number of means including the Urim and Thummim, the Nephite plates, and revelation.

While the Delaware chief was leery of the missionaries at first, he responded to this connection with his heritage. A religious book? Not interested. A history of *my* people, of *my* ancestors, of *my* bloodline? Yes! Oliver Cowdery's understanding that the *Book of Mormon* was a genuinely translated historical record opened hearts and doors that would otherwise have been locked.

Was Joseph Smith a Treasure Digger?

Recalling the animosity leveled against the Prophet and his family because he claimed to have seen visions, Joseph Smith remembered that, "rumor with her thousand tongues was all the time employed in circulating falsehoods about my father's family, and about myself. If I were to relate a thousandth part of them, it would fill up volumes."[27] Surprisingly, progressive historians have adopted those old rumors and reshaped them as "new verified facts." For example, some progressive historians declare their belief that Joseph Smith was involved in "treasure-digging activities." The scholars who wrote the introduction to the Joseph Smith Papers' volume, *Revelations and Translations, Volume 3: Printer's Manuscript of the Book of Mormon*, argue that Joseph Smith deceptively or artfully avoided addressing his supposed treasure digging activities because, they suggest, he was afraid it would tarnish his reputation in the Church:

❪❪ The Smiths and many in their community drew upon long-established traditions of what some scholars have termed **folk religion** or **folk magic** . . . Faced with rumors that he was an **active** or even **leading participant** in local **treasure-digging** activities and concerned that his **history might prove an obstacle** for some to accepting his religious message, Joseph Smith rarely mentioned

27   Joseph Smith—History 1:61.

his participation in treasure digging and never in great detail. But **neither did he deny** his early activities.... The caution with which Joseph Smith wrote about his **involvement in treasure digging** suggests that he was mindful of an audience largely skeptical of such activities.[28]

If Oliver Cowdery were here today, he would no doubt laugh, or perhaps cry, at the ignorant claims made by these historians. In 1834, Oliver Cowdery specifically detailed his own refutation of the allegations that Joseph Smith was a treasure digger:

*❧ ...a gentleman [Josiah Stowell] from the south part of the State, (Chenango County,) **employed** our brother [Joseph Smith] as a **common labourer**, and accordingly he visited that section of the country; and had he not been accused of digging down all, or nearly so, the mountains of Susquehannah [sic], or causing others to do it by some art of necromancy, I should leave this, for the present, unnoticed.... Some forty miles south, or down the river, in the town of Harmony, Susquehannah [sic] county, Pa. is said to be a cave ... such is said to be the case,—when a company of Spaniards, a long time since, when the country was uninhabited by white settlers, excavated from the bowels of the earth ore, and coined a large quantity of money; ... Enough however, was credited of the Spaniard's story, to excite the belief of many that there was a fine sum of the precious metal being coined in this subterraneous vault, among whom was our employer [Stowell]; and accordingly our brother [Joseph Smith] was **required to spend a few months** with some others in excavating the earth, in pursuit of this treasure.[29]*

Oliver Cowdery pointed out that Joseph was employed as a "common labourer" by Josiah Stowell who *required* him to work with other men digging and searching for an old Spanish mine. Stowell believed the legends of Spanish treasure circulating about the area, and had begun

---

28   "Introduction to Revelations and Translations: Volume 3 - Printer's Manuscript of the Book of Mormon," in *The Joseph Smith Papers: Revelations and Translations, Volume 3, Part 1: Printer's Manuscript of the Book of Mormon, 1 Nephi 1-Alma 35*, vol. 3 (Church Historian's Press, 2013); emphasis added.

29   Oliver Cowdery, "Letter VIII," *Messenger and Advocate* 2 (October 1835): 200-201; emphasis added.

digging for the mine *before* Joseph was hired. In the end, Joseph finally succeeded in convincing Stowell to "give up" the venture. Joseph Smith explained:

❞ In the month of October, 1825, I hired with an old gentleman by the name of Josiah Stoal, who lived in Chenango county, State of New York. He had heard something of a silver mine having been opened by the Spaniards in Harmony, Susquehanna county, State of Pennsylvania; and had, **previous to my hiring to him**, been digging, in order, if possible, to discover the mine. After I went to live with him, he took me, with the rest of his hands, to dig for the silver mine, at which I continued to work for nearly a month, without success in our undertaking, and **finally I prevailed with the old gentleman to cease digging after it**. Hence arose the very prevalent story of my having been a money-digger.[30]

Both Joseph Smith and Oliver Cowdery attest that the claims suggesting that Joseph Smith had a career in treasure digging, or that he ever led such expeditions, guided by his seer stone in search of "lost objects" and "lost treasure," were nothing more than "false and slanderous reports."[31]

Oliver Cowdery's Testimony in 1848

Sadly, Oliver Cowdery fell away and was excommunicated from the Church in 1838. However, four years after the death of the Prophet Joseph Smith, Oliver Cowdery traveled to Winter Quarters, Nebraska where he humbly asked to be re-baptized. In 1848, Brother Cowdery spoke at a conference in Iowa. Reuben Miller, one of the members present at that meeting, recorded Oliver Cowdery as he shared his eyewitness testimony of the coming forth of the *Book of Mormon*:

❞ Friends and brethren my name is Cowdery, Oliver Cowdery, In the early history of this Church I stood Identified with her. And one in her councils. . . . [I was called] to fulfil the purposes and will of god he called me to a high and holy calling, I wrote with

---

30   Joseph Smith—History 1:56; emphasis added.

31   Oliver Cowdery, "Letter VIII," *Messenger and Advocate* 2 (October 1835): 200.

my own pen the intire [*sic*] Book of Mormon (save a few pages) as it fell from the lips of the prophet. As he **translated** it by the gift and power of god, By the **means of the urim and thummim**, or as it is called by that book **holy Interpreters.**

I beheld with my eyes, And handled with my hands the gold **plates from which it was translated.** I also beheld the **Interpreters.** That book is true. Sidney Rigdon did not write it. Mr Spaulding did not write it. I wrote it myself as it fell from the lips of the prophet.

... It contains principles of salvation And if you will walk by its light and obey [its?] precepts you will be saved in the everlasting Kingdom of god.[32]

- More than 150 years later, Oliver Cowdery's testimony is stirring and unforgettable. The transcription of Oliver's words have been carefully scrutinized. Historian Richard Lloyd Anderson has said:

// The Miller journal can be tested by comparing it with official records of the Cowdery speeches, and it is clearly accurate. Thus the above words are likely to be Cowdery verbatim.[33]

Throughout his life Oliver Cowdery never referred to a translation process involving a seer stone or a "stone in a hat." He spoke extensively of the plates and of the use of the Urim and Thummim during the translation process. He explained that they were called by the Nephites, "Interpreters." Moreover, Oliver Cowdery never retracted his testimony. Therefore, we submit to the jury that Oliver Cowdery's testimony carries the commensurate weight of one who witnessed the translation closer than anyone else other than the translator (Joseph Smith) himself. His testimony remained constant and unchanged despite his temporary estrangement with the translator-prophet, Joseph Smith, and his intimate details and unwavering testimony of the translation process position him as a solid and sound witness of the translation of the *Book of Mormon*.

---

32   Reuben Miller journals, 1848-1849; Journal, 1848, 15; Church History Library, https://catalog.lds.org/assets/22222322-f4fe-41e3-aa86-bfc54b94df92/0/14 (accessed: July, 2018); emphasis added.

33   Richard Lloyd Anderson, "By the Gift and Power of God," *Ensign*, September 1977.

9

MORMONISM UNVAILED: HURLBUT ON TRIAL

A review of the testimony given by the Lord, the ancient prophets, the Prophet Joseph Smith, and his principal scribe, Oliver Cowdery, unanimously and harmoniously testify that Joseph Smith translated the Nephite plates by studying the engravings. He translated the characters by means of the Urim and Thummim, which consisted of two transparent stones set in the rim of a bow fastened to a breastplate. No credible statements support the notion that Joseph Smith used a seer stone at any time for the translation.

Since the testimonies of these eyewitnesses are clear and consistent, what was the origin of the seer stone narrative? Why do progressive historians claim we should rewrite Latter-day Saint history to reflect a "new narrative"?

To answer this question, and to properly present our defense against the charges brought by the plaintiff, we next submit for evaluation some of the sources—the books, papers, and footnotes of publications that advocate and popularize the seer stone hypothesis today. This list includes books such as *Joseph Smith: Rough Stone Rolling* (Richard L. Bushman), *Joseph Smith's Seer Stones* (Michael Hubbard MacKay and Nicholas J. Frederick), and research papers such as *A Pathway to Prophethood: Joseph Smith Junior as Rodsman, Village Seer, and Judeo-Christian Prophet* (Mark Ashurst-McGee). A careful analysis of these sources reveals that one book appears repeatedly as a "source" of the new narrative: *Mormonism Unvailed* [sic] published in 1834 by E. D. Howe.

For example, in the book *Joseph Smith's Seer Stones*, authors MacKay and Frederick write:

// . . . Willard Chase was also interested in divination and money digging, and it is quite possible that Joseph **found one of his seer stones** with him on the Chase family property.[1]

Footnote #11 leads the reader to *"Mormonism Unvailed*, 240-45." Similarly, author and professor Alexander L. Baugh uses *Mormonism Unvailed* to support the same Willard Chase claim that "The young prophet obtained a seer stone, described as dark brown in color, while digging a well for Willard Chase around 1822."[2]

In *A Pathway to Prophethood*, Mark Ashurst-McGee claims:

// The modes of **divination employed by Joseph Smith Senior** [father of the Joseph Smith] are **better documented.** . . . In 1833, Peter Ingersoll, whose farm adjoined the Smith farm, reported that he had seen father Smith divine with "a small stick in his hand" in the spring of 1822 or 1823 and on another occasion sometime before 1827.[3]

Ashurst-McGee's footnote #76 refers to "Peter Ingersoll, statement, Palmyra, New York, 2 December 1833, quoted in Howe, *Mormonism Unvailed*, 232-34."

In Richard Bushman's work, *Joseph Smith: Rough Stone Rolling*, Bushman makes the extraordinary claim, "Magic and religion melded in Smith family culture."[4] His footnote #86 includes "Peter Ingersoll, William Stafford, Willard Chase, and Henry Harris, Affidavits (1833); Abigail Harris, Statement (1833), all in *MoU* [Mormonism Unvailed], 232-34, 238, 239, 242, 251-53."

---

1   Michael Hubbard MacKay and Nicholas J. Frederick, *Joseph Smith's Seer Stones* (Provo, UT: BYU Religious Studies Center, 2016), 8; emphasis added.

2   Alexander L. Baugh, "How Joseph Smith Received Visions Through Seer Stones and the Urim and Thummim," December 12, 2017, accessed January 2019, http://www.ldsliving.com/How-Joseph-Smith-Received-Visions-Through-Seer-Stones-and-the-Urim-and-Thummim/s/87263.

3   Mark Ashurst-McGee, *A Pathway to Prophethood: Joseph Smith Junior as Rodsman, Village Seer, and Judeo-Christian Prophet*, Master's thesis, Utah State University, 2000, 74; emphasis added.

4   Richard L. Bushman, *Joseph Smith: Rough Stone Rolling* (New York: Alfred A. Knopf, 2005), 51.

References to *Mormonism Unvailed* continue throughout the book, each mimicking the pseudo claim that the Smith family was lazy, involved in magic and treasure digging, and so forth. *Mormonism Unvailed* also perpetuates the claim that Joseph Smith dictated the *Book of Mormon* by reading from a seer stone in a hat:

❝ The translation finally commenced. They [the plates] were found to contain a language not now known upon the earth, which they termed 'reformed Egyptian characters.' The plates, therefore, which had been so much talked of, were found to be of **no manner of use**. After all, the Lord showed and communicated to him every word and letter of the Book. **Instead of looking at the characters** inscribed upon the plates, the prophet was obliged to resort to the **old 'peep stone,'** which he **formerly used in money-digging**. This he placed in a hat, or box, into which he also thrust his face. Through the stone he could then discover a single word at a time, which he repeated aloud to his amanuensis [scribe], who committed it to paper, when another word would immediately appear, and thus the performance continued to the end of the book.[5]

The manner in which he pretended to read and interpret, was the **same as when he looked for the money-diggers,** with the **stone in his hat**, and his hat over his face, while the Book of Plates were at the same time **hid in the woods!**[6]

The seer stone plaintiff in this case has introduced *Mormonism Unvailed* as an exhibit in this trial. As defendants of the "traditional narrative," we challenge the authenticity of this evidence, first, due to the scandalous character of its authors, specifically Doctor Philastus Hurlbut and E. D. Howe, and second, due to the demonstrably false accusations made therein. We submit that the "testimony" presented in *Mormonism Unvailed* is unreliable hearsay.

What does *Mormonism Unvailed* represent and should Latter-day Saints view this work as a credible authority on the life of Joseph Smith and his family?

---

5   Eber D. Howe, *Mormonism Unvailed* (Painesville, 1834), 18; emphasis added.
6   Ibid, 265; emphasis added. (Isaac Hale Affidavit)

Doctor Philastus Hurlbut: Membership and Excommunication

Mormonism Unvailed was among the first known "anti-Mormon" publications and represents the first significant published opposition to the Prophet Joseph Smith and the Restoration. First released in 1834 by Eber D. Howe, *Mormonism Unvailed* included affidavits and research collected by Latter-day Saint dissenter, Doctor Philastus Hurlbut.

Eber D. Howe was the founder and editor of the *Painesville Telegraph* in Painesville, Ohio. Howe's wife, Sophia, and her sister, Harriet became members of The Church of Jesus Christ of Latter-day Saints, known previously as the Church of Christ, or The Church of the Latter Day Saints, and Sophia even donated money in 1834.[7] That same year, her husband connected with an excommunicated member of the Church, Doctor Philastus Hurlbut, to publish an expose of Joseph Smith and the Restoration. He titled that work, *Mormonism Unvailed*.

Doctor Philastus Hurlbut was not a doctor of medicine or anything else, but rather, carried the name, "Doctor" as his given first name. The Prophet Joseph Smith rightly labeled him, "not so much a doctor of physic, as of falsehood, or by name."[8] Hurlbut joined the Church sometime in 1832-33 and was ordained an elder by Sidney Rigdon on March 18, 1833.[9] His membership was short lived as less than two months later, on June 3, 1833, Hurlbut "was accused of unchristian conduct with the female sex while on a mission to the east." His "commission [was] taken from him" and he was excommunicated from the Church.[10]

Hurlbut was absent during the June 3, 1833 trial, and upon returning to Kirtland claimed that, "Strict justice was not done me."[11] Hurlbut appealed the decision whereon a "re-hearing" was held on June 21, 1833. Hurlbut "begged to be forgiven, made every promise that a

7 Joseph Smith, "Joseph Smith Jrs Book for Record," Journal, 30 April 1834, 84, The Joseph Smith Papers.

8 Joseph Smith to "the Elders of the Church of the Latter Day Saints," 30 Nov. 1835-1 Dec. 1835, 228, The Joseph Smith Papers. Published in the *Messenger and Advocate* 2 (December 1835): 228.

9 Minute Book 1, 18 March 1833, 12, The Joseph Smith Papers.

10 Minute Book 1, 3 June 1833, 12, The Joseph Smith Papers.

11 Minute Book 1, 21 June 1833, 21, The Joseph Smith Papers.

man could make that he would from that day live a virtuous life."[12]
The Council decided to accept and trust Hurlbut's plea. According
to minutes from the trial:

❧ ... Brother Hurlbut's case was laid before the Court & the testimony
against him given by Orson Hyde & Hyrum Smith and duly
investigated. It was decided that Brother Hurlbut should be
forgiven because of the liberal confession which he made. This
council decided that the Bishop's council **decided correctly before**,
and that Brother Hurlbut's crime was **sufficient to cut him off**
from the church, but on his confession, he was restored—Joseph
Smith Jr[13]

While the council believed the sincerity of Hurlbut's confession and
his promises, the Prophet Joseph Smith was not moved. The Prophet's
cousin, George A. Smith, was present at the June 21, 1833 meeting
and remembered:

❧ As soon as this Council had made this decision upon Hurlburt
[*sic*], Joseph arose, and said to the Council, he is **not honest**, and
what he has promised he will not fulfil; what he has confessed are
not the thoughts and intents of his heart, and time will prove it.[14]

Some may have felt the Prophet was being too harsh or overly
judgmental, but just two days later, his forewarning proved accurate.
Hurlbut's case reopened and he was again excommunicated from the
Church after he was caught bragging that "he had **deceived Joseph
Smith**; **God**, or the Spirit by which he is actuated." Hurlbut was
convicted by the corroborated testimony of Brothers Solomon "Gee
of Thompson" and Curtis Hodges.[15] George A. Smith later recalled
Hurlbut's boast:

---

12   George A. Smith, "Historical Discourse," in *Journal of Discourses*, vol. 11
(Liverpool, 1867), 8.

13   Minute Book 1, 21 June 1833, 21, The Joseph Smith Papers; emphasis added;
spelling modernized.

14   George A. Smith, "Historical Discourse," in *Journal of Discourses*, vol. 11 (Liverpool, 1867), 8; emphasis added.

15   Minute Book 1, 21-23 June 1833, 22, The Joseph Smith Papers; emphasis
added.

❙❙ I [Hurlbut] have proved that Council has **no wisdom**, I told them I was sorry I confessed and they believed it to be an honest confession, **I deceived the whole of them** and made them restore me to the Church.[16]

It should be noted that Hurlbut did not repent of his immoral conduct; his conscience was seared and past feeling. On May 27, 1839, Sidney Rigdon reported in a letter that "After his [Hurlbut's] exclusion, he swore—for he was vilely profane—that he would have revenge, and commenced his work."[17]

Hurlbut Incites Persecution Against Joseph Smith

Following Hurlbut's excommunication, the Prophet Joseph Smith and the other brethren were no doubt hopeful that this would be the last they would hear of the lying schemer, Doctor Hurlbut. However, Hurlbut became bitter and began circulating lies and threatening violence against the Prophet. On August 18, 1833, the Prophet wrote a letter to church leaders in Jackson County, Missouri:

❙❙ ... the harder the persecution the greater the gifts of God upon his church yea all things shall work together for good to them who are willing to lay down their lives for Christ sake we are suffering **great persecution** on account of one man by the name of Doctor **Hurlbut** who has been expelled from the church for **lude and adulterous** conduct and to **spite us** he is **lying** in a wonderful manner and the people are running after him and giving him money to break down Mormonism which much **endangers our lives** at present but **God will put a stop to his career** soon and all will be well ...[18]

While persecution was intensifying in Ohio, the Prophet began receiving word of violent acts being committed against the Saints in Missouri. On July 20, 1833, the Latter-Day Saint printing office

---

16   George A. Smith, "Historical Discourse," in *Journal of Discourses*, vol. 11 (Liverpool, 1867), 8; emphasis added.

17   James Henry Flanigan, *Mormonism Triumphant!* (Liverpool, 1849), 10.

18   Joseph Smith to Leaders in Jackson County, Missouri, 18 Aug. 1833, 3, The Joseph Smith Papers; emphasis added; spelling modernized.

in Independence was destroyed.[19] On November 4, 1833, three men were killed in a confrontation known as the Battle of Crooked Creek, and several Church leaders were imprisoned.[20] By November 8, 1833, members of the Church were fleeing the land they had envisioned would become the New Jerusalem in Jackson County, Missouri. Later that month, Joseph Smith received word that the mobs had successfully expelled the Latter-day Saints.[21] Heartbroken and unable to render any assistance, Joseph encouraged the brethren to seek redress for their grievances:

❝ … It is your privilege [*sic*] to use every lawful means in your power to seek redress for your grievances of your enemies and prosecute them to the extent of the Law but it will be impossable [*sic*] for us to render you any assistance in a temporal point of view as our means are already exhausted and are deeply in debt and know no means whereby we shall be able to extricate ourselves.

The inhabitants of this county **threaten our destruction** and we know not how soon they may be permitted to follow the examples of the Missourians but our trust is in God and we are determined by his grace assisting us to maintain the cause and hold out faithful unto the end that we may be crowned with crowns of celestial glory and enter into that rest that is prepared for the children of God.[22]

The Church in Kirtland was penniless, unable to send assistance, and Joseph was running for his life in the face of threatened violence from various men, including Hurlbut. On December 21, 1833, Joseph Smith was compelled to file a complaint with Kirtland Justice of the Peace, John Dowen, explaining that he had "reason to fear that Doctor

---

19　"To His Excellency, Daniel Dunklin, Governor of the State of Missouri," *The Evening and Morning Star* (December 1833): 228.

20　Joseph Smith History, volume A-1, 4 November 1833, 368-370, Joseph Smith Papers.

21　Joseph Smith, "Joseph Smith Jrs Book for Record," Journal, 25 November 1833, 28, The Joseph Smith Papers.

22　Joseph Smith History, volume A-1, 5 December 1833, 388-389, Joseph Smith Papers. See also, Letter to Edward Partridge, 5 December 1833, p. 65, The Joseph Smith Papers; emphasis added.

P. Hurlbut would Beat wound or kill him or injure his property."[23]
Joseph's cousin, George A. Smith, later recalled:

/ / In consequence of the persecution which raged against the Prophet
Joseph and the constant threats to do him violence it was found
necessary to keep **continual guard** to **prevent his being murdered**
by his enemies, who were headed by Joseph H. Wakefield and **Dr.
P. Hurlbert** ... during the fall and winter I took part of this service
going 2½ miles to guard at President Rigdon's.[24]

Thankfully, Justice Dowen did act by allowing the issuance of a
warrant for the arrest of Hurlbut, requesting that he be apprehended
and brought before Painesville Justice of the Peace, William Holbrook.[25]

Meanwhile, Hurlbut had been busy stirring the public against the
Church and against the Smith family. After his excommunication, he
began delivering oppositional lectures against the Church in Kirtland
and collecting donations from "many leading citizens of Kirtland
and Geauga Co."[26] The donors wanted Hurlbut to "obtain affidavits
showing the bad character of the Mormon Smith family."[27] Hurlbut
didn't need to be asked twice. He swore that "he would wash his hands
in Joseph Smith's blood."[28]

23   Docket Entry, between 4 and 15 January 1834 [State of Ohio v. D. P. Hurl-
but], 432, The Joseph Smith Papers.

24   George A. Smith papers, 1834-1877, p. 12; Autobiographical Writings; Mem-
oirs of George A. Smith, circa 1860-1882; Church History Library, https://catalog.
lds.org/assets/4c08ca0f-21d3-4f93-bce3-907010163446/0/19 (accessed: March 9,
2019)

25   John C. Dowen, Statement, January 2, 1885, Chicago Historical Society, 3.

26   Howe, Eber D. Statement to Arthur B. Deming, dated April 8, 1885. Original
in Arthur B. Deming file, Mormon Collection, Chicago Historical Society Library.

27   Ibid.

28   George A. Smith, "Historical Discourse," in *Journal of Discourses*, vol. 11
(Liverpool, 1867), 8.

10

MORMONISM UNVAILED: HURLBUT'S AFFIDAVITS

Hurlbut traveled throughout New York, Pennsylvania, and Ohio gathering statements from neighbors and other locals who claimed to have known Joseph Smith and his family. By December 11, 1833, he had collected 14 statements but his "research" was anything but unbiased and honest.

Hurlbut was being paid to produce antagonistic material. The committee commissioning Hurlbut announced on January 31, 1834, that they were about to publish evidence that would "prove" the *Book of Mormon* to be a "work of fiction and imagination" and would "completely divest Joseph Smith of all claims to the character of an honest man, and place him at an immeasurable distance from the high station which he pretends to occupy."[1] Ironically, two weeks before, a preliminary hearing had determined that there was sufficient evidence (of Hurlbut threatening violence to the Prophet Joseph Smith) to send the case to the county court.[2] Apparently the committee publishing Hurlbut's material didn't mind the sketchy character and background of the reporter.

How did Hurlbut gather the claimed "evidence" that would "completely divest Joseph Smith" of all honor, character, and virtue? One neighbor later remembered, "He [Hurlbut] came to me, but he could not get out of me what he wanted; so he went to others."[3] This

---

1   "To the Public," *Painesville Telegraph* (Geauga County), January 31, 1834.

2   Gordon A. Madsen, Jeffrey N. Walker, and John W. Welch, *Sustaining the Law: Joseph Smith's Legal Encounters* (Provo, UT: BYU Studies, 2014), 145.

3   Benjamin Saunders, interview by William H. Kelley, *Miscellany*, 1884, 19.

statement comes to us from Benjamin Saunders, the brother-in-law of Willard Chase, an occultic Methodist minister who had led many escapades with the intent to steal the plates while Joseph Smith was living in New York in 1827-28.[4] Apparently, however, Benjamin was not willing to perjure himself as the others did.

It would be inaccurate to say that all of Joseph Smith's former neighbors and acquaintances were negative and antagonistic to the Smith family. In order to produce the materials he needed, Hurlbut had to conduct selective research. Oliver Cowdery also interviewed many of those who knew the Smith family:

// By some he [Joseph Smith] is said to have been a lazy, idle, vicious, profligate fellow. These I am prepared to contradict, and that too by the testimony of **many persons** with whom I have been intimately acquainted, and know to be individuals of the strictest veracity, and unquestionable integrity. All these strictly and virtually agree in saying, that he was an **honest, upright, virtuous, and faithfully industrious young man.**

And those who say to the contrary can be influenced by no other motive than to destroy the reputation of one who never injured any man in either property or person. While young, I have been informed he was afflicted with sickness; but I have been told by those for whom he has labored, that he was a young man of **truth and industrious habits.**[5]

A review of Hurlbut's "affidavits" reveal that some contain entirely baseless, fabricated slanders, while others report distorted events, manipulated to deprecate the Prophet Joseph Smith. For example, David Stafford reportedly told Hurlbut that Joseph Smith once attacked him after drinking too freely:

// Previous to his going to Pennsylvania to get married, we worked together making a coal pit. While working at one time, a dispute arose between us (he having drinked a little too freely), and some hard words passed between us, and as usual with him at such times,

4   Lucy Mack Smith, History, 1845, 108, 116-117, The Joseph Smith Papers.
5   Oliver Cowdery, "Letter VIII," *Messenger and Advocate* 2 (October 1835): 200; emphasis added.

was for fighting. He got the advantage of me in the scuffle, and a gentleman by the name of Ford interfered, when Joseph turned to fighting him. We both entered a complaint against him, and he was fined for the breach of the peace.[6]

The Prophet responded to Stafford's accusation during a dinner in 1843. Contrary to Stafford's dramatic narrative, Joseph explained that in reality Stafford had allowed his hog to invade the Smith cornfield. The Smith family watchdog "bit off an ear" of the hog and Stafford responded by cruelly shooting the dog. A scuffle ensued between Joseph and Stafford and his gang of violent friends:

▌▌ ... while supper was preparing, Joseph related an anecdote. While young, his father had a fine large watchdog which bit off an ear from David Stafford's hog, which **Stafford had turned into** [the] **Smith cornfield**. Stafford **shot the dog**, and with six other fellows **pitched upon him unawares** and Joseph whipped the whole of them and escaped unhurt, which they swore to as recorded in **Hurlbut's or Eber Howe's book** ...[7]

Stafford's misrepresentation of history was only one of the so-called "affidavits" that Hurlbut eagerly snatched up. There were those who supported the Smiths and considered them honest, hard-working and devout, while others were eager to ridicule. This was in fulfillment of prophecy and has ever been the case. The Prophet was told at age seventeen that:

▌▌ [His] name should be had for **good** and **evil** among **all** nations, kindreds, and tongues, or that it should be both good and evil spoken of among **all** people.[8]

In other words, upon close acquaintance with the Prophet, each individual either hates him or loves him, either fights him or defends him. The choice is darkness or light.

---

6   Eber D. Howe, "Testimony of David Stafford," *Mormonism Unvailed* (Painesville, 1834), 249.

7   Joseph Smith, "President Joseph Smith's Journal," Journal, Book 1, 1 January 1843, 34, The Joseph Smith Papers; spelling and punctuation modernized; emphasis added.

8   Joseph Smith History, volume A-1, 5, Joseph Smith Papers; emphasis added.

Jonathan H. Hale visited Palmyra, New York in 1835, recording in his journal:

// We went about in the Neighborhood from house to house to inquire the Character of Joseph Smith jr previous to his receiving the Book of Mormon The amount was that his **Character was as good** as young men in General. this was on the 30 day of May 1835.[9]

When John S. Carter, a member of the Church, traveled through Palmyra, New York shortly before Hurlbut would make the same trip, he recalled:

// the people [were] greatly opposed to the work of God. Talked with many of them, & found them **unable to make out anything against Joseph Smith** altho [sic] they talked hard against him.[10]

Several men and women who knew the Smith family before the organization of the Church, but did not accept the Restoration of the Gospel, remembered the Smiths as hard-working, industrious and honest:

// My father owned a farm near that of the Smith family, in New York. My parents were friends of the Smith family, which was **one of the best** in that locality—**honest, religious and industrious**, but poor. The father of the family was **above the average in intelligence.** I have heard my parents say that he bore the appearance of having descended from royalty. Mrs. Smith was called "Mother Smith" by many. **Children loved to go to her home.**

My father loved young Joseph Smith and often hired him to work with his boys. I was about six years old when he first came to our home. I remember going into the field on an afternoon to play in the corn rows while my brothers worked. When evening came, I was too tired to walk home and cried because my brothers refused

---

9   Jonathan H. Hale, "Jonathan H. Hale Reminiscences and Journals, 1837-1840," Church History Catalog, pp. 6-7, accessed February 2019, https://catalog.lds.org/assets/711eb3cd-b800-4113-92a0-447619d09f72/1/5; emphasis added.

10   Diary of John S. Carter, in Davis Bitton, *Guide to Mormon Diaries and Autobiographies* (Provo, UT: Brigham Young University Press, 1977), 62.

to carry me. Joseph lifted me to his shoulder, and with his arm thrown across my feet to steady me, and my arm about his neck, **he carried me to our home.**

I remember the excitement stirred up among some of the people over Joseph's First Vision, and of hearing my father contend that it was only the sweet dream of a pure minded boy. One of our church leaders came to my father to remonstrate against his allowing such close friendship between his family and the 'Smith Boy,' as he called him. My father defended his own position by saying that **Joseph was the best help he had ever found.** He told the churchman that he always fixed the time of hoeing his large field to that when he could secure the services of Joseph Smith, because of the **influence that boy had over the wild boys** of the neighborhood, and explained that when these boys, or young men, worked by themselves much time would be spent in arguing and quarreling, which often ended in a ring fight. But when Joseph Smith worked with them, the **work went steadily forward,** and he got the full worth of the wages he paid.

I remember the churchman saying, in a very solemn and impressive tone, that the very influence the boy carried was the danger they feared for the coming generation, that not only the young men, but all who came in contact with him, would follow him, and he must be put down.

Not until Joseph had had a second vision and begun to write a book which drew many of the best and brightest people of the churches away did my parents come to a realization of the fact that their friend, the churchman, had told them the truth. Then, my family cut off their friendship for all the Smiths, for all the family followed Joseph. Even the father, intelligent man that he was, could not discern the evil he was helping to promote.

My parents then lent all the aid they could in helping to crush Joseph Smith; but it was too late. He had run his course too long. He could not be put down. There was **never a truer, purer, nobler boy than Joseph Smith,** before he was led away by superstition."[11]

---

11   Hyrum L. Andrus and Helen Mae Andrus, eds., They Knew the Prophet (Salt Lake City: Bookcraft, 1974), 1–2; emphasis added. Also "Stories from

Thomas H. Taylor reported to missionaries for the *Reorganized Church of Jesus Christ of Latter-day Saints*:

❦ ❦ To our inquiries if he was acquainted with the Smiths, and the early settlers throughout that part sometimes called Mormons, Mr. Taylor said:

Yes, I knew them very well. They were very nice men, too. The only trouble was they were **ahead of the people**; and the people, as in every such case, turned out to abuse them, because they had the **manhood to stand for their own convictions**. I have seen such work all through life.

What did the Smiths do that the people abused them so?

They did not do anything. Why! these rascals at one time took Joseph Smith and ducked him in the pond that you see over there, just because he preached what he believed, and for nothing else. And if Jesus Christ had been there, they would have done the same to Him. Now I don't believe like he did; but every man has a right to his religious opinions, and to advocate his views, too. If people don't like it, let them come out and meet him on the stand, and show his error. Smith was always ready to exchange views with the best men they had.

"Why didn't they like Smith?"

To tell the truth, there was something about him they could not understand. Some way he knew more than they did, and it made them mad.

But a good many tell terrible stories, about them being rogues, and liars, and such things. How is that?

Oh! they are a set of d- - - - d liars. I have had a home here, and been here, except when on business, all my life—ever since I came to this country—and I know these fellows. They make these lies on

---

the Notebook of Martha Cox, Grandmother of Fern Cox Anderson," Church Historian's Library, Salt Lake City, Utah. Also Lee C. LaFayette, "Recollections of Joseph Smith," Church Historian's Library, Salt Lake City, Utah.

Smith, because they love a lie better than the truth. I can take you to a great many old settlers here who will substantiate what I say.

Well, that is very kind, Mr. Taylor, and fair; if we have time we will call around and give you the chance; but we are first going to see these fellows who, so rumor says, know so much against them.

All right; but you will find they don't know anything against those men when you put them down to it. They could never sustain anything against Smith.[12]

It is important to note that Hurlbut shared no supportive statements from those who knew the Smith family in his collection. He only gave voice to those who were willing to criticize and slander the Smith family. When Hurlbut returned from his trip to the East, he began broadcasting the lies and slanders he had compiled against Joseph Smith and the Church. However, it wasn't long before he was arrested and put on trial for threatening the life and safety of the Prophet.

Violence Against the Latter-day Saints

On January 4, 1834, Kirtland Constable Stephen Sherman arrested Hurlbut and held him in custody for a few days.[13] Joseph Smith prepared for the preliminary hearing by turning to the Lord and pleading for deliverance. On the evening of January 11, 1834, Joseph Smith united in prayer with Frederick G. Williams, Newel K. Whitney, John Johnson, Oliver Cowdery, and Orson Hyde to petition the Lord for protection from his enemy. The transcript of this prayer reads:

❝ That the Lord would grant that our brother Joseph might prevail over his enemy, even Docter [*sic*] P. Hurlbut, who has **threatened** his **life**, whom brother Joseph has caused to be taken with a precept; that the Lord would fill the heart of the Court with a spirit to do justice, and cause that the law of the land may be magnified in bringing him to justice. [14]

---

12   Interview with E. L. and William H. Kelley, March 1881, published in *Saint's Herald* XXVIII (June 1, 1881): 167; *Juvenile Instructor* 17, no. 19 (October 1, 1882): 302; emphasis added.

13   Docket Entry, between 4 and 15 January 1834 [State of Ohio v. D. P. Hurlbut], 431, The Joseph Smith Papers.

14   Joseph Smith History, volume A-1, 416-417, Joseph Smith Papers.

Threats of violence became increasingly serious. On January 6, 1834, B. F. Norris, a non-member, wrote a letter describing the threats being made against Joseph Smith and the Latter-day Saints:

❦❦ It is said that the inhabitants have threatend [*sic*] mobing [*sic*] them. They are now **arming** themselves with instruments of war such as guns sords [*sic*] dirks spontoons &c Smith has four or five armed men to gard [*sic*] him every night they say they are not going to be drove away as they ware [*sic*] at missory [Missouri] they will fight for there [*sic*] rights.[15]

Two days later, they heard a cannon fired, which Oliver Cowdery reported was meant "to alarm us, but no one was frightened, but all prepared to defend ourselves if they made a sally upon our houses."[16]

Hurlbut on Trial

When the day of Hurlbut's preliminary hearing arrived (January 13-15, 1834), witnesses appeared before the judge, some on behalf of Hurlbut and others on behalf of Joseph Smith. One of those who spoke in defense of Hurlbut was a man named Leman Copley. Two years later, Leman visited the Prophet Joseph Smith and confessed that during the Hurlbut trial, he had lied and borne "false testimony" against the Prophet:

❦❦ Friday th [*sic*] 1st day of April 1836 At home most of the day, many brethren called to see me. some on temporal & some on Spiritual buisiness [*sic*], among the number was Leeman [*sic*] Copley, who testified against me in a suit I brought against Doctor P. Hulburt [*sic*] for threatening my life, he confessed that he **bore a false testimony** against me, in that suit but verily thought at the time that he was right but on calling to mind all the circumstances connected with the things that transpired at that time he was **convinced that he was wrong**, and humbly confessed it and asked my forgiveness, which was readily granted, he also wished

---

15   B. F. Norris to Mark Norris, January 6, 1834, Detroit Public Library, Detroit, Michigan.

16   Oliver Cowdery to W. W. Phelps and John Whitmer, January 21, 1834, Oliver Cowdery Letter Book, Huntington Library, San Marino, California.

to be received into the church again by baptism, and was received according to his desire, he gave me his confession in writing.[17]

In spite of those men who spoke against the Prophet, the court determined that Joseph Smith did have:

▌▌ reason to fear that **Doctor P. Hurlbut would Beat wound or kill him or injure his property** as set forth in his complaint and it is the consideration of the Court that the defendant enter into a recognizance to keep the peace generally and especalley [sic] towards the Complainant, and also to appear before the Court of Common Pleas on the first day of the term thereof next to be holden [sic] in and for said County and not depart without leave, or stand committed till the judgement of the Court be complied with.[18]

The hearing's decision against Hurlbut resulted in some measure of peace for the Church. The First Presidency (consisting of Joseph Smith, Sidney Rigdon, and Frederick G. Williams) addressed a letter to the Church in Clay County, Missouri, on January 22, 1834, describing Hurlbut's activities and the aftermath of the trial:

▌▌ There is not quite so much danger of a Mob upon us as there has been. The hand of the Lord has thus far been stretched out to protect us,

Doctor P Hurlbut an apostate Elder from this Church has been to the State of New York and gathered up all the **rediculous** [sic] **stories that could be invented and some affidavits** respecting the character of Bro Joseph and the Smith family and he exhibeted [sic] them to numerous congregations in Chagrin Kirtland Mentor and Painesville and **fired the minds of the people with much indignation** against Bro Joseph and the Church.

Hurlbut also made **many harsh threats** &c that he would **take the life of Bro Joseph** if he could not distroy [sic] Mormonism

17   Joseph Smith, "Sketch Book for the use of Joseph Smith, jr.," Journal, 1 April 1836, 190-191, The Joseph Smith Papers; emphasis added.

18   Docket Entry, between 4 and 15 January 1834 [State of Ohio v. D. P. Hurlbut], 432, The Joseph Smith Papers; emphasis added.

without. Bro Joseph took him with a peace warrant and after 3 days trial and investigating the merits of our religion in the town of Painesville by able attorney on both sides he was bound over to the County Court. thus his influence was pritty [*sic*] much distroyed [*sic*], and since the trial the spirit of hostility seames [*sic*] to be broken down in a good degree but how long it will continue so we cannot say.[19]

On January 28, 1834, the Prophet recorded in his journal some reflections on Hurlbut's history and his gratitude toward the Lord for deliverance:

On the 13th of March A.D. 1833, Docter [*sic*] P. Hurlbut came to my house; I conversed with him considerably about the book of Mormon. . . . According to my best recollection, I heard him say, in the course of conversing with him, that if he ever became convinced that the book of Mormon was false, he would be the **cause of my destruction**, &c. . . .

. . . He was finally cut off from the church . . . and then saught [*sic*] the **distruction** [*sic*] of the **sainst** [*sic*] in this place and more particularly **myself** and **family** and as the Lord has in his mercy Delivered me out of his hand. till the present and also the church that he has not prevailed viz th 28 day of Jany 1834 for which I offr [*sic*] the gratitud [*sic*] of my heart to Allmighty [*sic*] God for the sam [*sic*] and on this night Bro Olivr [*sic*] and bro Frederick and my self bowed before the Lord being agred [*sic*] and united in pray that God would continu [*sic*] to deliver me and my brethrn [*sic*] from him that he may not prevail again [*sic*] us in the law suit [*sic*] that is pending . . .[20]

After the preliminary hearing referred the case against Hurlbut to the county court, Hurlbut was called to stand before the Geauga County Court of Common Pleas. As the day of Hurlbut's April 1834 trial approached, the Prophet continued to exert faith that the Lord

---

19   Letter to the Church in Clay County, 22 January 1834, in Letterbook 1, p. 81, The Joseph Smith Papers; emphasis added.

20   Joseph Smith, "Joseph Smith Jrs Book for Record," Journal, 28 January 1834, 48-51, The Joseph Smith Papers; emphasis added.

would influence the natural course of events so that those who were attempting to dig the pit would themselves fall therein:[21]

*// My soul delighteth in the law of the Lord, for He forgiveth my sins, and will confound my enemies. The Lord shall destroy him who has lifted his heel against me, even that **wicked man Dr. Philastus Hurlbut**; He will deliver him to the fowls of heaven, and his bones shall be cast to blasts of the wind, for he lifted his arm against the Almighty, therefore the Lord shall destroy him.[22]*

Hurlbut's trial commenced on April 2, 1834. On Monday, April 7, 1834, the Prophet again knelt in humble prayer, joined by his friends, Newel K. Whitney, Oliver Cowdery, Frederick G. Williams, and Heber C. Kimball:

*// ... met in the council room, and bowed down before the Lord, and prayed ... that I might prevail against that **wicked man, Hurlburt**, and that he might be put to shame ...[23]*

As Hurlbut's trial began, one reporter described the courtroom:

// The court house was filled, almost to suffocation, with an eager and curious crowd of spectators, to hear the Mormon trial, as it was called.[24]

Finally, after over six months of fear and harassment, the Court determined that Hurlbut was indeed guilty of the charges brought against him. Joseph Smith had been justified in his fear that Hurlbut "would wound beat or kill him or destroy his property" and Hurlbut was bound over to pay $200 bail and charged to keep the peace:

---

21   1 Nephi 14:3.

22   Joseph Smith, "Joseph Smith Jrs Book for Record," Journal, 1 April 1834, 68-69, The Joseph Smith Papers; spelling and punctuation modernized, emphasis added.

23   Joseph Smith History, volume A-1, 7 April 1834, 450, Joseph Smith Papers; emphasis added.

24   "Mormon Trial," *Chardon Spectator and Geauga Gazette*, April 12, 1834, https://contentdm.lib.byu.edu/digital/collection/BOMP/id/854.

▌▌ April 9 1834 - "This day comes the Prosecuting Attorney for the County, and also the said defendant; and the Court having heard the said complaint, and all the testimony adduced by the said complainant, and also by the said defendant, and having duly considered the same, are of opinion that the said complainant had **ground to fear that the said Docter P. Hulbut [*sic*] would wound beat or kill him, or destroy his property**, as set forth in said complaint. Whereupon it is ordered and adjudged by the Court, that the said Doctor P. Hulbut [*sic*] enter into a new recognizance, with good and sufficient security in the sum of two hundred dollars, hereafter to keep the peace and be of good behaviour to the citizens of the State of Ohio generally, and to the said Joseph Smith Jr. in particular, for the period of six months; and it is further ordered that the said Doctor P. Hulbut [*sic*] pay the costs of this prosecution to be taxed.[25]

The Prophet Joseph Smith recorded the outcome of the trial in his journal as follows:

▌▌ ... after an impartial trial, the court decided that the said Hurlbut was bound over under 200 dollars' bond to keep the peace for six months and pay the cost, which amounted to near three hundred dollars, all of which was in answer to our prayer, for which I thank my Heavenly Father.[26]

Nearly four years previously, the Lord promised the Prophet Joseph Smith that those who attempted to use legal measures against him would be "cursed by the law" and that the Lord would "smite" Joseph's opponents in His own due time:

▌▌ And it shall come to pass that whosoever shall lay their hands upon you by violence, ye shall command to be smitten in my name; and, behold, I will smite them according to your words, in mine own due time. And whosoever shall go to law with thee shall be cursed by the law.[27]

---

25   Docket Entry, Ruling, 9 April 1834 [State of Ohio v. D. P. Hurlbut], 193, The Joseph Smith Papers; emphasis added.

26   Joseph Smith, "Joseph Smith Jrs Book for Record," Journal, 7–9 April 1834, 70-71, The Joseph Smith Papers; spelling and punctuation modernized.

27   Doctrine and Covenants 24:16-17.

11

MORMONISM UNVAILED:
REACTION TO PUBLICATION

Hurlbut's "time" had partially come. In addition to being found guilty of threatening the Prophet's life, he became further humiliated when his wife was caught in an affair with Orris Clapp, a leading member of the Mentor Baptists.[1] Unwilling to relinquish his scheme to destroy the Church and the Prophet Joseph Smith, Hurlbut paid E. D. Howe, publisher of the *Painesville Telegraph*, a visit. Howe later remembered that Hurlbut "came to me to have the evidence he had published. I bargained to pay him in books."[2]

Hurlbut paid his visit to Howe sometime before February 4, 1834. Soon thereafter, Howe began preparing for publication, and in November of that year, published Hurlbut's "research" accompanied by material gathered or written by Howe.

Impact of *Mormonism Unvailed*

One of *Mormonism Unvailed*'s chief complaints against the Prophet Joseph Smith lay in the characterization of the Smith family as treasure

---

1   *Elders' Journal* 1 (August 1838): 59. "While Hurlburt was held in bounds by the church, and made to behave himself, he was denounced by the priests as one of the worst of men, but no sooner was he excluded from the church for adultery, than instantly he became one of the finest men in the world, old deacon [Orris] Clapp of Mentor ran and took him and his family into the house with himself, and so exceedingly was he pleased with him, that purely out of respect to him, he went to bed to his wife. This great kindness and respect, Hurlburt did not feel just so well about but the pious old deacon gave him a hundred dollars and a yoke of oxen, and all was well again."

2   Arthur B. Deming, *Startling Revelations! Naked Truths about Mormonism* (Oakland, Calif.: n.p., 1888), 3.

diggers who employed the dark arts to lead their followers on hunts for "hidden treasures." The first chapter of *Mormonism Unvailed* begins by going straight for the jugular:

> // All who became intimate with them [the Smith family] during this period, unite in representing the general character of old Joseph and wife, the parents of the pretended Prophet, as **lazy**, **indolent**, **ignorant** and **superstitious** -- having a firm belief in **ghosts** and **witches**; the telling of **fortunes**; pretending to believe that the earth was filled with **hidden treasures**, buried there by Kid or the Spaniards. Being miserably poor, and not much disposed to obtain an honorable livlihood [*sic*] by labor, the energies of their minds seemed to be mostly directed towards finding where these treasures were concealed, and the best mode of acquiring their Possession.
>
> Joseph. Jun. in the mean time [*sic*], had become very expert in the arts of **necromancy**, **jugling** [*sic*], the use of the divining rod, and looking into what they termed a "**peep-stone**," by which means he soon collected about him a gang of idle, credulous young men, to perform the labor of digging into the hills and mountains, and other lonly [*sic*] places, in that vicinity, in search of gold. . . . His business was to point out the locations of the treasures, which he did by looking at a **stone placed in a hat**.[3]

When Richard Bushman wrote his first biography of Joseph Smith, the prelude to *Joseph Smith: Rough Stone Rolling*, he suggested that the activity described by *Mormonism Unvailed* was, in Joseph Smith's day, "no more scandalous than say gambling" and that no one should really care whether or not he engaged in ritual magic and hunting for lost treasure. Why? Because everyone was doing it and no "serious Christian" cared:

> // . . . it became evident that these practices were commonplace in the 17th century in all levels of society [and] in the 18th and 19th century, among common people in the lower classes. So that once you spread out this process, so that Joseph Smith is not a peculiarly weird version of treasure seeking but that it was widely

---

3   Eber D. Howe, *Mormonism Unvailed* (Painesville, 1834), 11-12; emphasis added.

practiced, suddenly, it was **no longer a blot** on his character, his family's character. It was **no more scandalous than say gambling**, playing poker today. A little bit discredited and slightly morally disreputable but **not really evil**. And when it was found that all sorts of **treasure seekers were also serious Christians**, why not the Smiths too? So, instead of being a puzzle or a contradiction, it was just one aspect of Smith family culture and **not really anything to be worried about**.[4]

Is Bushman accurate in his assertion that *Mormonism Unvailed's* accusations were trifling and inconsequential, essentially no big deal? On the contrary, when Hurlbut first began spreading the scandalous reports he had gathered from disaffected neighbors back in New York and Pennsylvania, the First Presidency reported that Hurlbut's claims "fired the minds of the people with much indignation" against Joseph Smith and the Church. "The people" were incensed! No good Christian in Joseph Smith's day heard Hurlbut and thought, "Those Smiths are kind of weird but no big deal":

❘❘ Doctor P Hurlbut an apostate Elder from this Church has been to the State of New York and gathered up **all the rediculous [*sic*] stories that could be invented and some affidavits** respecting the character of Bro Joseph and the Smith family and he exhibeted [*sic*] them to numerous congregations in Chagrin Kirtland Mentor and Painesville and fired the minds of the people with **much indignation** against Bro Joseph and the Church.[5]

Why were the minds of the people "fired with indignation" if, as Bushman claims, this occultic activity was simply normal for the time and "all sorts of treasure seekers were also serious Christians?"

On the contrary, when "serious Christians" in Joseph Smith's day— and this is true as well for serious Christians today—heard that Joseph Smith was "expert in the arts of necromancy" and that he had spent his boyhood "digging into the hills and mountains"[6] searching

---

4   Richard L. Bushman, "Joseph Smith Miscellany by Richard Bushman," YouTube video, 1:00:34, posted by Fair Mormon, October 8, 2012, https://www.youtube.com/watch?v=5g_JBRiDms4; emphasis added.

5   Letter to the Church in Clay County, Missouri, 22 January 1834, in Letterbook 1, p. 81, The Joseph Smith Papers; emphasis added.

6   Eber D. Howe, *Mormonism Unvailed* (Painesville, 1834), 12.

for gold, it destroyed any interest in the Restoration of the Gospel. Viewed as "blots" on the character of the young Prophet, most of the persecution leveled against the Church in 1834 was rooted firmly in these scandalous tales.

Testimonies that might have been were never had because of the false reports. Why should we expect a different outcome today? A man or woman with true faith in God, or in other words, any "serious Christian" should and will be extremely disturbed upon being confronted with the accusations in *Mormonism Unvailed*. If there were any truth in the accusations that Joseph Smith was involved in the occult or pursued a career in money digging or that his family was lazy and indolent, the foundation of the Restoration would be as sand. We confidently declare that these accusations are false.

Latter-day Saints Respond to Hurlbut

Unlike current progressive historians who express an eagerness to embrace Hurlbut's nonsense by creating a "new narrative," Church leaders and faithful members in Joseph Smith's day refuted such drivel, and defended the Prophet against those false reports. These early Saints endeavored to expose Hurlbut as the "illegitimate author"[7] or ghost-writer of *Mormonism Unvailed*, and they shared facts revealing Hurlbut's true character. One example comes to us in the form of an editorial published in the *Elders' Journal of the Church of Latter Day Saints* in August 1838:

❝ This is the Hurlburt, that was author of a book which bears the name of E D. Howe, but it was this said Hurlburt that was the author of it; but after the **affair of Hurlburt's wife and the pious old deacon,** the persecutors thought it better to put some other name as author to their book than Hurlburt, so E. D. Howe substituted his name.

The change however was not much better. Asahel Howe one of E. D.'s. brothers who was said to be the likeliest of the family, served a prenticeship [*sic*] in the work house [*sic*] in Ohio, for **robbing**

7   "To the Elders of the Church of the Latter Day Saints," *Messenger and Advocate* 2 (December 1835): 228. "... the illegitimate author of 'Mormonism Unvailed,' in order to give currency to the publication, as Mr. Hurlburt, about this time, was bound over to court, for threatening life."

the post office. And yet notwithstanding all this, all the pious priests of all denominations, were found following in the wake of these mortals.

Hurlburt and the Howe's, are among the **basest of mankind,** and **known to be** such; and yet the priests and their coadjutors hail them as their best friends, and publish their lies, speaking of them in the highest terms. And after all this, they want us to say, that they are pious souls and good saints. Can we believe it? surely men of common sense will not ask us to do it.

Good men love to associate with good men; and bad men with bad ones; and when we see men making friends with drunkards, thieves, liars, and swindlers, shall we call them saints? If we were to do it, we might be justly charged with "partaking of their evil deeds."

Therefore until we have more evidence than we have now, we shall always think when we see men associating with scoundrels, that they themselves are scoundrels.[8]

In response to false statements circulating in 1834, the Prophet Joseph Smith wrote a letter to Oliver Cowdery, published in December of that year. In the letter Joseph warned Oliver that many people claimed to "know him" although there was no true acquaintance:

❝ ... I have been induced to give you [Oliver Cowdery] the time and place of my birth; as I have learned that many of the opposers of those principles which I have held forth to the world, **profess** a personal **acquaintance** with me, though when in my presence, **represent me to be another person in age, education, and stature**, from what I am. . . .

During this time [age 10-21], as is common to most, or all youths, I fell into many vices and follies; but as my accusers are, and have been forward to accuse me of being guilty of gross and outragious [*sic*] violations of the peace and good order of the community, I take the occasion to remark, that, though, as I have said above, "as is common to most, or all youths, I fell into many vices and

---

8   *Elders' Journal* 1, no. 4 (August 1838): 59-60; emphasis added.

follies," I have **not**, neither can it be sustained, in truth, been **guilty of wronging or injuring any man or society of men;** and those imperfections to which I alude [*sic*], and for which I have often had occasion to lament, were a light, and too often, vain mind, exhibiting a foolish and trifling conversation.

This being **all**, and the **worst**, that my accusers can substantiate against my moral character . . . ⁹

Joseph concluded his letter with profuse apologies for ever indulging in being a little too exuberant, boisterous or trifling at times, clarifying that he never professed perfection. One has to ask, is this truly the same man that progressive evangelists such as Bushman, McGee, Gardner, and others attempt to depict as dabbling in the occult? The man whose *worst fault* was exhibiting a little "foolish" and "trifling" conversation in his teens? Can any man or woman alive today begin to hold themselves to the same standard? Perhaps it would be well to remember: "Thou hypocrite, first cast out the beam out of thine own eye; and then shalt thou see clearly to cast out the mote out of thy brother's eye."¹⁰ It is ironic that it was Hurlbut, a man who struggled with immorality, deceit, and as we shall see later, likely murder, who aspired to become the Prophet's judge.

During the translation of the *Book of Mormon*, the Lord commanded Oliver Cowdery to "stand by my servant Joseph, faithfully, in whatsoever difficult circumstances he may be for the word's sake."¹¹ In 1834, as *Mormonism Unvailed* began circulating, hot off the press, Oliver Cowdery took it as his responsibility "to convince the public of the incorrectness of those scurrilous reports which have inundated our land, or even but a small portion of them." He expressed his confidence that "before HIM [God] I must stand and answer for the deeds transacted in this life."¹²

Oliver Cowdery wrote a series of letters to W. W. Phelps, which were published in the periodical *Messenger and Advocate* in December

---

9   Joseph Smith to Oliver Cowdery, *Messenger and Advocate* 1 (December 1834): 40; emphasis added.

10   Matthew 7:5.

11   Doctrine and Covenants 6:18.

12   Oliver Cowdery, "Letter III," *Messenger and Advocate* 1 (December 1834): 42. Also Oliver Cowdery, "Letter III," Joseph Smith History, December 1834, 58, The Joseph Smith Papers.

1834. He urged his readers to "hear before they judge, and understand both sides of this matter before they condemn."[13] In his last letter, Oliver addressed claims that the Prophet was a "lazy, idle, vicious, profligate fellow." After confirming that he had spoken with "many persons" who could all testify to the honesty, virtue, and industry of Joseph Smith, he bore his own testimony and condemned Joseph's critics to "crumble to dust":

❝ ... I have been told by those for whom he has labored, that he was a young man of **truth and industrious habits**. And I will add further that it is my conviction, if he never had been called to the exalted station in which he now occupies, he might have passed down the stream of time with ease and in respectability, without the foul and hellish tongue of slander ever being employed against him.

It is no more than to be expected, I admit, that men of corrupt hearts will try to traduce his character and put a stop upon his name: indeed, this is according to the word of the angel; but this does not prohibit me from speaking freely of his merits, and **contradicting those falsehoods**—I feel myself bound so to do, and I know that my testimony, on this matter, will be received and believed while those who testify to the contrary are crumbled to dust, and their words swept away in the general mass of lies, when God shall purify the earth![14]

Oliver recognized that the mass persecution against the name and character of Joseph Smith was simply a fulfillment of Moroni's prophecy:

❝ God had a work for me [Joseph] to do; and that my name should be had for good and evil among all nations, kindreds, and tongues, or that it should be both good and evil spoken of among all people.[15]

Joseph's obedience to the Lord was followed by intense hatred from the adversary. Rumors began flying and Joseph recalled that "If I were to relate a **thousandth part** of them [the falsehoods], it would **fill up**

---

13   Ibid.

14   Oliver Cowdery, "Letter VIII," *Messenger and Advocate* 2 (October 1835): 200; emphasis added.

15   Joseph Smith—History 1:33.

volumes."[16] What are the falsehoods and the rumors to which Joseph referred? Today, progressive historians engage in rewriting Church history in order to give credence and voice to all of the reports and all of the perspectives, including those of Joseph's enemies, whether true or false. Why should we embrace the testimonies of the present-day scribes, pharisees, and Judas Iscariots?

Oliver Cowdery did not. In fact, he testified of Joseph Smith and his family's righteous character and nature:

❝ Connected with this, is the character of the family: and on this I say as I said concerning the character of our brother [Joseph Smith]—I feel myself bound to defend the innocent always when opportunity offers. Had not those who are **notorious for lies and dishonesty**, also assailed the character of the family, I should pass over them here in silence; but now I shall not forbear.

It has been industriously circulated that they were **dishonest, deceitful** and **vile**. On this I have the testimony of responsible persons, who have said and will say, that this is **basely false**; and besides, a **personal acquaintance for seven years**, has demonstrated that all the difficulty is, they were once poor, (yet **industrious,**) and have now, by the help of God, arisen to note, and their names are like to, (indeed they will,) be handed down to posterity, and had among the righteous. They are **industrious honest, virtuous and liberal** to all.

This is their character; and though many take advantage of their liberality, God will reward them; but this is the fact, and this testimony shall shine upon the records of the Saints, and be recorded on the archives of heaven to be read in the day of eternity, when the wicked and perverse, who have **vilely slandered them without cause or provocation**, reap their reward with the unjust, where there is weeping, wailing and gnashing of teeth—if they do not repent.[17]

---

16   Joseph Smith, "History of Joseph Smith," *Times and Seasons* 3 (May 2, 1842): 772; emphasis added.

17   Oliver Cowdery, "Letter VIII," *Messenger and Advocate* 2 (October 1835): 199; emphasis added.

Shortly after Hurlbut was convicted by the county court, Oliver Cowdery endeavored to publish the facts relative to Hurlbut's case. He explained that Hurlbut had "threatened the life of Brother Joseph Smith" but that many desired Hurlbut to "escape justice":

> ❝ ... a number of those who doubtless desired that Hurlbut might escape justice, (some whose oaths were sufficient evidence of the feelings of their hearts,) indulged themselves in **conjectures**, and **rumors**, raising and spreading them to their own shame, or at least, to the shame of every good citizen who has the smallest regard for truth and righteousness, or peace and harmony in society; and by these means, created considerable feelings on the subject, as far as their influence could extend; trying to excite unfavorable impressions against [Joseph Smith] by every **foolish report that ignorance could believe, or malice could invent**. However, their exertions were in vain ... they could not screen Hurlbut from the punishment due his crime: the evidence was so positive, notwithstanding the great exertion to invalidate the testimony on the part of the State, that they failed in every attempt to save him from the force of the law; and the Court, after a patient hearing of all the witnesses, has holden Hurlbut to bail under bonds of two hundred dollars for his good behavior.
>
> This is as it should be-all idlers who seek to obtain a support from the public, by threatening the lives, and assailing the characters of innocent men, ought to be brought to justice, or be exposed to the view of all ...

Oliver went on to describe the reports which had been spread abroad before the court convicted Hurlbut. Many of Hurlbut's defenders had confidently proclaimed that the only reason Hurlbut was brought to trial was so that "the lawyers might have a fair opportunity of ridiculing, and scandalizing, Jo. Smith." However, their dreams were dashed when Hurlbut was convicted. Oliver observed that he hoped Hurlbut would begin "labor[ing] honestly with his own hands for his support"[18] rather than taking money from honest citizens in his attempt to destroy the reputation of Joseph Smith.

---

18   Oliver Cowdery, *The Evening and Morning Star* 2 (April 1834): 298; emphasis added.

12

MORMONISM UNVAILED: DEMISE & REBIRTH

It is unfortunate that Hurlbut did not take Oliver Cowdery's advice to begin laboring honestly for his support. Some believe that Hurlbut was responsible for the robbing and murder of Garrit Brass of Mentor, Ohio who died on November 25, 1837. This story begins with Arthur B. Deming, a critic of the Church, who, like Hurlbut, gathered affidavits antagonistic to the Prophet Joseph Smith and the Church nearly five decades later during the 1880s. Along the way, Deming also gathered statements that revealed inconvenient stories and troubling inconsistencies surrounding the character and integrity of Doctor Hurlbut. Historian Dale Morgan wrote to Fawn Brodie, another detractor of the Prophet Joseph Smith and author of *No Man Knows My History*:

> The Chicago Historical Society has some further affidavits collected by Deming which he didn't publish in the first two issues of his paper and which thus remained unpublished. . . . Deming also had half a dozen statements bearing on Hurlbut in 1836-37, which he may have kept unpublished because they weren't especially helpful to his anti-Mormon crusade—they had to do with **accusations of theft made against Hurlbut** at that time . . .[1]

According to Deming's affidavits, Esther Scott, the daughter of the man who was killed [Mr. Brass], told Arthur B. Deming in 1885 that

---

1   Dale Lowell Morgan, *Dale Morgan on Early Mormonism Correspondence and a New History*, ed. John Phillip Walker (Salt Lake City, UT: Signature Books, 1986), 142-143; emphasis added.

her father's home was found burnt while several hundred dollars, known to be in his possession, were missing. Esther's brother believed the malefactor was Hurlbut, especially considering a suspicious conversation their sister claimed to have had with Hurlbut soon after the murder:

> In the late fall or early winter of 1837 his [Garrit Brass'] house was found on fire, in which was found his remains partly consumed. No trace of feathers from his bedding being found, and no money of which he was known to have, several hundred dollars in gold and silver, part of which was paid to him a few days before by a neighbor, and his pension money received the day before. . . . My brother always believed it and thought that a man living in Mentor was the guilty person, by the name of Hulburt, whom it was learned on the night of the murder moved away, going west.
>
> I had a sister at that time living in Michigan, Mrs. Bronson, who said that a man stopped at her house for a meal and during the conversation with him she learned he was from Geauga Co., Ohio, and asked him if he was acquainted in Mentor, and if he knew a Mr. Bras[s] there that was murdered, and that it was near her father, after which he seemed uneasy, acted strangely and soon left. It so impressed her that he knew something about it, she wrote back with a description of him which satisfied my brother that it was the same Hurlbut that left Mentor, and it helped to strengthen and confirm them in their previous suspicions.[2]

Calvin Ingersoll is believed to have told Deming that Hurlbut worked for him, but after the Garrit Brass murder, Hurlbut was caught by citizens of Mentor with "various articles which he had stolen":

> Doctor P. Hurlbut sometimes worked for me cutting and splitting rails during the year . . . He lived at the time in Judge Clapp's house. Hurlbut's wife enticed a wealthy citizen to go to bed with her. When this party was in the act of getting into bed, Hurlbut, who was secreted under the bed, caught him by the legs. Hurlbut began a lawsuit for damages, which was settled by the defendant without trial. . . . I was at the ruins of his [Garrit Brass'] cabin

---

2   Esther Scott statement, Chicago Historical Society (Ill.) collection of manuscripts about Mormons. Church History Library, The Church of Jesus Christ of Latter-day Saints, Salt Lake City, Utah.

the morning after it was burned. Hurlbut, who lived in Henry Munson's house, moved west the night Mr. Bras[s] was burned with his cabin. He was pursued by citizens of Mentor who recovered from him various articles which he had stolen.[3]

Calvin Ingersoll mentioned to Arthur Deming that Hurlbut lived with a man by the name of Henry Murson or Munson. Henry's cousin, Mrs. J. D. Barber, confirmed Ingersoll's story, adding that Hurlbut was caught with several stolen items including "carpets, chains," and "farming tools":

// D.P. Hurlbut, who lived in my cousin's, Harry [Henry?] Munson's house, in Mentor, moved west the night of the fire. He was pursued and overtaken by citizens who recovered from him carpets, chains, farming tools, and other things which he had stolen from them. . . . My cousin missed two pillows after Hurlbut moved. . . . There was much comment among the people of Mentor about Hurlbut's thefts, and the facts of his leaving in the night when Mr. Bras[s] was murdered, robbed and burned.[4]

Another statement collected by Arthur Deming claimed that a neighbor of Garrit Brass, Mrs. Alvors, remembered Hurlbut frequently visiting the Brass cabin before the crime. She also seemed convinced that Hurlbut was connected to the robbing and murder of Garrit Brass:

// I have many times seen D. P. Hurlbut at Brass' house. Geo. M. Dickey, who bought John Bras's farm on which GenL. Bras's cabin stood, and Samuel Hodges our neighbor(s); in conversation with father, I have several times heard discuss the probable reason why Hurlbut spent so much time at Gen. Bras's. They advanced various reasons, and said he might be trying to make a Morman of him. Mr. Brass was known to have money, and he received his pension a few days before his cabin was burned. I have heard Mrs. J. D. Barber's

---

3   Calvin Ingersoll statement, Chicago Historical Society (Ill.) collection of manuscripts about Mormons. Church History Library, The Church of Jesus Christ of Latter-day Saints, Salt Lake City, Utah.

4   Statement of Mrs. J. D. Barker, Chicago Historical Society (Ill.) collection of manuscripts about Mormons. Church History Library, The Church of Jesus Christ of Latter-day Saints, Salt Lake City, Utah.

statement read and believe it is true, as did our neighbors at the time. I went to school to Mrs. Esther Scott, his [Brass'] daughter.[5]

Commenting on the affidavits collected by Deming and other negative sources on Hurlbut, Matthew Roper at Brigham Young University commented:

// The evidence available so far, however, does not allow us to establish Hurlbut's culpability beyond dispute. What we can say is that Latter-day Saints were scarcely the only people who held Hurlbut in low esteem.[6]

In 1840, Benjamin Winchester, a member of the Church who began as a zealous defender, but sadly later apostatized, printed "a short biography of Dr. P. Hurlbert [sic]" in Philadelphia. He also claimed that Hurlbut was guilty of "stealing for a livelihood." Winchester reported:

// Those who were anxious that Mr. Hulbert's [sic] work should come out, discovered it would not do to publish it in his name, his reputation was too rotten; they advised him therefore, to sell it to Mr. E. D. Howe, of Painesville, Ohio, for five hundred dollars. Mr. H[urlbut]. got the money, and gave up his manuscript, thus Mormonism Unvailed, became the adopted offspring of Mr. Howe; indeed Hulbert's [sic] name was canceled in many places. These are the facts, and can be proven by hundreds of unimpeachable witnesses in that region of country.

Mr. Hulbert [sic] with his ill gotten gains, went to Erie county, Pa., in the township of Girard, Miller Settlement, and bought a farm, and married a wife, soon became a confirmed drunkard, spent every cent of his inglorious gain, was reduced to beggary, took to stealing for a livelihood, was detected in stealing a log chain, fled the country to escape justice, and that is the last of him, so far as I know.[7]

---

5   Mrs. Alvor's Statement, Chicago Historical Society (Ill.) collection of manuscripts about Mormons. Church History Library, The Church of Jesus Christ of Latter-day Saints, Salt Lake City, Utah; spelling modernized. Duplicate wording found in original document was removed for this publication.

6   Matthew Roper, "The Mythical 'Manuscript Found,'" FARMS Review 17/2 (2005): 7–140.

7   Benjamin Winchester, Origin of the Spaulding Story (Philadelphia: Brown,

Sidney Rigdon also stated that before Hurlbut joined the Church, he had previously been "excluded" from the Methodist Church "for immoralities."[8] Orson Hyde wrote to George Adams, June 7, 1841:

❝ ... it fell to my lot to travel with him [Hurlbut] to preach the gospel; and it was at my instance that a charge was preferred against him before the Council of the Church for an attempt at seduction and crime. He was expelled; and from personal knowledge I am prepared to say, that Mr. Winchester and Mr. Rigdon have told the truth concerning him, and the character which he sustains. ... [9]

In 1846 Hurlbut became an elder for the United Brethren Church[10] and in 1847 he became a member of the board of trustees of Otterbein College. However, by 1851 the United Brethren Church had charged Hurlbut with similar improprieties to those the Methodists and the Latter-day Saints had previously witnessed. His actions, which included, "charges of gross improprieties toward the opposite sex, lying ...." led finally to his entire excommunication. One of the ministers of the United Brethren Church wrote a letter to Joseph Smith III in 1884 relating:

❝ Here, both in the conference and in the church, there was a **constantly growing uneasiness** about his **improprieties**; until the fall of 1851, when he was held before the Sandusky Annual Conference of said church, for a trial on charges of **gross improprieties toward the opposite sex, lying, and intemperance**. Each charge; to wit, First, improprieties toward the opposite sex; Second, lying; Third, intemperance, was **clearly and fully sustained**; and he was **suspended** from the ministry one year; and as that year he grew from **bad to worse**, he was entirely excommunicated at the next session of the conference which was held in the fall

Bicking and Guilpert, 1840), 11.

8   Sidney Rigdon to the *Quincy Whig*, 27 May 1839; *Quincy Whig*, 8 June 1839.

9   Orson Hyde to George Adams, 7 June 1841, London.

10   Basil Meek, ed., *Yearbook of the Sandusky County Pioneer and Historical Association* (Fremont: Sandusky County Pioneer and Historical Association, 1915), 327. Mentioned in Dale W. Adams, "Doctor Philastus Hurlbut: Originator of Derogatory Statements About Joseph Smith, Jr.," *The John Whitmer Historical Association Journal* 20:86, 2000, 86, http://www.jstor.org/stable/43200133.

of 1852.... And we all came to the same conclusion, that he was a **very bad man**, and **guilty of each charge** made against him.[11]

Hurlbut came to an inglorious end when he finally died in Gibsonburg, Ohio, June 16, 1883.

What Happened to Eber D. Howe?

Eber D. Howe died two years after Hurlbut on November 10, 1885, after having forsaken the Christian faith and embracing Spiritualism. He defended his beliefs in an 1878 pamphlet titled, *Autobiography and Recollections of a Pioneer Printer,* wherein he stated:

// In this [Spiritualism] I believed, and still believe, and why? Simply because I could not help it, without ignoring and casting far from me every vestige of common sense and my reasoning faculties . . . The phenomena of the spiritual science is now pretty generally admitted.[12]

What is Spiritualism? This religious movement is identified as beginning in the 1840s in upstate New York, where two sisters, Kate and Margaret Fox, claimed to have established contact with a spirit that communicated through rapping noises. The Fox sisters told others that the spirit claimed to have once been a peddler until he was murdered. Kate and Margaret began acting as mediums for this "spirit," taking questions from visitors. They became instant sensations. The idea that spirits were able to communicate with the living through mediums exploded like wildfire on the world's religious stage with converts estimated in the millions. As the Fox sisters' fame as accomplished mediums spread, they began conducting séances for hundreds of eager spectators. Believers in Spiritualism claimed to have "spirit guides" and millions swore to the reality of the phenomena. So pervasive was this movement that President Brigham Young felt moved to address these experiences, teaching church members that the power of the devil was real and fully able to make objects move, including the creation of rapping noises and other phenomenon:

11   "Hiram Rathbun to Joseph Smith III, Lansing, Michigan, 17 July 1884," *Saints Herald* 31 (August 2, 1884): 492; emphasis added.

12   Eber D. Howe, *Autobiography and Recollections of a Pioneer Printer* (Painesville, 1878), 54-55.

// There are many Elders in this house who, if I had the power to Mesmerize that vase and make it dance on that table, would say that it was done by the power of God; and I expect that some of them would begin to shout, and that some of the sisters would shout, "Glory be to God, hallelujah." Who could tell whether it was done by the power of God or the power of the devil? No person, **unless he had the revelations of Jesus Christ within him.**

I suppose you are ready to ask brother Brigham if he thinks the power of the devil could make the vase dance. Yes, and could take it up and carry it outdoors, just as easy as to turn up a table and move it here and there, or to cause a rap, rap, rap, or to bake and pass around pancakes, or to get hold of a person's hand, and make him write in every style you can think of, imitating George Washington's, Benjamin Franklin's, Joseph Smith's, and others' autographs. Can you tell whether that is by the power of God or by the power of the devil? No, **unless you have the revelations of Jesus Christ.**[13]

It is perhaps an important point to note that Spiritualism's recognized birthplace (Hydesville, New York) is less than 15 miles from the Hill Cumorah. Speaking of the rise of false and alternative counterfeits of the truth, Joseph Smith taught:

// ... false prophets **always arise to oppose** the true prophets, and they will prophesy so very near the truth that they will deceive almost the very chosen ones ... in relation to the Kingdom of God— the devil always **sets up his Kingdom at the very same time in opposition to God ...**[14]

It is no coincidence that Spiritualism, a perfect counterfeit to the Gospel of Jesus Christ and true revelation, was established less than 15 miles from where Joseph Smith received the Nephite plates that would become the *Book of Mormon*, and less than 25 miles from the birthplace of The Church of Jesus Christ of Latter-day Saints, in Fayette, New York.

---

13   Brigham Young, "The Necessity of the Saints Having the Spirit of Revelation," in *Journal of Discourses*, vol. 3 (London, 1856), 157. Discourse given on May 6, 1855; emphasis added.

14   Joseph Smith, Discourse, 12 May 1844, as Reported by Thomas Bullock, 1, The Joseph Smith Papers; emphasis added.

Howe rejected Joseph Smith, he rejected the Gospel of Jesus Christ, he rejected the spirit of true revelation, and according to the teachings of Brigham Young, this left him vulnerable to be seduced by the spirits of the adversary:

❞ It was revealed to me that **if the people did not receive the spirit of revelation that God had sent** for the salvation of the world, **they would receive false spirits, and would have revelation.** Men would have revelation, women would have revelation, the priest in the pulpit and the deacon under the pulpit would have revelation, and the people would have revelation enough to damn the whole nation, and nations of them, unless they would hearken to the voice of God.

It was not only revealed to Joseph, but to your humble servant [Brigham Young], that false spirits would be as prevalent and as common among the inhabitants of the earth as we now see them. ... We receive revelation from Heaven, you [Spiritualists] receive your revelations from every foul spirit that has departed this life, and gone out of the bodies of mobbers, murderers, highwaymen, drunkards, thieves, liars, and every kind of debauched character, whose spirits are floating around here, and searching and seeking whom they can destroy; for they are the servants of the devil, and they are permitted to come now to reveal to the people.[15]

President Brigham Young taught, that before the Restoration of the Gospel, the Lord did not allow the adversary to administer false revelation to the same extent as after "Jesus revealed his Priesthood":

❞ It was not so once, anciently or formerly, when there was no Priesthood on the earth, no revelations from Heaven. Then the Lord Almighty shut up this evidence, and all intercourse between men on the earth and the foul spirits, so that the latter could not deceive and destroy the former with their revelations. But God has spoken now, and so has the devil; Jesus has revealed his Priesthood, so has the devil revealed his, and there is quite a difference between the two.

---

15   Brigham Young, "The Word of Wisdom—Spiritualism," in *Journal of Discourses*, vol. 13 (London, 1871), 280-281. Discourse given on October 30, 1870; emphasis added.

One forms a perfect chain, the links of which cannot be separated; one has perfect order, laws, rules, regulations, organization; it forms, fashions, makes, creates, produces, protects and holds in existence the inhabitants of the earth in a pure and holy form of government, preparatory to their entering the kingdom of Heaven. The other is a rope of sand; it is disjointed, jargon, confusion, discord, everybody receiving revelation to suit himself.[16]

Howe embraced what Brigham Young called the "rope of sand." In his autobiography, Howe declared his belief that spirits were "determined to be seen, heard and felt." It is interesting that Howe accused Joseph Smith of witchcraft: he accused Joseph Smith of being a diviner, a necromancer, a soothsayer, an astrologer, and on and on, while the truth was, and is, that Howe was the true villain of his own story. E. D. Howe was the man who lived a life of darkness and thus communed with spirits of darkness. Howe became an evangelist for Spiritualism, which is, in fact, Satanism. Howe celebrated the growing tide and success of Spiritualism throughout the world in these words:

❙❙ In spite of all the obstacles and impediments thrown in its [Spiritualism's] way, what do we now see? We see the denizens of the upper spheres [disembodied spirits] constantly at work devising new plans to make themselves known and respected among their dear ones left behind. They are determined to be seen, heard and felt ... There are now more believers in this new dispensation, after an exhibition of thirty years, than there were in the Christian religion for the first five hundred after its advent. It is "marching on" in its glorious career, and has already encircled the entire globe. Its numbers are computed by millions.[17]

In addition to his embracing Spiritualism, Howe acknowledged a belief in Darwinian Evolution: "I believe that man, physically, was evolved from the animal kingdom."[18,19]

---

16   Ibid, 281.

17   Eber D. Howe, *Autobiography and Recollections of a Pioneer Printer* (Painesville, 1878), 55.

18   Ibid, 56.

19   President Joseph Fielding Smith pronounced Darwinian Evolution as "Satan's chief weapon in this dispensation in his attempt to destroy the divine mission of Jesus Christ." (Joseph Fielding Smith, *Man, His Origin and Destiny*, 184.) President

Howe's rejection of the Gospel led him to embrace false revelation and false science. And yet, in spite of Howe's professed confidence in the "common sense" of Spiritualism, he admitted that he had no sure knowledge, no witness that any of his beliefs were correct. Howe pronounced his relativistic philosophy in these words, "I do not promise to believe to-morrow exactly what I believe to-day, and I do not believe to-day exactly what I believed yesterday . . . ."[20]

This is the origin, the root and stalk, of the famous, or rather infamous, *Mormonism Unvailed*, to which so many of today's progressive scholars turn. Hurlbut's and Howe's slander is heralded as historic "proof" that Joseph Smith and his family engaged in treasure digging, ritual magic, and that the Prophet used a seer stone to "translate" the *Book of Mormon*. How can it be that the historians and authors in the Church advance the writings, ideas and narrative of E. D. Howe and Doctor Philastus Hurlbut?

The Resurrection of *Mormonism Unvailed*

After its publication, *Mormonism Unvailed* served as a basis for many derogatory works on the life and teachings of the Prophet Joseph Smith.[21] For many decades, faithful Latter-day Saint historians considered Hurlbut's affidavits and Howe's publications nothing more than the "false and scandalous reports" that the Prophet Joseph Smith repudiated while he was alive. However, by the mid-1970s, an eerie shift began

---

Ezra Taft Benson identified Charles Darwin as one of the five chief anti-Christs in our day (Ezra Taft Benson, "Strengthening the Family," Conference Report [October 1970] 21-25) and nearly every President of the Church has taught that Darwinism is destructive to faith and contrary to the doctrines of the Gospel of Jesus Christ. ("Why have the Presidents of the Church consistently taught against Darwinism?," Latter-day Answers, accessed February 2019, http://ldsanswers.org/why-have-the-presidents-of-the-church-consistently-taught-against-darwinism/.) President Nelson termed belief in Darwinian Evolution as "incomprehensible." (Elder Russell M. Nelson in an interview with the Pew Forum, May 16, 2007. Interview conducted by Robert Ruby, Senior Editor, Pew Forum on Religion & Public Life, http://www.pewforum.org/PublicationPage.aspx?id=3838.)

20   Eber D. Howe, *Autobiography and Recollections of a Pioneer Printer* (Painesville, 1878), 56.

21   Ibid, 45. Eber D. Howe proudly noted in his autobiography, "In 1834 I wrote and compiled a book of 290 pages, which was entitled 'Mormonism Unveiled,' which contained a succinct and true history of the rise and progress of the sect up to that time, as I verily believed. It has now been out of print more than forty years, but which I have reason to believe has been the basis of all the histories which have appeared from time to time since that period touching that people."

to appear when Richard Bushman was working as a professor of early American history. Bushman decided the "traditional" Latter-day Saint narrative needed to change and later recalled:

❘❘ The response of Mormon historians in the 1970s was to deny almost everything. Beyond the Josiah Stowell incident, they argued, all the money digging stories were fabrications of Joseph Smith's enemies. They claimed that the sources for the stories were corrupted and therefore not to be trusted. . . . Most of the accounts came from a set of affidavits collected by Philastus Hurlbut . . . Church historians thought Hurlbut's motives were too suspect to trust his findings. What reason was there to believe him?[22]

Indeed, what reason was there to believe a man who had lied repeatedly and finally been excommunicated from the Church for immorality and blasphemy against God? What reason was there to trust the man who threatened violence against Joseph Smith and traveled throughout the country making it his mission to destroy the Gospel of Jesus Christ? Should the character of Joseph Smith and the history of our Church be based upon the words of a man who was excommunicated from the Methodists and United Christian Brethren for immorality and lying, and who was known for his thievery—a man who almost certainly murdered and robbed an old, helpless gentleman? No true Latter-day Saint in the Prophet's day considered Hurlbut a credible witness, so why would we do so today? For over 100 years the "traditional" narrative honored the name and character of Joseph Smith and his family, while more recently, the "reconstructed narrative"[23] places the dogma of Hurlbut and his comrades on a pedestal:

❘❘ The first thing I [Bushman] decided was that I could not dismiss all of Hurlbut's affidavits with a wave of a hand. Academic historians had taken them seriously, and so should I. . . . As I read the Hurlbut affidavits, I picked up clues that not only the Smiths but also many of their neighbors were looking for treasure in Palmyra in the

---

22   Richard L. Bushman, "Joseph Smith and Money Digging," in *A Reason for Faith: Navigating LDS Doctrine & Church History*, ed. Laura H. Hales (Provo, UT: Religious Studies Center, Brigham Young University, 2016), 2.

23   "Richard and Claudia Bushman," YouTube video, 1:56:30, "Blake Bishop," June 12, 2016, https://www.youtube.com/watch?v=MA0YS8LWWX4.

1820s.... The Smiths may have been subscribing to folk religion, but in this they were part of a culture found virtually everywhere among Yankees of their generation. It may not have been the most uplifting activity, and some scoffed, but it was something like reading astrological charts today--a little goofy but harmless.[24]

By Bushman's own admission, his contribution to Latter-day Saint history, as published in his works, *Joseph Smith and the Beginnings of Mormonism* and *Joseph Smith: Rough Stone Rolling*, was to take Hurlbut's research seriously and to teach this generation of Latter-day Saints that not only was Hurlbut credible, but that his slanders were trivial. So it is, the same man who threatened Joseph Smith's life and was convicted in court, the same man who Oliver Cowdery, Joseph Smith, and other faithful members fought and prayed for deliverance from, this same man was now being given the red carpet among the scholars in the Church.

Have Bushman and the progressives of the new narrative succeeded? In 2016, Bushman celebrated his achievement in convincing Latter-day Saints to accept Hurlbut's perspective as credible history:

I occasionally hear of people who are still offended by a prophet who dealt in treasure seeking, but very few. The most important issue when I began to write in the 1970s has faded in importance. Even highly orthodox Latter-day Saints are not offended by treasure seeking and seer stones ....[25]

Have we reached a time in the Church where we delight in promoting scandalous and maligning stories about the Prophet Joseph Smith and his family? Are we more "advanced" and "literate" because we are accepting what Joseph Smith once called "all the ridiculous stories that could be invented and some affidavits"[26]? Do we seek the praise of academia at the expense of betraying our Prophet as we embrace the

---

24   Richard L. Bushman, "Joseph Smith and Money Digging," in *A Reason for Faith: Navigating LDS Doctrine & Church History*, ed. Laura H. Hales (Provo, UT: Religious Studies Center, Brigham Young University, 2016), 2-3.

25   Ibid, 4.

26   Joseph Smith History, volume A-1, 22 January 1834, 420, Joseph Smith Papers; spelling modernized.

"testimony of traitors"[27]? Should we be celebrating the writings of a man who swore he would "wash his hands in Joseph Smith's blood"[28]?

When the Prophet Joseph Smith languished in Liberty Jail, the Lord encouraged him by promising that while the "fools" of the earth would mock and ridicule his character and name, while the Hurlbuts and the Howes would hold him in derision, the Lord's true Saints would never turn against him:

// The ends of the earth shall inquire after thy name, and **fools** shall have thee in **derision**, and **hell** shall **rage** against thee;

While the **pure in heart**, and the **wise**, and the **noble**, and the virtuous, shall seek counsel, and authority, and blessings constantly from under thy hand.

And **thy people shall never be turned against thee by the testimony of traitors.**[29]

Ladies and gentlemen of the jury, where are the Prophet Joseph's people today? Where are the "pure in heart," "the wise," "the noble," and "the virtuous"? Where do *you* stand?

---

27   Doctrine and Covenants 122:3.

28   George A. Smith, "Historical Discourse," in *Journal of Discourses*, vol. 11 (Liverpool, 1867), 8. Discourse given on November 15, 1864.

29   Doctrine and Covenants 122:1-3; emphasis added.

13

David Whitmer: Friend or Foe?

The testimony of the only two men who thoroughly *witnessed* and *participated* in the translation process of the Nephite plates both presented clear testimony that the Urim and Thummim was the means by which Joseph Smith translated the Nephite plates. Even Oliver Cowdery, who failed in his attempt to translate, remained unwavering in his affirmation that the Nephite record was translated using the Jaredite—Nephite interpreters, or Urim and Thummim.

The question then becomes, from whence did the claim arise that Joseph Smith translated the Nephite record utilizing a dark chocolate-colored—or any other colored—seer stone? According to research utilizing all known sources to date, every historically viable statement indicating that Joseph Smith translated the *Book of Mormon* using a seer stone in a hat, originates from one of two antagonistic sources—a disaffected member or a hostile nonmember.

There is one question the jury—each one of us individually—must consider. How serious should Latter-day Saints take the accounts of these hostile, disaffected members and non-members? The answer will likely depend upon how we view the claims of those who have turned against the Gospel of Jesus Christ, as it was delivered to the Prophet Joseph Smith.

David Whitmer Contradicts Joseph Smith

We now prepare to cross-examine and challenge the integrity of a claimed witness for the "seer stone" petitioner, David Whitmer. Whitmer was one of the most significant advocates of the seer stone narrative. While many Latter-day Saints recognize him as one of the original Three Witnesses of the Nephite plates and *Book of Mormon* record, few are aware of the "rest of the story."

In 1887 Whitmer published a pamphlet entitled, *An Address to All Believers in Christ*. Whitmer's address denounced The Church of Jesus Christ of Latter-day Saints, claiming that Joseph Smith was a fallen prophet. He charged Joseph Smith of "drift[ing] into many errors," becoming a "stumbling-block to many," "listen[ing] to the persuasions of men," setting up "idols" in his heart, dividing believers in the *Book of Mormon*, committing "grievous error," and introducing "doctrines, ordinances and offices in the church, which are in conflict with Christ's teachings." Whitmer was angry that "the people of the church put too much trust in him [Joseph Smith]—in the man—and believed his words as if they were from God's own mouth." Whitmer claimed that Joseph Smith's demise fulfilled *New Testament* passages which spoke of individuals, "giving heed to seducing spirits and doctrines of devils." In summary, Whitmer professed that Joseph Smith failed in his calling and caused untold damage to the Gospel of Jesus Christ in the Latter-days.[1]

In the midst of this epithet against the Prophet, Whitmer provided his own description of the translation process:

    I will now give you a description of the manner in which the Book of Mormon was translated. Joseph Smith would put the **seer stone into a hat**, and put his face in the hat, drawing it closely around his face to exclude the light; and in the darkness the spiritual light would shine. A piece of something resembling **parchment** would **appear**, and on that appeared the **writing. One character at a time** would appear, and under it was the **interpretation** in **English**. Brother Joseph would read off the English to Oliver Cowdery, who was his principal scribe, and when it was written down and **repeated** to Brother Joseph to see if it was **correct**, then it would **disappear**, and another character with the interpretation would appear. Thus the Book of Mormon was translated by the gift and power of God, and not by any power of man.[2]

---

1   David Whitmer, *An Address to All Believers in Christ by a Witness to the Divine Authenticity of The Book of Mormon* (Richmond, 1887).

2   Ibid, 12; emphasis added.

On another occasion, David Whitmer emphatically stated, "He [Joseph Smith] **did not use the plates in translation.**"[3]

With David Whitmer's description, Joseph Smith is completely taken out of the picture as a translator. The translation, in David Whitmer's view, happened despite the weaknesses and folly of Joseph Smith. With the seer stone narrative, Joseph Smith's righteousness, or in this case, wickedness, was not an integral factor.

Here we encounter two conflicting narratives. The testimony of the Lord Jesus Christ in the *Doctrine and Covenants*, the *Book of Mormon* prophets, including the Jaredite prophets, the Prophet Joseph Smith and his principal scribe, Oliver Cowdery, all unitedly affirm that the *Book of Mormon* was translated using engravings on ancient plates, and that the means of interpretation was through the use of two transparent stones fastened to a breastplate, known as the Urim and Thummim, or Jaredite—Nephite interpreters.

On the other hand, David Whitmer claimed that Joseph Smith placed a seer stone in a hat into which he looked until writing appeared. Whitmer was emphatic that the Prophet did not even use the plates during translation, and he made no mention of the Urim and Thummim. Interestingly, Whitmer's claims were eerily similar to the defamations included in *Mormonism Unvailed*, published over 50 years earlier:

❝ The plates, therefore, which had been so much talked of, were found to be of no manner of use. After all, the Lord showed and communicated to him every word and letter of the Book. Instead of looking at the characters inscribed upon the plates, the prophet was obliged to resort to the old "**peep stone,**" which he **formerly used in money-digging.** This he **placed in a hat,** or box, into which he also thrust his face. Through the stone he could then **discover a single word at a time,** which he repeated aloud to his amanuensis [scribe] who committed it to paper, when **another word would immediately appear,** and thus the performance continued to the end of the book.[4]

Should we attempt to harmonize the claims of David Whitmer (and *Mormonism Unvailed*) with the testimony of Joseph Smith? Is harmonization even possible? Further, most modernists reject the

---

3   *Kansas City Daily Journal,* June 5, 1881; emphasis added.
4   Eber D. Howe, *Mormonism Unvailed* (Painesville, 1834), 18; emphasis added.

statements of Joseph Smith while clinging to those of David Whitmer, Martin Harris, and Emma Smith Bidamon.

David Whitmer's Excommunication

During the early days of the Church, David Whitmer was privileged to stand beside Oliver Cowdery when an angel of the Lord presented to their view the Nephite plates, the Urim and Thummim, and other Nephite artifacts. Whitmer was commanded to offer his testimony as one of the Three Witnesses. Tragically, eight short years after the Church was organized, David Whitmer betrayed the Prophet and became his sworn enemy, and an antagonizer toward the Saints. Although tradition holds that Whitmer never denied his testimony, some suggest that he did, and he certainly did in part.

In January 1838, Joseph Smith and Sidney Rigdon fled Kirtland, Ohio with their families. The Kirtland Safety Society bank had closed the previous year and many unjustly blamed the Prophet for financial losses they incurred. With tensions high there were many members of the Church in the Kirtland, Ohio area who turned against Joseph. Unfortunately, a disaffected David Whitmer was excommunicated during the period of the Kirtland apostasy.

Members and Church leaders alike struggled with their testimonies during those difficult times. The Prophet Joseph Smith later remembered that only *two* of the members of the original Quorum of the Twelve remained faithful to him: Brigham Young, and Heber C. Kimball. Every other member of the Quorum of the Twelve, at one time or another, turned his back and lifted his heel against the Prophet:

❘❘ Of the first Twelve Apostles chosen in Kirtland and ordained under the hands of Oliver Cowdery, David Whitmer, and myself, there have been but two, but what have lifted their heel against me, namely Brigham Young and Heber C. Kimball.[5]

David Whitmer: the "Dumb Ass"

Tragically, David Whitmer not only deserted the Prophet and the Church, he became a hostile enemy. While enduring starvation,

---

5   Joseph Smith History, volume D-1, 28 May 1843, 1563, The Joseph Smith Papers. Printed in *History of the Church*, vol. 5, 412.

loneliness, sickness, fatigue, bitterly cold conditions, and unjust incarceration in Liberty Jail, Joseph Smith wrote a letter to "the church in Caldwell County, Missouri." On December 16, 1838, the Prophet chastised David Whitmer, describing him as a "dumb ass" comparable to Biblical dissenters and corrupted "prophets" such as Baalam, Korah, Dathan, and Abiram. The Prophet reprimanded those who were associating with Whitmer, and who sought to become their own light and follow their own god. Speaking particularly of W. W. Phelps, who testified against the Prophet Joseph Smith in a legal hearing in Missouri and "helped establish the case that committed the Mormon leaders to prison,"[6] the Prophet warned:

/ / This poor man [W. W. Phelps] who professes to be much of a prophet has no other **dumb ass** to ride but David Whitmer to forbid his **madness** when he goes up to **curse Israel** . . . he [David Whitmer] **brays out cursings** instead of blessings.[7]

Why did Joseph Smith refer to David Whitmer as a "dumb ass"? This wasn't a moment of bad language for the Prophet; he was referencing the story of Balaam and his donkey in the *Old Testament*. Balaam, an apostate prophet who practiced witchcraft and magic (essentially the occult or Satanism),[8] was commissioned by the King of Moab to curse Israel. However, Balaam was intercepted by an angel with a drawn sword standing in his path. The Bible records that Balaam could not see the angel, but his donkey could. With the animal's tongue unloosed in a miraculous way, it began to plead with Balaam to abandon his destructive mission. In contrast, Joseph Smith noted in his 1838 letter to the Latter-day Saints in Missouri that in the instance of the donkey "David Whitmer," Whitmer could only "bray out cursing[s] instead of blessings." Sadly, there was no donkey to warn W. W. Phelps.

Korah, Dathan, and Abiram

The Prophet Joseph Smith then prophesied that whoever chose to follow the "dumb ass" David Whitmer would see Whitmer "and his

6   Joseph Smith, *The Personal Writings of Joseph Smith*, ed. Dean C. Jessee (Salt Lake City: Deseret Book, 2002), 471-472.

7   Letter to the Church in Caldwell County, Missouri, 16 December 1838, 2, The Joseph Smith Papers.

8   Joshua 13:22; Number 22-24.

rider perish." The Prophet indicated that they would be destroyed in like manner to another group of ancient Israelites who were condemned for rebelling against the Lord's servant, Moses:

// Poor ass whoever lives to see it will see **him and his rider perish** like those who perished in the gainsaying of Core [Korah], or after the same condemnation.

Now as for these and the rest of their company we will not presume to say that the world loves them but we presume to say that they love the world and we **classify** them in the error [of] **Balaam** and in the gainsaying of **Core** [Korah] and with the company of **Cora** [Korah] and **Dathan** and **Abiram.**[9]

Who were Korah, Dathan, and Abiram? These three Israelites led a revolt against Moses while the children of Israel were wandering in the desert. These coveters of priesthood authority and office desired to pull down the revered Moses from his pedestal. The account of their dissent and subsequent destruction is recorded in Numbers 16. The parallels with David Whitmer and the apostasy in Kirtland are striking, as are the parallels with modern scholars who seek to prop up David Whitmer today. By doing so, they unite in their effort to pull down the Prophet Joseph Smith from his pedestal.

Joseph Smith as the Latter-day Moses

In order to understand the correlation between the adversaries of both the Prophet Joseph Smith and Moses, it is necessary to establish that Joseph Smith was and is the Latter-day Moses, as foretold throughout the standard works. Joseph Smith was given a blessing in Kirtland, wherein he was called to "lead Israel . . . even as Moses led him in days of old . . ."[10] Moses conferred the keys he held upon the Prophet a few months later, after the Kirtland Temple was dedicated in 1836.[11] Some of the early brethren, including Wilford Woodruff referred to Joseph Smith as their "Moses."[12] In the *Doctrine and Covenants*, the

9   Letter to the Church in Caldwell County, Missouri, 16 December 1838, 2, The Joseph Smith Papers; emphasis added.

10   Joseph Smith History, volume B-1, 21 January 1836, 695, The Joseph Smith Papers.

11   Doctrine and Covenants 110:11.

12   See example in Scott G. Kenney, ed., *Wilford Woodruff's Journal*, January 10,

Lord referred to Joseph Smith as holding a position similar to that of the ancient lawgiver, Moses.[13] In Section 103, the Lord promised, "I will raise up unto my people a man, who shall lead them like as Moses led the children of Israel."[14] A few verses later, He defined the "man" as the Prophet Joseph Smith.[15] The *Joseph Smith Translation* of Genesis 50 records ancient prophecies of Joseph of Egypt wherein he paralleled the life and mission of Moses and Joseph Smith. In addition to ancient Joseph's prophecy, a study of the life of Moses and the past, present, and future mission of the Prophet Joseph Smith (as documented in history and foretold in patriarchal blessings), reveals important parallels between these two leaders. Joseph Smith's patriarchal blessing speaks of his future mission in overseeing and enacting Latter-day destructions.[16] This and many other evidences offer a compelling witness that Joseph Smith is indeed, the Latter-day Moses that "prophets, priests, and kings"[17] looked forward to with joyful anticipation millennia after millennia.

David Whitmer Covets Joseph Smith's Priesthood Office as Korah Coveted Moses' Office

If we understand that Joseph Smith is the Latter-day Moses, it would make sense to look for the equivalent Latter-day Korahs, Dathans, and Abirams. During the Kirtland era, and perhaps earlier, David Whitmer and other leaders became jealous of Joseph's position as Prophet, Seer, Revelator, Translator, and President.[18] David Whitmer, in particular, resented members looking "to Joseph Smith as lawgiver." He would later bitterly lament that "the people of the church put too much trust in him" and "believed his words as if they were from God's

---

1837 (Midvale, Utah: Signature Books, 1983), 86; also, June 20, 1839, 339. See also original lyrics of The Spirit of God, Hymn 90, *A Collection of Sacred Hymns for the Church of the Latter Day Saints*, 120, The Joseph Smith Papers.

13   See Doctrine and Covenants 28:2; 101; 103.

14   Doctrine and Covenants 103:16.

15   Doctrine and Covenants 103:21-22.

16   Blessing from Joseph Smith Sr., 9 December 1834, 3, The Joseph Smith Papers. See also Blessing from Oliver Cowdery, 22 September 1835, 15, The Joseph Smith Papers.

17   Joseph Smith History, vol. C-1, 2 May 1842, 1327, The Joseph Smith Papers.

18   Revelation, 6 April 1830 [D&C 21], in Revelation Book 1, 28–29, The Joseph Smith Papers.

own mouth."[19] In fact, during the Kirtland apostasy, a conspiracy surged with the intent to denounce Joseph Smith and sustain David Whitmer as President of the Church in his stead.[20]

David Whitmer and others disdained the fact that on the day the Church was organized the Lord gave a revelation describing how the Church could weather the storms that lay ahead. This revelation, given on the day the Church was organized, is the charter, the commission, the Constitution of the Church:

// Wherefore, meaning the church, thou shalt **give heed unto all his** [Joseph Smith's] **words and commandments** which he shall give unto you as he receiveth them, walking in all holiness before me . . .[21]

The Lord continued by answering the question so often asked by true Saints, "How can I survive through the darkness, the destruction, the despair that has and will envelop the earth in the latter-days?":

// For his [Joseph Smith's] word ye shall **receive, as if from mine own mouth,** in all patience and faith. For by doing these things the **gates of hell shall not prevail** against you; yea, and the Lord God will **disperse the powers of darkness** from before you, and cause the heavens to **shake for your good,** and his name's glory.[22]

The Lord had previously established the Prophet's position of revelatory authority, when a year before the Church was organized (in March 1829), He explained that this dispensation would receive God's word through His prophet, Joseph Smith: "... this generation shall have my word though [Joseph Smith]."[23,24]

---

19   David Whitmer, *An Address to All Believers in Christ by a Witness to the Divine Authenticity of The Book of Mormon* (Richmond, Virginia, 1887), 4, 34.

20   Brigham Young, *Manuscript History of Brigham Young, 1801–1844,* ed. Elden J. Watson (Salt Lake City: Smith Secretarial Service, 1968), 16–17.

21   Doctrine and Covenants 21:4; emphasis added.

22   Doctrine and Covenants 21:5-6; emphasis added.

23   Doctrine and Covenants 5:10.

24   Bruce R. McConkie and other leaders have made it clear that God's word comes to this dispensation through Joseph Smith. "... the generation of which we speak is this era or period of time. It is the dispensation in which we live; it is the time from the opening of our dispensation down to the second coming of the Son of Man; and for that allotted period of the earth's history, the word of the Lord, the word of salvation, the word of light and truth are going to the world through

One of David Whitmer's primary complaints was that some Latter-day Saints were receiving Joseph Smith's words "as if from mine [the Lord's] own mouth." He castigated these revelations as false and uninspired.[25] As Korah had conspired to overthrow Moses, Whitmer and other defectors sought to pull Joseph Smith down from his pedestal, his place of prominence established not by man, but by God. In the Prophet's place they hoped to usurp his position for themselves.

What made this even more disconcerting was the fact that Whitmer was not only a member of the Church, he was a leader. David Whitmer was acting as President of the High Council in Zion and one of the original Three Witnesses of the Nephite plates and the Urim and Thummim. Likewise, the Bible reveals that Korah was a Levite,[26] the only tribe of the House of Israel permitted to be ordained as priests, perform sacrifices, and serve in the Tabernacle.[27] Korah's position of authority gave him influence among the people, but it did not excuse him for revolting against Moses:

> And the earth opened her mouth, and swallowed them [Korah, Dathan, Abiram] up, and their houses, and all the men that appertained unto Korah, and all their goods. They, and all that appertained to them, went down alive into the pit, and the earth closed upon them: and they perished from among the congregation.[28]

As a result of Korah's insurrection against Moses, fire was sent from heaven and burned Korah and 249 of his supporters. When the "congregation of . . . Israel" grumbled because of the seemingly harsh judgement against Korah, a deadly plague destroyed 14,700 members of Israel's congregation.[29]

Joseph Smith, and in no other way and through no one else." Bruce R. McConkie, "'This Generation Shall Have My Word through You,'" *Ensign*, June 1980, https://www.lds.org/study/ensign/1980/06/this-generation-shall-have-my-word-through-you?lang=eng.

25   David Whitmer, *An Address to All Believers in Christ by a Witness to the Divine Authenticity of The Book of Mormon* (Richmond, Virginia, 1887), 31.

26   Exodus 6:19-21.

27   Joshua, Elijah, Isaiah, Jeremiah, Lehi, Ezekiel and other prophets throughout Israel's history held the Melchizedek Priesthood but this holy order was not generally among the people.

28   Numbers 16:32.

29   Numbers 16:41-50.

Joseph Smith knew the history of the *Old Testament* and he deliberately chose to liken Whitmer and other apostates at the time "in the error [of] Balaam" (a false occultic prophet) "and in the gainsaying of [Korah] and with the company of Cora [Korah] and Dathan and Abiram" (apostate Church leaders rebelling against Moses).[30] During the period of the Kirtland apostasy, and still today, David Whitmer represents one of the pre-eminent antagonists of the Prophet Joseph Smith, particularly in regard to the translation of the *Book of Mormon*. Moses cursed Korah, Dathan, and Abiram; Joseph Smith cursed David Whitmer.

Some modernists accuse Joseph Smith of alienating those around him, or of "defensiveness," while others say he let his temper get the best of him.[31] The Prophet addressed these very concerns in his letter written from Liberty Jail:

*❝ Perhaps our brethren may say because we thus write that we are offended at those characters, if we are, it is . . . because they have been the **means of shedding innocent blood**. Are they not **murderers then at heart**? Are not their **consciences seared as with a hot iron**? We confess that we are offended but . . . the saviour said that offences must come but woe unto them by whom they come, and again blessed are ye when **all men** shall **revile you** and speak **all manner of evil** against you **falsely** for my sake, rejoice and be exceeding glad for great is your reward in heaven for so **persecuted** they the **prophets** which were **before you**.[32]*

Why did Joseph Smith accuse David Whitmer and others of being the "means of shedding innocent blood"? Why did he call them "murderers at heart"?

Few are aware of the dark horrors, the genocide-like violence inflicted on the Latter-day Saints during the Missouri persecutions of the 1830s,

---

30 Numbers 16; 26:9-11.

31 Richard Lloyd Anderson, "Explaining Away the Book of Mormon Witnesses," FairMormon, accessed March 2019, https://www.fairmormon.org/conference/august-2004/explaining-away-the-book-of-mormon-witnesses. Also Richard L. Bushman, *Joseph Smith: Rough Stone Rolling* (New York: Alfred A. Knopf, 2005), 54. ". . . he [Joseph Smith] may have been tone-deaf to the spirit of his own words. Unable to bear criticism, he rebuked anyone who challenged him."

32 Letter to the Church in Caldwell County, Missouri, 16 December 1838, 2, The Joseph Smith Papers; emphasis added.

persecutions Whitmer and others played a major role in promoting. Joseph Smith described the crimes as "dark and blackening deeds .. . enough to make hell itself shudder."[33]

Hyrum Smith, brother of the Prophet Joseph Smith and later joint President of the Church, remembered that while incarcerated in Richmond Jail, they were forced to listen as men mockingly and boastfully described the atrocities:

> ❘❘ The same jury sat as a jury in the day time, and were placed over
> us as a guard in the night time; they tantalized and boasted
> over us, of their great achievements at Hauns mills, and at other
> places, telling us how many houses they had burned, and how
> many sheep, cattle and hogs they had driven off, belonging to the
> Mormons, and how many rapes they had committed, and what
> squealing and kicking there was among the damned bitches; saying
> that they lashed one woman upon one of the damned Mormon
> meeting benches, tying her hands and her feet fast and sixteen
> of them abused her as much as they a mind to, and then left her
> bound and exposed in that distressed condition. These fiends of
> the lower region boasted of these acts of barbarity, and tantalized
> our feelings with them for ten days. We had heard of these acts
> of cruelty previous to this time, but we were slow to believe that
> such acts of cruelty had been perpetrated. The lady who was the
> subject of their brutality did not recover her health, to be able to
> help herself for more than three months afterwards.[34]

Parley P. Pratt, a friend of the Prophet Joseph, added his account of the atrocities:

> ❘❘ ... one or two individual females of our society, whom they had
> forcibly bound, and twenty or thirty of them, one after another,
> committed rape upon. One of these females was a daughter of a
> respectable family, with whom I have been long acquainted, and
> with whom I have since conversed, and learned that it was truly
> the case. Delicacy at present forbids my mentioning the names.[35]

---

33   Doctrine and Covenants 123:10.

34   Joseph Smith History, vol. D-1, 1 July 1843, 1617, The Joseph Smith Papers.

35   Ibid, 1621.

Brigham Young further testified:

❝ A part of these mobs were painted like Indians and "Gillum," their leader, was also painted in a similar manner, and styled himself the "Deleware Chief" ... That there were Mormon citizens wounded and murdered by the army under the command of General Lucas, and he verily believes that several women were ravished to death by the soldiery of Lucas and Clark. ...

The next morning, General Lucas demanded and took away the arms of the Militia of Caldwell County, (which arms have never been returned), assuring them that they should be protected; but so soon as they obtained possession of the arms, they commenced their ravages by plundering the citizens of their bedding, clothing, money, wearing apparel, and every thing of value they could lay their hands upon; and also attempting to violate the chastity of the women in sight of their husbands and friends— under the pretence of hunting for prisoners and arms.[36]

Sidney Rigdon also testified of the vile horrors:

❝ I heard a party of them one night telling about some female whose person they had violated and this language was used by one of them: "The damned bitch, how she yelled." Who this person was, I did not know; but before I got out of prison, I heard that a widow, whose husband had died some few months before, with consumption, had been brutally violated by a gang of them, and died in their hands, leaving three little children, in whose presence the scene of brutality took place.

After I got out of prison, and had arrived in Quincy Illinois, I met a strange man in the street, who was inquiring and inquired of me respecting a circumstance of this kind— saying he had heard of it, and was on his way going to Missouri to get the children if he could find them. He said the woman thus murdered was his Sister, or his wife's sister. I am not positive which. The man was in great agitation. What success he had I know not.[37]

---

36   Ibid, 1626-1627.

37   Joseph Smith History, 1838–1856, volume E-1, 1 July 1843, 1649-1650, The Joseph Smith Papers.

Lyman Wight remembered:

❦ . . . Sarah Ann Higbee who had been sick of chills and fever for many months; and another of the name of Keziah Higbee, who was under the most delicate circumstances, lay on the bank of the river, without shelter, during one of the most stormy nights I ever witnessed while torrents of rain poured down during the whole night, and streams of the smallest size were magnified into rivers. The former was carried across the river, apparently a lifeless corpse.— The latter [sic] was delivred [sic] of a fine son, on the bank, within twenty minutes after being carried across the river, under the open canopy of heaven, and from which cause, I have every reason to believe, she died a premature death. The only consolation they received from the mob, under these circumstances, was "God damn you, do you believe in Joe Smith now?"[38]

Joseph Smith's own family did not escape inhumane treatment at the hands of the mob. Emma Smith was specifically targeted and violent activity was attempted. His sister-in-law, Agnes Moulton Coolbrith, barely escaped from her burning home and was forced to wade through three inches of snow and a waist-deep river with her two children (an infant and toddler). She traveled in these conditions for three miles before finding help.[39] According to recollections of the grand-daughter of George A. Smith (Joseph Smith's cousin), Eliza R. Snow, who later became a plural wife of the Prophet, may have been gang raped in Missouri, carrying the scars of that brutality for the rest of her life.[40]

---

38   Joseph Smith History, vol. D-1, 1 July 1843, 1631, The Joseph Smith Papers.

39   Ibid, 1606, The Joseph Smith Papers. ". . . the wife of my brother, the late Don Carlos Smith, came in to Col. Wight's about eleven O'Clock at night, bringing her two children along with her, one about two years and a half old, the other a babe in her arms. She came on foot, a distance of three miles and waded Grand River, the water was then waist deep and the snow 3 inches deep. She stated that a party of the Mob, a gang of ruffians, had turned her out of doors, had taken her household goods and had burnt up her house, and she had escaped by the skin of her teeth.— Her husband at that time was in Tennessee and she was living alone."

40   "Shocking historical finding: Mormon icon Eliza R. Snow was gang-raped by Missouri ruffians," The Salt Lake Tribune, March 17, 2016, accessed November 2017, https://archive.sltrib.com/article.php?id=3613791&itype=CMSID. See also, "Eliza R. Snow As a Victim of Sexual Violence: What One Historian Learned," LDS Living, accessed November 2017, http://www.ldsliving.com/Eliza-R-Snow-as-a-Victim-of-Sexual-Violence-What-One-Historian-Learned/s/81509.

While the Prophet's people fled Missouri, leaving a trail of blood and horror behind them, Joseph Smith was helplessly incarcerated in Liberty Jail. The jailers attempted to feed him human flesh, while the stench of human filth and smoke was overwhelming.

Was Joseph Smith over-reacting when he condemned the disloyal apostates who enabled the torment and suffering of these faithful saints? Or, was he instead declaring righteous judgement on the "murderers at heart"[41]?

The men who had turned on the Prophet and betrayed their own people enabled the barbaric persecution at the hands of the Missouri mob. Although they were not the only guilty parties, according to Joseph Smith, they had enabled the deaths of innocent men, women, and children. David Whitmer had his hands stained by the blood of these atrocities:

❛❛ ... in the campaign when the militia was ordered to drive the Mormons from the state at the point of the bayonet, he [David Whitmer] **drove** one of the **military** baggage-**wagons** to Far West.[42]

Incredibly, David Whitmer had betrayed his own people even more profoundly than Benedict Arnold had during America's struggle for independence, acting in several particulars like Judas of old, driving the baggage wagons of the Saints' militant exterminators.

Joseph Smith decried these men, including David Whitmer, as being "the means of shedding innocent blood. Are they not murderers then at heart? Are not their consciences seared as with a hot iron?"[43] Joseph Smith would later teach, when discussing the redemption of King David following his enabling of the murder of Uriah, that those who "shed innocent blood ... cannot be forgiven, until they have paid the last farthing":

❛❛ If the ministers of religion had a proper understanding of the doctrine of eternal judgment, they would not be found attending the man who had forfeited his life to the injured laws of his

---

41 Letter to the Church in Caldwell County, Missouri, 16 December 1838, 2, The Joseph Smith Papers.

42 "The Book of Mormon," *Chicago Daily Tribune* (Chicago), December 17, 1885, 3; emphasis added.

43 Letter to the Church in Caldwell County, Missouri, 16 December 1838, 2, The Joseph Smith Papers.

country by shedding innocent blood; for such characters cannot be forgiven, until they have paid the last farthing. The prayers of all the ministers in the world could never close the gates of hell against a murderer.[44]

Continuing with Joseph Smith's 1838 letter, he lamented:

❚❚ Such characters as [William E.] McLellin, John Whitmer, **D[avid] Whitmer**, O[liver] Cowdery, Martin Harris . . . are **too mean to mention** and we had **liked to have forgotten them.**[45]

To understand what Joseph Smith meant by the term, "mean," we turn to *Webster's 1828 Dictionary*, the resource contemporaneous with Joseph's letter:

❚❚ [Definition #1] **Wanting dignity**; low in rank or birth; as a man of mean parentage, mean birth or origin.

[Definition #2] Wanting dignity of mind; **low minded; base; destitute of honor;** spiritless.

[Definition #3] **Contemptible; despicable.**

[Definition #4] Of little value; low in worth or estimation; worthy of little or no regard.[46]

In other words, David Whitmer was among those who, after betraying the Gospel of Jesus Christ, fell until he was destitute of honor, too base, too despicable, too contemptible to even mention. Understandably, Joseph Smith wished he could have forgotten this enemy of Christ. Why have we not forgotten this enemy, rather than promoting his beliefs?

Most modern historians now choose David Whitmer's words over those of the Prophet Joseph Smith. It has become popular among members to describe Joseph Smith as an "ordinary man with an extraordinary calling." Some believe that perhaps he said many things with deviant motives and in fits of passion. However, as early as 1831, the Lord entrusted Joseph Smith with the power to curse, the power to bless, and even the power to retain or remit sin:

---

44   *Times and Seasons* 2 (June 1, 1841): 430.

45   Letter to the Church in Caldwell County, Missouri, 16 December 1838, 6, The Joseph Smith Papers; emphasis added.

46   Noah Webster, *An American Dictionary of the English Language*; emphasis added.

❧ ... whosesoever **sins** you [Joseph Smith] **remit** on earth shall
be **remitted** eternally in the **heavens**; and whosesoever **sins** you
retain on earth shall be **retained** in **heaven**. And again, verily
I say, whomsoever you **bless I will bless**, and whomsoever you
curse I will curse, saith the Lord; for I, the Lord, am thy God.[47]

Current scholarship estimates that *Doctrine and Covenants* Section
132 may have been revealed as early as 1831 while Joseph Smith was
only 25 or 26 years old. We have no record of the Lord entrusting
any other man with this Godlike responsibility since the days of the
Prophet Joseph Smith.

David Whitmer and the Prophet Joseph Smith's neighbors accused
Joseph Smith of Satanic activity. Would the Lord grant someone who
had been dabbling in occultic practices this remarkable sealing and
cursing power, the power to retain or to remit sin? Such a thought
is patently ludicrous! Joseph Smith remarked on this gift given him
from God:

❧ The Lord once told me that what I **asked** for I should **have**. I
have been **afraid** to ask God to kill my enemies, lest some of them
should, peradventure, **repent**.

I asked a short time since for the Lord to **deliver** me out of the hands
of the Governor of Missouri, and if it ... must be to accomplish
it, to **take him away**; and the next news that came pouring down
from there was, that Governor Reynolds had **shot himself.**[48]

The Lord has placed His stamp of approval upon the words and the
character of the Prophet Joseph Smith. In contrast, He has cursed
David Whitmer.

While in Kirtland, David Whitmer became deeply involved in the
occult, committing some of mankind's most grievous sins. Lucy Mack
Smith recorded:

❧ ... a certain **young woman**, who was **living at David Whitmer's**
uttered a prophecy; which she said was given her, by **looking
through a black stone** that she had found. This prophecy gave

---

47 Doctrine and Covenants 132:46-47; emphasis added.

48 Joseph Smith, Discourse, 10 March 1844, as Reported by Wilford Woodruff,
p. 211, The Joseph Smith Papers; emphasis added.

some altogether a **new idea of things.** She said, the reason why one third of the church would turn away from Joseph was, because that he was in transgression himself; and would fall from his office on account of the same;[49] that David Whitmer or Martin Harris would fill Joseph's place: and that the one, who did not succeed him, would be councillor to him who did.[50]

The witch's prophecy was partly fulfilled. William E. McLellin[51] was an excommunicated member of the Church and a former member of the Quorum of the Twelve who organized his own congregation in Kirtland, Ohio. He believed, for a time, that David Whitmer was Joseph Smith's designated successor and in 1847 he encouraged Whitmer to come forward and to lead his church. Whitmer agreed and gathered others to his cause, including fellow *Book of Mormon* witnesses, Oliver Cowdery, Martin Harris, Hiram Page, and John

---

49   Lucy Mack Smith, History, 1844-1845, Page [8], bk. 14-Page [9], bk. 14, The Joseph Smith Papers. According to Lucy's 1844-1845 rough draft, David Whitmer requested the witch to provide this revelation. "David Whitmer requested her to look through this stone and tell him what Joseph meant by one third of the church turning against him . . ."

50   Lucy Mack Smith, History, 1845, 235-236, The Joseph Smith Papers; spelling modernized; emphasis added.

51   William E. McLellin was originally a member of the Quorum of the Twelve but was excommunicated on May 11, 1838. While Joseph was imprisoned, McLellin, "went into Brother Joseph's house and commenced searching over his things and Sister Emma asked him why he had done so and his answer was because he could. He took all the jewelry out of Joseph's box and took a lot of bed clothes and in fact, plundered the house and took the things off and while Brother Joseph was in prison, he suffered with the cold, and he sent home to his wife Emma to send him some quilts or bed clothes, for they had no fire there and he had to have something to keep him from the cold. It was in the dead of winter. My wife [wife of John L. Butler] was up there when the word came, and she said that Sister Emma cried and said that they had taken all of her bed clothes, except one quilt and blanket and what could she do." John L. Butler autobiography, circa 1859; Autobiography, circa 1859, p. 26; Church History Library, accessed March, 2019, https://catalog.lds.org/assets/8e634e8e-51e5-4db2-b2e6-1b20a56d034a/0/54

Note this account taken from "History of Brigham Young": "McLellin also took part in persecuting the Latter-day Saints in Missouri. "While Joseph was in prison at Richmond, Missouri, McLellin, who was a large and active man, went to the sheriff and asked for the privilege of flogging the Prophet. Permission was granted on condition that Joseph would fight. The sheriff made known to Joseph McLellin's earnest request, to which Joseph consented, if his irons were taken off. McLellin then refused to fight unless he could have a club, to which Joseph was perfectly willing; but the sheriff would not allow them to fight on such unequal terms." "History of Brigham Young," *Millennial Star* 26 (December 17, 1864): 807-808, accessed March 2019, https://contentdm.lib.byu.edu/digital/collection/MStar/id/27892.

Whitmer. David Whitmer would later announce, after breaking with McLellin and organizing his own church, that Joseph Smith was a fallen prophet because of transgression.[52] His address is often quoted by progressive historians who promote the "seer stone in a hat" hypothesis because Whitmer endorses the seer stone translation therein. David Whitmer was attempting to fulfill the words of the witch who pronounced prophecies from a black seer stone. Is it merely a coincidence that David Whitmer helped instigate the pernicious idea that it was Joseph Smith who used a dark occultic seer stone to translate the *Book of Mormon*, when in fact it was David Whitmer who received revelations for his own church through the use of a dark occultic seer stone? Returning to Lucy Mack Smith's account of the witch in Kirtland:

// This girl soon became an object of great attention among those who were disaffected. . . . [They] held their **secret meetings** at **David Whitmer's**; and when the young woman, who was their instructress was through giving what **revelations** she intended for the evening, she would **jump out of her chair** and **dance over the floor, boasting** of her **power** until she was **perfectly exhausted**. Her **proselytes** would also, in the most vehement manner, proclaim their purity and holiness, and the **mighty power** which **they were going to have**.[53]

Imagine the following scene as it is played out in Kirtland. David Whitmer, formerly one of the witnesses of the *Book of Mormon*, now collaborates with a witch who receives revelations through a dark, occultic peep stone. But the witch and her disciples are not just receiving Satanic revelations, they are dancing, jumping, hopping around the room, and boasting about how powerful they are going to be! It is no wonder Joseph Smith likened David Whitmer and those who followed him to the occultic prophet, Balaam and his donkey.

Given David Whitmer's involvement with the occult and his witch who used dark seer stones, some interesting questions are raised regarding the origin of Whitmer's own "seer stone translation" myth.

---

52   David Whitmer, *An Address to All Believers in Christ by a Witness to the Divine Authenticity of The Book of Mormon* (Richmond, Virginia, 1887), 36-38, 43.

53   Lucy Mack Smith, History, 1845, 236-237, The Joseph Smith Papers; spelling modernized; emphasis added.

The record reveals that as David Whitmer drifted further and further into darkness, he began promoting conflicting historical accounts of the translation that contradicted the testimonies of Joseph Smith, the Lord, the prophets in the *Book of Mormon*, Lucy Mack Smith, and Oliver Cowdery. (See chapter in this volume, "David Whitmer vs. David Whitmer.") Moreover, Whitmer supported many of the slanders published by nefarious characters such as Hurlbut and Howe in *Mormonism Unvailed*.

It is as if a dark pall had settled over David Whitmer; he could not deny that he had certain experiences with the *Book of Mormon*, he knew there was something there, but at the same time, he had lost all reason as to the sacred nature of the *Book of Mormon* and how it truly came about.

According to historian D. Michael Quinn, a stone located in the research library and archives of the *Community of Christ* (formerly *Reorganized Church of Jesus Christ of Latter Day Saints*) is believed to have been owned and possibly used as an occultic seer stone by David Whitmer and/or others in his disaffected church. David's brother John (one of the Eight Witnesses to the *Book of Mormon* who later apostatized) may have also possessed and used an occultic seer stone(s):

> David Whitmer . . . **may have possessed one of his own** [seer stones], and authorized a later spokesman for his own religious organization to **obtain revelations through a stone.**
>
> . . . David Whitmer's seer stone, [was] **used in his church** organization during the 1870s and 1880s by his grandson George Schweich.
>
> . . . **John Whitmer possessed a seer stone** which his descendants preserved.[54]

When David Whitmer was excommunicated from the Church and cut off from the blessings of the Gospel of Jesus Christ, he was charged with slandering the mission and character of the Prophet Joseph Smith, according to the report of the event:

---

54 Michael Quinn, *Early Mormonism and the Magic Worldview* (Signature Books, 1998), 233.

❙❙ The following Charges were prefered [*sic*] against **David [Whitmer]** before the high Council which assembled on the 13th of April 1838 for the purpose of attending to such Charges. Which Charges are as follows

1st For not observing the words of wisdom,

2nd For unchristianlike conduct in neglecting to attend to meetings in uniting with and possesing [*sic*] the same spirit of the desenters [*sic*]

3rd In writing letters to the desenters [*sic*] in Kirtland **unfaivorable** [*sic*] to the **Cause**, and to the **Character of Joseph Smith Jr.**

4th In neglecting the duties of his calling and seperating [*sic*] himself from the Church while he has a name among us.

5th. For **Signing himself Pres. of the Church** of Christ after he had been cut off, in an insulting, letter to the High Council . . .

The Council considered the charges sustained and Consequently Considred [*sic*] him [David Whitmer] no longer a member of the Church of Jesus Christ of Latterday [*sic*] Saints.[55]

Notice that during the proceedings, David Whitmer was charged with and found guilty of slandering the character of the Prophet Joseph, yet years later, he would accuse Joseph Smith:

- of being a stumbling block to the Church,[56]
- of promoting false doctrine,[57]
- of violating his promise to Moroni and showing the plates to men and women the Lord had not approved,[58]
- of translating the *Book of Mormon* using magic seer stones (though the Lord, Joseph Smith, and Oliver Cowdery

55   Joseph Smith, "The Scriptory Book—of Joseph Smith Jr.—President of The Church of Jesus Christ, of Latterday Saints In all the World," 13 April 1838, 31, The Joseph Smith Papers; emphasis added.

56   David Whitmer, *An Address to All Believers in Christ by a Witness to the Divine Authenticity of The Book of Mormon* (Richmond, 1887), 4.

57   Ibid, 37-38, 43.

58   "The Book of Mormon," *Chicago Tribune*, December 17, 1885, 3.

repeatedly insisted that the *Book of Mormon* was translated using the Nephite Urim and Thummim),[59]

- of giving false revelations from the devil[60]

- and even "tattling the secrets of the work among his neighbors," sacred details the Lord did not want revealed.[61]

David Whitmer was not alone in his slanderous activities. The Prophet Joseph made it clear that both he and his family were the victims of the most bitter and severe persecution of the age:

❝ ... rumor with her thousand tongues was all the time employed in circulating falsehoods about my father's family [Joseph Smith Sr. and Lucy Mack Smith family], and about myself. If I were to relate a thousandth part of them, it would fill up volumes.[62]

Some historians purport that Joseph Smith and those who remained loyal to him were deceptive and that David Whitmer, William E. McLellin, and other apostates were the "whistleblowers"—those allegedly telling the truth. It remains for each Latter-day Saint to survey the fruits of these individuals and answer the question: who is telling the truth, Joseph Smith or David Whitmer?

David Whitmer denounced the Prophet in the publication, *An Address to All Believers in Christ,* only a few pages before Whitmer described the translation process:

*❝ Joseph Smith **drifting into errors** after translating the Book of Mormon, is a **stumbling-block** to many ... They [the Mormons or Latter Day Saints] have **departed in a great measure** from the faith of the CHURCH OF CHRIST as it was first established ...[63]*

Essentially, Whitmer claimed that in the beginning, Joseph Smith was an inspired prophet, but after the publishing of the *Book of Mormon,*

---

59   Ibid.

60   David Whitmer, *An Address to All Believers in Christ by a Witness to the Divine Authenticity of The Book of Mormon* (Richmond, 1887), 35, 37, 41.

61   "The Book of Mormon," *Chicago Tribune*, December 17, 1885, 3.

62   Joseph Smith—History 1:61.

63   David Whitmer, *An Address to All Believers in Christ by a Witness to the Divine Authenticity of The Book of Mormon* (Richmond, 1887), 35, 37, 4; emphasis added.

and even before, he led many Saints astray. According to Whitmer, the Prophet's demeanor darkened and he guided the Church into apostasy:

// [The Church] departed . . . by heeding revelations given through Joseph Smith, who, after being called of God to translate his sacred word — the Book of Mormon — **drifted** into many **errors** and gave many revelations to introduce doctrines, ordinances and offices in the church, which are in **conflict with Christ's teachings.**[64]

David Whitmer rejected many elements of the Restoration, including priesthood offices,[65] celestial marriage,[66] and even the name of the Church, "The Church of Jesus Christ of Latter-day Saints."[67] Whitmer claimed that God Himself had revealed to him that Joseph Smith had led the Church astray:

// If you believe my testimony to the Book of Mormon, if you believe that God spake to us three witnesses by his own voice, then I tell you that in June, 1838, **God spake to me again by his own voice** from the heavens and told me to "**separate myself from among the Latter Day Saints,** for as they sought to do unto me, so it should be done unto them."[68]

David Whitmer never returned to the Church. Many Latter-day Saints continue to quote Whitmer's 1887 description of the translation process unaware that in the very same address Whitmer claims to have received revelation denouncing the Church and the Prophet Joseph Smith. Should we cherry pick Whitmer's statements? Can we count him as a credible witness?

The life of David Whitmer is a tragic example of a man called but who failed to live up to his calling. He lost his position, his blessings, and everything that could have been. Lucy Mack Smith remembered meeting David Whitmer in Richmond, Missouri. The Prophet's mother was traveling to raise money to "buy out the mobbers in . . . Missouri."[69]

---

64   Ibid; emphasis added..
65   Ibid, 35, 37, 62.
66   Ibid, 35, 37, 38-45; emphasis added.
67   Ibid, 9, 60, 73.
68   Ibid, 27; emphasis added.
69   Lucy Mack Smith, History, 1845, 318, The Joseph Smith Papers.

❯❯ Whilst waiting for this boat we had an interview with David
Whitmer. He had not confidence to look us in the face, for he
had become our enemy. . . ."[70]

Perhaps we should ask ourselves, should we ride on what Joseph Smith
referred to as the "dumb ass" of David Whitmer? When reviewing
original documents and primary sources, many progressive scholars give
deference and preferential treatment to David Whitmer over Joseph
Smith and the revelations he received. David Whitmer is considered
one of, if not the primary witness of the "seer stone in a hat" myth.
The growing number of those who choose to ride this donkey are
those adventurers who are seeking a new narrative for Church history.

Before deciding what confidence we should place in the history as
depicted by David Whitmer, we should consider what might have
been the story told by Judas Iscariot, fifty years after the original
events. If he had lived to describe the Lord's final days, do you think
his account would mirror the testimony borne by the Lord's loyal
Apostles or would he present a tale tainted by the darkness into which
he fed when he fell away?

In the *Book of Mormon* the unconverted descendants of Laman
and Lemuel loathed the Nephites for generations because they were
taught Laman and Lemuel's side of the story. Lehi's rebellious sons
indoctrinated their children to believe that the Lamanites had been
wronged, and that Nephi had stolen their birthright. For generations
the Lamanites hated their Nephite kin for allegedly robbing Laman
and Lemuel's "right" to the government.[71] Generations of *defective
history*, told through the lens of Laman and Lemuel, drove the Lamanite
population to destroy Nephite records and Nephite culture,[72] initiating
massacre after massacre of Nephite men, women, and children. The
Book of Mormon emphasizes repeatedly that when Lamanites were
finally converted to the Gospel, they recognized the wicked traditions
of their fathers.[73]

History is **not** neutral. The *Book of Mormon* explains the definition
of "truth" as:

---

70   Ibid, 319.

71   Alma 54:17.

72   Enos 1:14.

73   Alma 9:16-17, 17:9,15, 23:3,5; Helaman 15:4,7,15; Mosiah 10:12.

❙❙ . . . the Spirit speaketh the truth and lieth not. Wherefore, it speaketh of things as they **really are**, and of things as they **really will be** . . .[74]

No man or woman can fully understand truth or reality without the Spirit of the Lord. Those who break sacred Priesthood covenants lose the Spirit, critically impairing their worldview, their belief system, their judgment, and their memory.

At the end of the day, the decision is ours. Who is telling the truth: Joseph Smith or David Whitmer? The Lord Jesus Christ or David Whitmer? Who will you trust? The Nephite and the Jaredite prophets or David Whitmer?

During the crisis in Kirtland, when many Latter-day Saints and even members of the Quorum of the Twelve wavered in their allegiance to the Prophet in favor of David Whitmer, one man bravely took a stand for the Prophet Joseph Smith—Brigham Young:

❙❙ On a certain occasion several of the **Twelve**, the **witnesses** to the Book of Mormon, and others of the **Authorities** of the Church, held a council in the **upper room of the Temple.** The question before them was to ascertain how the Prophet Joseph could be **deposed**, and **David Whitmer appointed President of the Church.** Father John Smith, brother Heber C. Kimball and others were present who were opposed to such measures.

I rose up, and in a plain and forcible manner told them that **Joseph was a Prophet**, and **I knew it**, and that they might rail and slander him as much as they pleased, they could not destroy the appointment of the Prophet of God, they could only destroy their own authority, **cut the thread that bound them to the Prophet and to God and sink themselves to hell.**

Many were highly enraged at my decided opposition to their measures, and Jacob Bump (an old pugilist [boxer]) was so exasperated that he could not be still. Some of the brethren near him put their hands on him, and requested him to be quiet; but he writhed and twisted his arms and body saying, "How can I keep my hands off that man?" I told him if he thought it would give him any relief he might lay them on.

---

74 Jacob 4:13; emphasis added.

This meeting was broken up without the apostates being able to unite on any decided measures of opposition. This was a **crisis when earth and hell seemed leagued to overthrow the Prophet and Church of God.** The knees of many of the **strongest men in the Church faltered.**

During this siege of darkness I **stood close by Joseph**, and, with all the wisdom and power God bestowed upon me, put forth my **utmost energies to sustain the servant of God and unite the quorums of the Church.**[75]

The record shows that David Whitmer initially supported Joseph Smith in his prophetic calling, which gave him some proximity to the events of the translation. Without revelation, no one can know the mind and thoughts of another person directly, but we can judge Whitmer by his actions and his words, which demonstrate a bitter antagonism toward Joseph Smith and the Restoration. Whitmer was a member, if not the leader, in the vanguard sent to assail the Prophet during the Kirtland apostasy, and ever after sought to disparage the name of Joseph Smith. While once a friend, Whitmer now stands as foe of the blackest ilk, a man of unsteady character and unreliable testimony. The defense's next witness will pit David Whitmer as witness against David Whitmer.

---

75   Brigham Young, *Manuscript History of Brigham Young*, 1801–1844, ed. Elden J. Watson (Salt Lake City: Smith Secretarial Service, 1968), 16–17; emphasis added.

14

DAVID WHITMER VS. DAVID WHITMER

The plaintiff and others often quote David Whitmer as an authoritative "eyewitness" to the translation of the *Book of Mormon*. However, past researchers have made note that the "sketchy accounts . . . [David Whitmer] recorded much later in life were often contradictory."[1] One of the strengths of the Prophet Joseph Smith's testimony is that of consistency—that his expressions and the revelations of the Lord corroborate and harmonize together. David Whitmer's accounts, on the other hand, reveal many discrepancies with credible historical accounts and even his own statements. Furthermore, David Whitmer never participated in the translation process, nor did he ever serve as a scribe. We continue our cross-examination of David Whitmer's statements and testimony.

David Whitmer Interviews

David Whitmer's statements evaluated in this chapter come from interviews by various individuals and printed news sources from 1878 to 1909. Some of these interviews provide a variety of historical details related to the translation of the plates. The primary focus of this investigation lies in the details David Whitmer provided about how the translation occurred and his description of the instruments Joseph Smith used to translate the *Book of Mormon*. The reader can find the full text of each statement in the footnotes of a paper published on the *Joseph Smith Foundation* website.[2] These are provided for the benefit of those interested in evaluating the interviews in their entirety.

1 *Church History in the Fulness of Times: Religion 341–343 Student Manual* (Salt Lake City, UT: Church of Jesus Christ of Latter-day Saints, 2003), 58.

2 "David Whitmer: Man of Contradictions – An Analysis of Statements by David Whitmer on Translation of the Book of Mormon," Joseph Smith Foundation, February 10, 2019, accessed February 2019, https://josephsmithfoundation.org/

The Urim and Thummim

In one of David Whitmer's first published interviews (August 16, 1878), Whitmer provides a traditional description of the Jaredite—Nephite Urim and Thummim:

// The Urim and Thummim were **two white stones**, each of them cased in as **spectacles** are, in a kind of silver casing, but the **bow** between the stones was more heavy, and longer apart between the stones, than we usually find it in spectacles.[3]

In another Whitmer interview conducted in 1876 but published in 1879 by Thomas Wood Smith, Whitmer reaffirms that Joseph Smith used the Urim and Thummim in the translation process. Thomas Wood Smith was an apostle of the *Reorganized Church of Jesus Christ of Latter-day Saints*, the break-off church that remained in Nauvoo with Joseph Smith's widow, Emma, and her son, Joseph Smith III. This organization led the primary opposition against many doctrines and practices continued by President Brigham Young and the main body of the Church in Utah. Relating to the translation of the *Book of Mormon*, Thomas Wood Smith said:

// I **personally heard** him [David Whitmer] state in Jan 1876 in his own house in Richmond, Ray Co. Mo [Missouri] . . . . that he saw Joseph translate, by the **aid of the Urim and Thummim, time and again** . . .[4]

Thomas Smith reported that David Whitmer produced a manuscript that he claimed was:

// . . . written mainly by Oliver Cowdery and Martin Harris, as the translation was being read by the **aid of the Urim and Thummim** of the characters on the plates by Joseph Smith . . .[5]

---

papers/an-analysis-of-statements-by-david-whitmer-on-translation-of-the-book-of-mormon/.

3   P. Wilhelm Poulson, *Deseret Evening News*, August 16, 1878; emphasis added.

4   Thomas Wood Smith, *Fall River Herald*, March 28, 1879; reprinted in the *Saints' Herald* 26 (15 April 1879).

5   Ibid; emphasis added.

In this latter account, there are discrepancies. First, the manuscript shown by David Whitmer could not have been written in part by Martin Harris because Martin only helped with the translation up to the loss of the 116-page manuscript that he and Joseph produced. Additionally, when Orson Pratt and Joseph F. Smith examined David Whitmer's manuscript, they determined that the writing was primarily in the hand of Oliver Cowdery with only small sections attributed to Emma Smith, John Whitmer, and Christian Whitmer.[6]

We find another contradiction when comparing David Whitmer's interview with the *Kansas City Journal* from June 5, 1881,[7] wherein he states that the Urim and Thummim was taken from Joseph and never returned after the 116-page manuscript was lost. David did not meet Joseph until after the 116 pages were stolen. Why did David Whitmer claim in 1876 that "he saw Joseph translate, by the aid of the Urim and Thummim, time and again" if in 1881 he claimed that the Urim and Thummim was taken permanently from the Prophet before he ever met him? Five years later, David Whitmer reportedly shared yet another version claiming that "... [Joseph] had the Urim and Thummim, and a chocolate colored stone, which he used alternately, as suited his convenience..."[8] In still other accounts, David Whitmer claims Joseph used a seer stone in a hat to translate. Questions we need answered to settle this discrepancy include, did Joseph Smith use the Urim and Thummim or did he lose it after the 116 pages? Did Joseph use a seer stone? Did he use both seer stone and interpreters? David Whitmer seems to find it difficult to make up his mind.

Despite the discrepancies, Whitmer makes the point in 1876 that the Urim and Thummim was used in the translation. However, in an interview with David Whitmer, printed just three years later, on November 15, 1879, J. L. Traughber said:

> I, too, have seen the manuscripts and examined them. I, too, have heard Father [David] Whitmer say that he was present many times while Joseph was translating; but I never heard him say that

---

6   Andrew Jenson, ed., "The Three Witnesses," *Historical Record* 6 (May 1887): 216–17.

7   *Kansas City Daily Journal*, June 5, 1881.

8   Nathan A. Tanner Jr. to Nathan A. Tanner, February 17, 1909, 5, Church Archives; emphasis added. The interview took place on May 1886.

the translation was made by **aid of Urim and Thummim**; but in every case, and his testimony is always the same, he declared that Joseph first offered prayer, then took a **dark colored, opaque stone**, called a "seer-stone," and placed it in the crown of his hat, then put his face into the hat, and read the translation as it appeared before him.

Traughber stated further:

❚❚ With the sanction of David Whitmer, and by his authority, I now state that he does not say that Joseph Smith ever translated in his presence by **aid of Urim and Thummim**, but by means of **one dark colored, opaque stone**, called a "**Seer Stone**," which was placed in the crown of a hat, into which Joseph put his face, so as to exclude the external light. Then, a spiritual light would shine forth, and parchment would appear before Joseph, upon which was a line of characters from the plates, and under it, the translation in English; at least, so Joseph said.[9]

Traughber's comment that "at least, so Joseph said" is revealing in that either he or Whitmer questioned Joseph's account of the translation process. Advancing the seer stone hypothesis casts doubt on Joseph Smith's own testimony and narrative. Importantly, every individual who claimed that they witnessed Joseph Smith use a seer stone to translate the *Book of Mormon* either apostatized from the Church or was never a member. No man or woman who was familiar with the Prophet during the translation process and stayed true to the Gospel of Jesus Christ ever furthered the idea that Joseph Smith used a seer stone to "translate" the *Book of Mormon*. Only those who attempted to criticize the Prophet or impugn his character ever promoted the "seer stone in a hat" narrative.

Furthermore, it appears that Traughber was unaware of or chose to omit any of the numerous statements made by the Prophet Joseph Smith; he simply trusted the word of David Whitmer. Today, just as in Whitmer's day, "seer stone in a hat" advocates are either unaware of the Prophet Joseph Smith's statements and their consistency, or they discount the Prophet's statements altogether. The Prophet was

---

9   J. L. Traughber Jr., "Testimony of David Whitmer. Is it True or False?," *Saints' Herald* 26 (November 15, 1879): 341; emphasis added.

unambiguously clear that he used the Urim and Thummim and not a seer stone during the translation.

According to the timeline of historical documents, David Whitmer claimed that Joseph used the seer stone *after* David Whitmer claimed that Joseph used the Urim and Thummim. Why the apparent change in tune? One shift in David Whitmer's account occurred shortly after he reorganized his own Whitmerite "Church of Christ."[10] He claimed that Joseph Smith had violated the commands of the Lord and had become a fallen prophet, and that David Whitmer held the authority instead. About this same time, David Whitmer's narrative often fluctuated, as he seemed to have developed an aversion to the idea that the Urim and Thummim was used after the loss of the 116 pages. By advancing this claim, Whitmer could bolster his position that Joseph Smith had lost his privilege as a seer and translator, lost the right to use the Urim and Thummim/interpreters and the plates, and was left to rely on magic seer stones. According to David Whitmer, Joseph declined in spiritual gifts and moral character until he led the Church to "stumble."[11]

The Seer Stone in a Hat

The "seer stone in a hat" narrative, albeit an inconsistent narrative, began to dominate the David Whitmer interviews. Whitmer went so far as to require Thomas Wood Smith (January 1, 1880) to retract a previous account he had given, which had been printed on March 28, 1879 and to which a disconcerted Thomas recounted:

// Unless my interview with David Whitmer in January, 1876, was only a dream, or that I failed to understand plain English, I believed then, and since, and now, that he said that Joseph **possessed, and used the Urim and Thummim** in the translation

10   David Whitmer resurrected the Whitmerite Church of Christ in January 1876. In 1874, 1876 and 1878, interviews claim that David Whitmer reported Joseph Smith used the Urim and Thummim. However, in 1879, 1881, and later interviews Whitmer instead holds to a narrative describing stones being called a "seer stone" or at least resembling seer stone descriptions. There is an account in 1884 and 1886 that speak of the Urim and Thummim being used, even after the loss of the 116 pages. It is therefore extremely difficult to determine Whitmer's motivation behind his conflicting narratives.

11   David Whitmer, *An Address to All Believers in Christ by a Witness to the Divine Authenticity of The Book of Mormon* (Richmond, 1887), 39, 42.

of the inscriptions referred to, and I remember being much pleased with that statement as I had heard of the 'Seer stone' being used. And unless I dreamed the interview, or very soon after failed to recollect the occasion, he **described the form and size of the said Urim and Thummim**.

Referring to David Whitmer as "Father Whitmer," Thomas continued:

❝ ... that unless I altogether misunderstood "Father Whitmer" on this point, he said the translation was done by the **aid of the Urim and Thummim.** If he says he did not intend to convey such an impression to my mind, then I say I regret that I misunderstood him, and unintentionally have misrepresented him. But that I understood him as represented by me frequently I still affirm. If Father Whitmer will say over his own signature, that he never said, or at least never intended to say, that Joseph possessed or used in translating the Book of Mormon, the Urim and Thummim, I will agree to not repeat my testimony as seen in the Fall River Herald on that point.[12]

Although the account of translation through the use of the seer stone appears repeatedly in many interviews, the story is not consistent. In an interview with Eri B. Mullin, published on March 1, 1880, Mullin stated:

❝ Mr. D. Whitmer told me in the year 1874, that Joseph Smith **used the Urim and Thummim** when he was translating.... I for my part know he said that Joseph had the instrument **Urim and Thummim**. I asked him how they looked. He said they looked like **spectacles**, and he [Joseph] would put them on and look in a hat, or put his face in the hat and read.[13]

In this version of Whitmer's story, Joseph uses the Urim and Thummim, but instead of reading the plates with them, he looks into a hat, or places his face in a hat, to read words that appear therein.

---

12   Thomas Wood Smith, Letter to the editor, "'Seer Stone' or 'Urim and Thummim,'" *Saints' Herald* 27 (January 1, 1880): 13; emphasis added.

13   Eri B. Mullin, Letter to the editor, *Saints' Herald* 27 (March 1, 1880): 76; emphasis added.

David Whitmer's story shifted again when on June 19, 1881, David Whitmer wrote to the editor of the *Kansas City Journal*. Referencing one of his interviews published a few weeks previous on June 5, 1881, Whitmer said:

▌▌ I did not say that Smith used "two small stones," as stated nor did I call the stone "interpreters." I stated that "he used **one stone (not two) and called it a sun stone.**" The "interpreters" were as I understood taken from Smith and were not used by him after losing the first 116 pages . . .[14]

In this account David Whitmer denies that Joseph had two stones, but only one stone that he called a "sun stone." Then in October of that same year, Whitmer told the *Chicago Times* that:

▌▌ The tablets or plates were translated by Smith, who used a **small oval kidney-shaped stone, called Urim and Thummim**, that seemed endowed with the marvelous power of converting the characters on the plates, when used by Smith, into English . . .[15]

In many of David Whitmer's accounts, Whitmer used the term "interpreters" synonymously with "the Urim and Thummim," which he usually described as having two stones. However, in this account, Whitmer refers to a stone that he describes as being a "small oval kidney-shaped stone," calling it Urim and Thummim. On other occasions, however, he described the Urim and Thummim as having "two white stones,"[16] or, "two small stones of chocolate color,"[17] or "two transparent pebbles;"[18] very differing accounts in different interviews. In one interview alone, Whitmer talked about "stone spectacles," "the Urim and Thummim," "the magic stone," and a "strange oval-shaped chocolate-colored stone."[19] The inconsistencies in David Whitmer's

---

14   David Whitmer to the editor, *Kansas City Daily Journal*, June 19, 1881; emphasis added.

15   *Chicago Times*, October 17, 1881; emphasis added.

16   P. Wilhelm Poulson, *Deseret Evening News*, August 16, 1878.

17   *Kansas City Daily Journal*, June 5, 1881.

18   *St. Louis Republican*, July 16, 1884.

19   *Omaha Herald*, October 17, 1886. See also *Chicago Inter Ocean*, October 17, 1886; and *Saints' Herald* 33 (November 13, 1886): 706.

descriptions of the object used by Joseph Smith to translate the *Book of Mormon* raise significant issues regarding the credibility of all David Whitmer's testimonials about the translation of the *Book of Mormon*.

To summarize, in several interviews, David Whitmer claims that Joseph Smith used the Urim and Thummim, at least sometime during the translation: 1874,[20] 1876,[21] 1878,[22] June 1884,[23] July 1884,[24] and 1886.[25] However, on other occasions, Whitmer describes the translation device as a stone, often called the seer stone, but sometimes by other names, which he says Joseph placed in a hat: November 1879,[26] June 1881,[27] October 1881,[28] February 1884,[29] March 1884,[30] January 1885,[31] and sometime in 1887.[32] Whitmer's profusion of inconsistencies continues, as later in his life, he changed his narrative yet again when he described Joseph using the Urim and Thummim and a "chocolate colored stone" interchangeably.[33] If the reader is confused, so have been the authors, thus the title "David Whitmer vs. David Whitmer."

Although David Whitmer here states that the Urim and Thummim was not returned to Joseph Smith after the 116 pages were lost, Lucy Mack Smith quotes Joseph as saying the Urim and Thummim was returned after a period of sorrow. See chapter in this volume, "Witness #2 - Joseph Smith: Translation Instruments" and Lucy Mack Smith, History, 1845, 135, The Joseph Smith Papers.

20   Eri B. Mullin, Letter to the editor, *Saints' Herald* 27 (March 1, 1880): 76.

21   Thomas Wood Smith, *Fall River Herald*, March 28, 1879.

22   P. Wilhelm Poulson, *Deseret Evening News*, August 16, 1878.

23   E. C. Briggs, Letter to the editor, *Saints' Herald* 31 (June 21, 1884): 396–397.

24   *St. Louis Republican*, July 16, 1884.

25   M. J. Hubble, interview, November 13, 1886.

26   J. L. Traughber Jr., "Testimony of David Whitmer. Is it True or False?," *Saints' Herald* 26 (November 15, 1879): 341.

27   David Whitmer to the editor, *Kansas City Daily Journal*, June 19, 1881.

28   *Chicago Times*, October 17, 1881.

29   George Q. Cannon, February 27, 1884, George Q. Cannon Journal, Church Archives.

30   James H. Hart, "About the Book of Mormon," *Deseret Evening News*, March 25, 1884.

31   Zenas H. Gurley, "Questions Asked of David Whitmer," holograph, 1, 3, 4, Gurley Collection, Church Archives.

32   David Whitmer, *An Address to All Believers in Christ by a Witness to the Divine Authenticity of The Book of Mormon* (Richmond, 1887).

33   *Richmond Democrat*, January 26, 1888.

Who Saw the Translation Process?

To bolster his testimony, David Whitmer claimed that he and others witnessed the work of translation. In the *Kansas City Journal* interview (published June 5, 1881), Whitmer claimed that all of his father's family, along with Emma Smith, Oliver Cowdery, and Martin Harris were present during the translation.[34] In an interview recorded by the *Chicago Tribune* on December 17, 1885, he said that all of Joseph's collaborators (undesignated), the entire Whitmer household, and several of Joseph's relatives were present during the translation. He also says that the translation was performed in the family room of the Whitmer home where Joseph made no attempt to conceal the plates or the method of translation:

> In order to give privacy to the proceeding a **blanket**, which served as a portière, was stretched across the family living room to shelter the translators and the plates from the eyes of any who might call at the house while the work was in progress. This, Mr. Whitmer says, was the only use made of the blanket, and it was **not for the purpose of concealing the plates or the translator** from the eyes of the amanuensis. In fact, Smith was at **no time hidden** from his collaborators, and the translation was performed **in the presence of not only the persons mentioned, but of the entire Whitmer household and several of Smith's relatives** besides.
>
> The work of translating the tablets consumed about eight months, Smith acting as the seer and Oliver Cowdery, Smith's wife, and Christian Whitmer, brother of David, performing the duties of amanuenses, in whose handwriting the original manuscript now is. Each time before resuming the work all present would kneel in prayer and invoke the Divine blessing on the proceeding. After prayer Smith would sit on one side of a table and the amanuenses, in turn as they became tired, on the other. Those present and not actively engaged in the work seated themselves around the room and then the work began. After affixing the magical spectacles to his eyes, Smith would take the plates and translate the characters one at a time.[35]

---

34 *Kansas City Daily Journal*, June 5, 1881.

35 "The Book of Mormon," *Chicago Tribune*, December 17, 1885, 3.

The following similar accounts add to Whitmer's claim:

▌▌ ... as the translation was being read by the aid of the Urim and Thummim of characters on the plates by Joseph Smith, which **work of translation and transcription he [David Whitmer] frequently saw.**[36]

... I, too, have heard Father [David] Whitmer say that he was **present many times while Joseph was translating.**[37]

Did David Whitmer "frequently" see Joseph translating? Did the "entire Whitmer household and several of Smith's relatives" see the plates and the translation process? Was Joseph truly "at no time hidden from his collaborators"? Did Joseph violate his trust? The answers to these questions impacts significantly the relationship between Joseph Smith, Moroni, and the Lord.

When Moroni delivered the plates into the hands of Joseph Smith, the Prophet was commanded to:

▌▌ ... not show them [the plates] to any person; neither the breastplate with the Urim and Thummim; only to those to whom I should be commanded to show them; if I did I should be **destroyed.**[38]

In March 1829, the Lord revealed that Joseph Smith had **covenanted** with the Lord to not show the plates to anyone, except those the Lord had commanded:

▌▌ I have caused you that you should enter into a **covenant** with me, that you should **not show them** except to those persons to whom I commanded you; and you have no power over them except I grant it unto you.[39]

There are no credible statements that any individuals saw the plates except the Prophet, the Three Witnesses, and the Eight Witnesses.

---

36   Thomas Wood Smith, *Fall River Herald* (28 March 1879); reprinted in the *Saints' Herald* 26 (15 April 1879): 128.

37   Ibid; emphasis added.

38   Joseph Smith—History 1:59; emphasis added.

39   Doctrine and Covenants 5:3; emphasis added.

Why would David Whitmer promote the idea that Joseph Smith violated his covenant by allowing the "entire Whitmer household," "several of Smith's relatives," and who knows how many others to see the plates, the Urim and Thummim, and the translation process? What was his motivation?

/ / ... It seems that [Joseph] Smith, who was **puffed up** with his great importance as a confidential secretary to the Lord, **displeased the Master** by entering into some **carnal confab** in relation to the work. For this offense he was punished by having the celestial visitant, who first commissioned him to inaugurate the work, suddenly appear and carry off the plates and spectacles....

> ... Smith's **offense of tattling the secrets of the work among his neighbors** was less readily condoned [than Harris losing the 116 pages], and for a long time the work was suspended, the angel being in possession of the plates and spectacles. Finally, when Smith had fully repented of his **rash conduct**, he was forgiven. The **plates**, however, were **not returned** ...[40]

Did Joseph Smith break his covenant? Was he "destroyed"? On the contrary, the Lord is clear in later revelations that Joseph Smith succeeded in accomplishing the task required at his hands and that the Lord was well-pleased with Joseph's work.[41]

We know that David Whitmer charged Joseph Smith in 1887, less than two years after giving the statement above, with "drift[ing] into many errors," becoming a "stumbling-block to many," "listen[ing] to the persuasions of men," setting up "idols" in his heart, dividing believers in the *Book of Mormon*, committing "grievous error," and introducing "doctrines, ordinances and offices in the church, which are in conflict with Christ's teachings."[42] David Whitmer's account of the translation is tailored to support Whitmer's allegation that Joseph broke his covenants and became a fallen prophet, even before the Church was organized. If Joseph Smith had fallen as a prophet,

---

40   "The Book of Mormon," *Chicago Tribune*, December 17, 1885, 3; emphasis added.

41   For example, see Doctrine and Covenants 17.

42   David Whitmer, *An Address to All Believers in Christ by a Witness to the Divine Authenticity of The Book of Mormon* (Richmond, 1887).

if he had broken his covenants, if he was "puffed up" and caused the Church to "stumble," the Gospel of Jesus Christ would have been lost.

Does it matter whether the Prophet stayed faithful? President Heber J. Grant once remarked:

> In many places I have met people who have studied our faith. Some of them would say: "I could accept everything that you people teach were it not for this man Joseph Smith. If you would only eliminate him!"
>
> The day can never come when we will do that. As well might we undertake to **leave out Jesus Christ,** the Son of the living God.[43]
>
> The whole **foundation** of this **Church** rests firmly upon the inspiration of the living God through **Joseph Smith** the Prophet.[44]

President Gordon B. Hinckley taught that the entire Church, including the President, should continue to look to Joseph Smith for direction in "guiding this great Church":

> Though Joseph's life was taken at an early age, his testimony of the Eternal God and the risen Lord lives on with luster and eloquence. I look to him. I love him. I seek to follow him. I read his words, and they become the **standards to be observed in guiding this great Church** as it moves forward in fulfilling its eternal destiny.[45]

The adversary has always understood the importance of Joseph Smith to a degree that we do not comprehend. It is no accident that all those who have opposed the Prophet Joseph Smith have sought to disparage his faithfulness and besmirch his integrity. It has been said that if the history is changed, the doctrine will also change with it. Apparently, David Whitmer and other critics of the Prophet Joseph Smith understood this concept thoroughly. Instead of writing tedious, boring books on theology, they attempted to change the history; they presented a "new narrative" and thereby began chipping away at the

---

43   Heber J. Grant, *Gospel Standards* (Salt Lake City: Deseret Sunday School Union Board, 1942), 3; emphasis added.

44   Ibid, 83; emphasis added.

45   Gordon B. Hinckley, First Presidency Christmas Devotional, 7 December 2003; emphasis added.

foundation of the Church. What danger then awaits those who place their trust in the historical perspective and shifting postulations of David Whitmer?

Other Inconsistencies

Another inconsistency lies in David Whitmer's claims as to the length of the translation process at his father's home. In a discussion with the *Kansas City Journal*, David said it took one month, "from June 1 to July 1, 1829,"[46] which seems to be consistent with other reliable accounts. On another occasion, he said that it took "at least two months" in his father's home.[47] He also said it took about six months,[48] and finally, on two other occasions he said that it took eight months to complete the translation.[49] The last two accounts are unclear whether he is referring to the entire translation period, or only the portion completed in the Whitmer home but the discrepancies are clear enough to raise concern and confusion.

These inconsistencies, coupled with all of the other disparities in his accounts, make it difficult to give any credibility to Whitmer's claim to have witnessed the translation, including his claim that many other unauthorized viewers had also observed the translation process.

If David Whitmer was a witness of the translation process, we should expect David Whitmer and the other supposed witnesses to express a reasonably consistent and unified story describing the work of translation. Because David Whitmer stands as one of the Three Witnesses, and because he claimed to have been present many times during the translation, we should expect his own accounts of the translation to exhibit consistency. Since this is clearly not the case, should we consider any of David Whitmer's descriptions accurate?

---

46   *Kansas City Daily Journal*, June 5, 1881.

47   *St. Louis Republican*, July 16, 1884; emphasis added.

48   *Chicago Times*, October 17, 1881.

49   "The Book of Mormon," *Chicago Tribune*, December 17, 1885, 3. See also *Omaha Herald*, October 17, 1886. See also *Chicago Inter Ocean*, October 17, 1886; and *Saints' Herald* 33 (November 13, 1886): 706.

Was David Whitmer an Eyewitness?

Why was there a need for Three Witnesses, or for an additional Eight Witnesses if Joseph had not concealed the plates and the translators from the casual view of so many witnesses during the translation process in the Peter Whitmer home? If David Whitmer and others had been allowed to see the entire process, why did Whitmer specifically request permission from the Lord to be a special witness of what had previously been withheld from his view, specifically the plates and the Urim and Thummim?[50]

Recall that Joseph expressed great relief after being able to show the plates to certain witnesses that the Lord had selected:

> Father, mother; you do not know happy I am; the Lord has now caused the plates to be shown to **three more besides myself.**— they have seen an angel, who has testified to them; and they will have to bear witness to the truth of what I have said; for now they know for themselves, that I do not go about to deceive the people. And I feel as if I was relieved of a burden, which was almost to heavy for me to bear; and it rejoices my heart, that I am **not any longer to be entirely alone in the world.**[51]

The relief Joseph expressed and the Lord's previous strict charge not to show the plates, make a compelling case that neither David Whitmer nor Martin Harris had seen the plates or the angel prior to this experience. Thus, David Whitmer was not privy to the translation and therefore not an "eyewitness" of the translation process. Moreover, he did not serve as a scribe to the Prophet Joseph Smith.

By all accounts, the only true eyewitnesses to the translation include the Lord, Joseph Smith, the ancient prophets, and perhaps Oliver Cowdery. Based on the fact that David Whitmer contradicted Joseph Smith, and that he frequently contradicted himself, we submit to the jury that David Whitmer did not see all he claimed to have seen.

It is also interesting that Joseph showed a reluctance to share details regarding the translation of the *Book of Mormon*. At a church conference held October 25-26, 1831, in Orange, Ohio, Hyrum Smith (Joseph's brother) requested a firsthand account of the coming forth of the *Book*

50   Joseph Smith History, volume A-1, June 1829, 23, Joseph Smith Papers.

51   Lucy Mack Smith, History, 1845, 154, The Joseph Smith Papers; emphasis added.

of Mormon. Joseph stated simply: "It was not intended to tell the world all the particulars of the coming forth of the Book of Mormon."[52]

The details the Prophet did provide are included in the chapters, "Witness #2 - Joseph Smith: Translation Instruments," "Witness #2 - Joseph Smith: Translator or Reader?," and "Witness #2 - Joseph Smith: Book of Mormon Historicity." David Whitmer's detailed characterizations of the translation process go above and beyond, far exceeding that which the Prophet Joseph shared, and they often contradict the Prophet. These facts alone should cause us to pause and reconsider David Whitmer's credibility as a source on the translation of the *Book of Mormon.*

Table Documenting Whitmer's Contradictory Statements

The varied accounts of the translation include different instruments used in the translation, different descriptions of the instruments, and different methods of translation. Table 1 provides a summary of these various descriptions as found in David Whitmer's published interviews. Table 2 provides a summary of the different methods of translation described by David Whitmer.

Table 1. Various Descriptions of the Translation Instruments		
Date & Source	*Instrument used to Translate*	*Description of Instrument*
1878 P. Wilhelm Poulson[53]	Urim and Thummim	Two white stones cased in spectacles of silver, stones separated more than normal spectacles
1879 Thomas Wood Smith[54]	Urim and Thummim	

---

52   Minute Book 2, 25 October 1831, 10, The Joseph Smith Papers; emphasis added.

53   P. Wilhelm Poulson, *Deseret Evening News*, August 16, 1878.

54   Thomas Wood Smith, *Fall River Herald*, March 28, 1879.

Table 1. Various Descriptions of the Translation Instruments		
Date & Source (continued)	*Instrument used to Translate*	*Description of Instrument*
1879 J. L. Traughber Jr.[55]	Seer Stone	Dark colored, opaque stone placed in hat, put face in hat to exclude light
1880 Thomas Wood Smith[56]	Retraction of Urim and Thummim method described in interview with Thomas Wood Smith from 1876 [57]	
1880 Eri B. Mullin [58]	Urim and Thummim	Looked like spectacles
1881 Kansas City Journal[59]	Interpreters	Two small stones of chocolate color, egg shaped and perfectly smooth, not transparent
1881 David Whitmer to the Kansas City Journal[60]	Retracted the Kansas City Journal Story about the Interpreters and said Joseph used a "sun stone"	Not two stones, but one stone was used. Said he did not say Joseph used the interpreters.

55   J. L. Traughber Jr., "Testimony of David Whitmer. Is it True or False?," *Saints' Herald* 26 (November 15, 1879): 341.

56   Thomas Wood Smith, Letter to the editor, *Saints' Herald* 27 (January 1, 1880): 13.

57   Thomas Wood Smith, *Fall River Herald*, March 28, 1879.

58   Eri B. Mullin, Letter to the editor, *Saints' Herald* 27 (March 1, 1880): 76.

59   *Kansas City Daily Journal*, June 5, 1881.

60   David Whitmer to the editor, *Kansas City Daily Journal*, June 19, 1881.

Date & Source (continued)	Instrument used to Translate	Description of Instrument
Table 1. Various Descriptions of the Translation Instruments		
1881 Chicago Times[61]	Urim and Thummim	Small oval kidney-shaped stone called Urim and Thummim that had marvelous power converting characters on the plates when used by Smith
1882 William H. Kelley and G. A. Blakeslee[62]	*None*	Joseph translated the *Book of Mormon* by the inspiration of God from the plates of the Nephites.
1884 George Q. Cannon[63]	Stone	Placed stone in hat from which all light was excluded
1884 James H. Hart[64]	Seer Stone	Placed the seer stone in a deep hat, and placing his face close to it
1884 E.C. Briggs[65]	Urim and Thummim	Looked dark when not humble

61   *Chicago Times* October 17, 1881.

62   *Saints' Herald* 29 (March 1, 1882): 68.

63   George Q. Cannon, February 27, 1884, George Q. Cannon Journal, Church Archives.

64   James H. Hart, "About the Book of Mormon," *Deseret Evening News*, March 25, 1884.

65   E. C. Briggs, Letter to the editor, *Saints' Herald* 31 (June 21, 1884): 396–97.

Table 1. Various Descriptions of the Translation Instruments		
Date & Source (continued)	*Instrument used to Translate*	*Description of Instrument*
1884 St. Louis Republican[66]	Urim and Thummim	Two transparent pebbles set in the rim of a bow and fastened to a breastplate.
1885 Zenas H. Gurley[67]	Seers stone	Placed the stone in a hat into which he buried his face.
1885 Chicago Tribune[68]	Started with Urim and Thummim he also called "magical spectacles." Replaced by "seer's stone" after 116 pages were lost	Urim and Thummim: affixed them to his eyes and translated the plates. Seer's Stone: Oval or kidney form, Placed in hat and covered his face in the hat
1886 Omaha Herald[69]	Stone spectacles, Urim and Thummim, magic stone, strange stone	The strange stone was described as oval-shaped, chocolate-colored, about the size of an egg only more flat
1886 M. J. Hubble[70]	*None*	Pair of large bound spectacles

66   *St. Louis Republican*, July 16, 1884.

67   Zenas H. Gurley, "Questions Asked of David Whitmer," holograph, 1, 3, 4, Gurley Collection, Church Archives.

68   "The Book of Mormon," *Chicago Tribune*, December 17, 1885, 3.

69   *Omaha Herald*, October 17, 1886. See also *Chicago Inter Ocean*, October 17, 1886; and *Saints' Herald* 33 (November 13, 1886): 706.

70   M. J. Hubble, interview, November 13, 1886.

Table 1. Various Descriptions of the Translation Instruments

Date & Source (continued)	Instrument used to Translate	Description of Instrument
1887 by David Whitmer[71]	Seer stone	Seer stone was placed in a hat and Joseph put his face in the hat drawing it closely around his face to exclude the light
1888 Richmond Democrat[72]	Urim and Thummim. After the 116 pages were lost, Joseph was presented with a stone	Urim and Thummim: Pair of transparent stone spectacles Stone: strange oval-shaped, chocolate colored, about the size of an egg but more flat.
1909 Nathan A. Tanner, Jr.[73]	Joseph had both the Urim and Thummim and the "stone"	Stone was chocolate colored

Table 2. Various Descriptions by David Whitmer of the Method of Translation

Date & Source	Method of Translation
1878 David Whitmer	Examination of the Book of Mormon manuscripts determined that Oliver Cowdery wrote all but few pages that were in the handwriting of Emma Smith, John Whitmer, or Christian Whitmer.
1878 P. Wilhelm Poulson	Martin Harris, Oliver Cowdery, Emma Smith, John Whitmer wrote words from Joseph at different times

71   David Whitmer, *An Address to All Believers in Christ by a Witness to the Divine Authenticity of The Book of Mormon* (Richmond, 1887).

72   *Richmond Democrat*, January 26, 1888.

73   The Testimony of David Whitmer as related by Nathan Tanner, Jr, https://catalog.lds.org/assets/b1706c2e-766c-41ab-88cd-dbafd5079d9b/0/8 (accessed: February 9, 2019)

Table 2. Various Descriptions by David Whitmer of the Method of Translation	
Date & Source (continued)	*Method of Translation*
1876 (published 1879) Thomas Wood Smith	Read from the plates by Joseph Smith and written mainly by Oliver Cowdery and Martin Harris
1879 J. L. Traughber Jr.	Stone was placed in a hat into which Joseph put his face to exclude light. Parchment would appear in the hat with a line of characters and the English translation below them.
1880 Thomas Wood Smith	Retraction of Urim and Thummim method described in interview in footnote [8]
1880 Eri B. Mullin	Joseph put them (Urim and Thummim) on and looked in a hat with his face in the hat to read. The plates were not in the hat, but words would appear and not go away until spelled correctly, then another set of words would appear
1881 Kansas City Journal	Did not use the plates, held interpreters to his eyes and covered his face in a hat to exclude light, a parchment appeared with characters from plates in a line with English translation below. The Urim and Thummim was taken away from Joseph when the 116 pages were lost and never returned.
1881 David Whitmer to the Kansas City Journal	The interpreters were taken from Joseph when he lost the 116 pages
1881 Chicago Times	Joseph had no manuscript notes or other means of knowledge save the seer stone and the characters as shown on the plates. One character often would make two lines of manuscript, while others made but a word or two words.

Table 2. Various Descriptions by David Whitmer of the Method of Translation	
Date & Source (continued)	*Method of Translation*
1882 William H. Kelly and G. A. Blakeslee	David said Joseph translated the *Book of Mormon* by the inspiration of God from the plates of the Nephites. Joseph couldn't translate unless he was humble and possessed the right feelings towards everyone. Tells story about disagreement with Emma that he fixed and was then able to translate. Information is accurate in this interview
1884 E. C. Briggs	The Urim and Thummim would appear dark if Joseph was not humble. Otherwise, letters appeared on them in light, and would not go off until they were written correctly by Oliver.
1884 James H. Hart	"Joseph placed the seer-stone in a deep hat, and placing his face close to it, would see, not the stone, but what appeared like an oblong piece of parchment, on which the hieroglyphics would appear, and also the translation in the English language, all appearing in bright luminous letters."
1884 George Q. Cannon	"Joseph had the stone in a hat from which all light was excluded. In the stone the characters appeared and under that the translation in English and they remained until the scribe had copied it correctly."
1884 St. Louis Republican	Looked through them [Urim and Thummim] and dictated by looking through them to his scribes.
1885 Zenas H. Gurley	Joseph placed the "Seers stone" in a hat into which he "buried his face, stating to me [David Whitmer] and others that the original Character appeared upon parchment and under it the translation in English." The Interpreters were taken away because of transgression.

Table 2. Various Descriptions by David Whitmer of the Method of Translation	
Date & Source (continued)	*Method of Translation*
1885 Chicago Tribune	Using the Urim and Thummim, which David calls "the magical spectacles," the graven characters and translation in English would appear under them. Seer's stone: character and translation would appear on the stone. After the loss of the 116 pages, the plates "were not returned, but instead Smith was given by the angel a Urim and Thummim of another pattern, it being shaped in oval or kidney form. This seer's stone he was instructed to place in his hat, and on covering his face with the hat the character and translation would appear on the stone." The plates were never returned to Joseph.
1886 Omaha Herald	Joseph had to be humble in order to see the words in the stone/Urim and Thummim. The Urim and Thummim was taken away when the 116 pages were lost and after fervent prayer was presented with a strange stone which, it was promised, should serve the same purpose as the missing Urim and Thummim. With this stone all the present *Book of Mormon* was translated.
1886, M. J. Hubble	The Urim and Thummim was taken away after "a part of the book of Lehigh [Lehi] had been translated, about 150 pages" and was lost. Joseph was never allowed to see the plates again. David and Joseph "translated by means of a pair of large bound Spectacles ie the Book of Mormon, that the Characters would appear in the air & stay until correctly translated and then disappear."

Table 2. Various Descriptions by David Whitmer of the Method of Translation	
Date & Source (continued)	*Method of Translation*
1887 by David Whitmer	Joseph would "put the seer stone in a hat, and put his face in the hat, drawing it closely around his face to exclude the light; and in the darkness the spiritual light would shine. A piece of something resembling parchment would appear and on that appeared the writing. One character at a time would appear, and under it interpretation in English." Joseph would read it to Oliver who would then repeat it and if correct, the character would disappear. Translation was finished in the spring of 1830 before April 6th at which time Joseph gave the stone to Oliver and told David Whitmer and the "rest" that he was through with it.
1888 Richmond Democrat	Joseph put on the spectacles [identified as the Urim and Thummim] and "a few words of the text of the Book of Mormon would appear on the lenses. When these were correctly translated by Cowdery... these words would disappear and others take their place." After losing the 116 pages, Joseph "was presented with a strange oval-shaped, chocolate colored stone, about the size of an egg but more flat, which it was promised should answer the same purpose. With this stone all the present book was translated. The prophet would place the stone in a hat, then put his face in the hat and read the words that appeared thereon."

Table 2. Various Descriptions by David Whitmer of the Method of Translation	
Date & Source (continued)	*Method of Translation*
1909 Nathan A. Tanner, Jr.	Joseph "had the Urim and Thummim, and a chocolate colored stone, which he used alternately, as suited his convenience." David Whitmer believed that "Joseph could as well accomplish the translation by looking into a hat, or any other stone, as by the use of the Urim and Thummim or the chocolate colored stone." David believed Joseph had power with God to get any information he wished for and didn't believe either the Urim and Thummim or stone he had were essential. Joseph would "place the manuscript beneath the stone or Urim and Thummim, and the characters would appear in English, which he would spell out, and they would remain there until the word was fully written and corrected." Then it would disappear, and another take its place.

Conclusion

Because of David Whitmer's inability to present a consistent narrative, as well as his frequent contradiction of known historical facts, we cannot accept David Whitmer as a reliable witness of the translation process, nor can we accept as credible his description of the instrument nor its use in translating. No objective judge could in good conscience hold Whitmer's testimony of the translation process as credible. Because of the multitude of conflicting claims regarding Joseph Smith's translation instrument, from Urim and Thummim to the use of the "seer stone," and back again, we can safely say that Whitmer's claim that the seer stone was the instrument of translation is entirely unreliable.

Additional corroboration from members of the Reorganized Church of Jesus Christ of Latter-day Saints during the 19th century, while Joseph Smith III presided, confirm that David Whitmer's statements contain contradictions of fact and are not trustworthy:

❦❦ The statements of David Whitmer in his pamphlet are palpable and plain **contradictions of the accepted facts** of history.... I [R. M. Elvin] feel impressed to admonish those who are boosting the "Seer Stone" theory, that one sure way of destroying the value of testimony is to have the **witness cross himself**, thereby **impeaching his own evidence**, and thus have their testimony **thrown out** of court as not reliable.[74]

David Whitmer, we [W. W. Blair and others] repeat, was **not a competent witness** as to the "means" used by the Seer in translating the *Book of Mormon*. ... Whatever David Whitmer may or may not have said on this point, it should be remembered that he had little or nothing to do with the Church and its history since the spring of 1838—fifty long years—and it is not difficult, from this fact, to account for errors in memory and defects in judgement which have been painfully apparent of late. The fact that David Whitmer remained idle, comparatively, in ministerial matters, for about fifty years, should be accepted as clear proof that the Lord did not call him of late to set in order and correct either the history, the doctrine, the organization, or the government of the Church. And not having been called to that work, **it is both vexatious, misleading and dangerous to give heed to what purports to be his efforts in that direction.**[75]

In closing, the evidence and those most familiar with David Whitmer summarily dismiss his claims and assertions as unreliable at best, and as "vexatious, misleading, and dangerous" at worst. The evidence suggests that professing support for the "seer stone in a hat" translation of the *Book of Mormon* aligns one with the unsteady, vacillating character of David Whitmer, an opposer of Joseph Smith, and denier of the sacred instruments of translation.

---

74   R. M. Elvin, "Nephite Record.—No. 2.," *Saints' Herald* 35 (May 12, 1888): 299; emphasis added.

75   W. W. Blair, *Saints' Herald* 35 (March 3, 1888): 129; emphasis added.

15

Joseph Smith: "Village Seer"? Magic?

Joseph Smith: Rough Stone Rolling, the popular biography of Joseph Smith by Richard L. Bushman, claims that the Prophet was "involved in magic," while simultaneously receiving revelation from Heaven and restoring the Gospel of Jesus Christ. In his book, Bushman asserts:

❚❚ When he [Joseph Smith] married Emma Hale in 1827, Joseph was on the eve of realizing himself as a prophet. He may **still have been involved in magic**, but he was sincere when he told Emma's father that his treasure-seeking days were over. **Magic had served its purpose** in his life. In a sense, it was a **preparatory gospel.**[1]

Since the day the Church was organized and until recently, faithful members viewed Joseph Smith as a prophet of God, while his detractors viewed him as a prophet of the devil. Church leaders and faithful members were adamant to keep the diametrically opposed worldviews separate and entirely distinct. With the "new narrative," beginning around the 1970s and culminating over the past decade, this has changed. Bushman, Quinn, and other scholars have attempted to meld the magical worldview with the Gospel of Jesus Christ as revealed by the Prophet. Bushman explains:

❚❚ **Magic and religion melded in the Smith family** culture. . . . It may have taken four years for Joseph to purge himself of his **treasure-seeking greed.** Joseph Jr. never repudiated the stones

---

1   Richard L. Bushman, *Joseph Smith: Rough Stone Rolling* (New York: Alfred A. Knopf, 2005), 54; emphasis added.

or denied their power to find treasure. **Remnants of the magical culture stayed with him to the end.**[2]

Bushman is not the first to propose a coexistence of magic and the Gospel in the "Smith family culture." Those seeking to thwart Joseph Smith's mission since before the Church was organized in 1830 have frequently leveled accusations against the Prophet. The Angel Moroni prophesied that Joseph Smith's "name should be had for good and evil among all nations, kindreds, and tongues, or that it should be both good and evil spoken of among all people."[3] We see the fulfillment of this prophecy during the Prophet's lifetime, but perhaps even more so today, and at an ever increasing rate.

Folk Magic?

Our contemporary historians are quick to point out that Joseph Smith and his ancestors practiced what they term "folk magic." *FairMormon* calls it a "known fact":

▟▏ It is a **known fact** that Joseph's family believed in **folk magic**, and that Joseph himself used several different seer stones in order to **locate lost objects.**[4]

Bushman further commented:

▟▏ The Smiths may have been subscribing to **folk religion**, but in this they were part of a culture found virtually everywhere among Yankees of their generation. It may not have been the most uplifting activity, and some scoffed, but it was something like reading astrological charts today–a little goofy but harmless. . . . **Magic and Christianity did not seem at odds with one another.** . . . In Mormonism and for many Christians, **folk traditions and religion blend.** To call the two incongruous seems more like a matter of religious taste than a necessary conclusion.[5]

---

2   Ibid, 51; emphasis added.

3   Joseph Smith—History 1:33.

4   "The Origin of Joseph Smith's Spiritual Experiences," FairMormon, accessed February 02, 2019, https://www.fairmormon.org/answers/Joseph_Smith/Occult-ism_and_magic/Spiritual_experiences; emphasis added.

5   Richard L. Bushman, "Joseph Smith and Money Digging," in *A Reason for*

Today, the rise of textbooks, literature, historians, and so forth mischaracterizing the Christian colonists of early American history has become a global epidemic. Magic and Satanism were not countenanced by righteous Puritans, Pilgrims, Huguenots, Quakers, Covenanters and other reformed Christians, neither was it countenanced by their "humble" descendants.[6] Nephi saw the birth of America in vision[7] and pronounced that "the power of God was with" those "saints of God"[8] who laid the foundation of our nation.[9] Although the "Lamans" and the "Lemuels" of the colonies dabbled in magic and the occult, the "Nephis" and the "Lehis" despised these dark practices.

Anyone thoroughly familiar with the Smith family, particularly those who stayed faithful in the Gospel of Jesus Christ from before, during, and after the Restoration, knows that the Smith family culture abhorred darkness, and therefore, anything associated with ritual magic. The authors identify with and descend from this heritage.

In 1841, the Prophet's cousin, George A. Smith, and Wilford Woodruff excommunicated a member of the Church for "fortune Telling" and "magic":

❝ The President [of the conference, George A. Smith] then brought up the case of a Br Moumford, who was holding the office of a Priest, from whome [*sic*] fellowship had been withdrawn by the council of officers in consequence of his practizing [*sic*] **fortune Telling, Magic, Black art** &c & called upon Elders Woodruff & Cordon to express their feelings upon the subject when Elder Woodruff arose, & spoke Briefly upon the subject, & informed the assembly that we had **no such custom or practice in the Church**, & that we should **not fellowship** any individual who Practiced

---

Faith: Navigating LDS Doctrine & Church History, ed. Laura H. Hales (Provo, UT: Religious Studies Center, Brigham Young University, 2016), 3-4; emphasis added.

6   1 Nephi 13:15-16.

7   *For Our Day: Covenant on the Land*, dir. L. Hannah Stoddard and James F. Stoddard, III (2013), DVD. To learn more regarding America's foundation, see the *Joseph Smith Foundation* documentary, *For Our Day: Covenant on the Land* which presents inspiring history from the American colonization, paralleling the Puritans, Pilgrims and other righteous forebears with Lehi, Nephi and the first part of the *Book of Mormon*.

8   1 Nephi 13:16-18.

9   Note that Nephi did not have such kind words for us today. See 2 Nephi 28:3-32.

Magic fortune Telling, Black art &c for it was **not of God**. When It was moved & carried by the whole church that fellowship be withdrawn from Br Moumford.[10]

Continuing the Smith family tradition, Joseph Smith's nephew, President Joseph F. Smith, had this to say:

// No man or woman who enjoys the Spirit of God and the influence and power of the holy Priesthood can believe in these **superstitious notions**, and those who do, will **lose, indeed have lost, the influence of the Spirit of God** and of the Priesthood, and are become **subject to the witchery of Satan** . . .

It is a **trick of Satan** to deceive men and women, and to draw them away from the Church and from the influence of the Spirit of God, and the power of his holy Priesthood, that they may be destroyed. These **peepstone-men and women are inspired by the devil**, and are the real witches, if any such there be. **Witchcraft, and all kindred evils**, are solely the creations of the superstitious imaginations of men and women who are steeped in **ignorance**, and **derive their power over people from the devil**, and those who submit to this influence are deceived by him.

Unless they repent, they will be destroyed. There is absolutely no possibility for a person who enjoys the Holy Spirit of God even to believe that such influences can have any effect upon him. The enjoyment of the Holy Spirit is absolute proof against all influences of evil; you never can obtain that Spirit by seeking diviners, and men and women who "peep and mutter." That is obtained by imposition of hands by the servants of God, and retained by right living. If you have lost it, **repent and return to God**, and for your salvation's sake and for the sake of your children, **avoid the emissaries of Satan who "peep and mutter"** and who would lead you down to darkness and death. It is **impossible for anyone possessing the spirit of the gospel and having the power**

---

10   Wilford Woodruff journals and papers, 1828-1898; Wilford Woodruff Journals, 1833-1898; Wilford Woodruff journal, 1841 January-1842 December; Church History Library, https://catalog.lds.org/assets/28b53d73-2ba2-418b-8ef7-dafcc935bee3/0/58 (accessed: March 9, 2019); emphasis added.

of the holy Priesthood to believe in or be influenced by any power of necromancy.[11]

The terms "magic," "Satanism," and "occult" are strong words and carry negative connotations, especially for those who truly understand their meaning. Because of this, some progressive historians have repackaged the vocabulary to "help the medicine go down." As such, the popular terms used when promoting the "new narrative" are "folk magic" and "folk tradition" which Bushman argues "had an influence on [Joseph Smith's] outlook."[12]

To some, "folk magic" implies a mild or benign, non-threatening pastime, but let us consider the following train of logic. If we accept that Joseph Smith and his ancestors practiced folk magic, including the use of peep stones, rods, crystals, rituals, etc., then we must ask the following. When young Joseph looked into his peep stone and claimed to "discover" lost objects or treasure, was he:

1. deceiving those with whom he worked by pretending to see lost items, or

2. using the power or influence of the occult to find the objects? What force was displaying the items?

On the one hand, he was a liar. On the other hand, he was a sorcerer, soothsayer, astrologer, or necromancer. If Joseph Smith and his family followed prescribed rituals or ritualistic magic as the "scholars" purport, this poses a significant problem. Ritualistic magic effectively blasphemes sacred names, perverts sacred acts, and thereby seeks to obtain the favor of an unknown force, which is none other than the adversary and his devils. This is by no means a benign tradition. To blaspheme sacred words or to blasphemously act out sacred ritual is to attempt to gain favor with Lucifer, or in other words, to embrace Satanism. If one accepts that the power of the adversary is real, this must be our conclusion: that Joseph Smith was involved in Satanic practices. If on the other hand, we believe the devil and his power is not real, then

---

11   *Improvement Era* 5 (September 1902): 896-899, https://archive.org/details/improvementera0511unse/page/896; emphasis added.

12   Richard L. Bushman, "Joseph Smith and Money Digging," in *A Reason for Faith: Navigating LDS Doctrine & Church History*, ed. Laura H. Hales (Provo, UT: Religious Studies Center, Brigham Young University, 2016), 4.

we must admit that Joseph Smith was merely pretending, hoping to deceive his gullible and over-believing followers.

After following these two trains of logic to their conclusions, we must apply the same logic to the *Book of Mormon*. If Joseph Smith was involved in magic and after recognizing the Satanic influence behind magic, how do we know the *Book of Mormon* is not the adversary's own arch-deception? If magic is not real, and the devil has no power, then we must accept the young Joseph as an arch-deceiver and the *Book of Mormon* itself as his own masterwork, his arch-deception.

We must allow for this line of thinking if we accept the scholars' claim regarding the young Joseph and his family. Thankfully, however, as many faithful past prophets and historians point out, and as many devoted Latter-day Saints throughout our history testify, there is no real evidence and there are no credible sources showing that Joseph Smith ever practiced folk magic, used "peep stones," or relied on the influence of the occult. President Gordon B. Hinckley commented:

> **❐❐** ... the fact that there were superstitions among the people in the days of Joseph Smith is **no evidence whatever** that the Church came of such superstition.[13]

In this chapter, we address, from a doctrinal perspective, the basic question, "Could Joseph Smith have dabbled in magic at *any* time in his life and at the same time have been a true prophet of God?"

Each and every member of the Church is left with a critical decision; "Is the new Latter-day Saint history, the neo-Mormonism promoted by the intellectuals, accurate?" In contrast, can we accept as inspired the traditional teachings of leaders of the Church, such as the testimony of President Gordon B. Hinckley?

What is "Magic"?

The *Webster's 1828 Dictionary*, contemporary with the Prophet Joseph Smith's era, defines "magic" as:

> **❐❐** The art or science of putting into action the **power of spirits**; or the science of producing wonderful effects by the aid of **superhuman beings**, or of **departed spirits; sorcery; enchantment.**

---

13 Gordon B. Hinckley, "Lord, Increase Our Faith," *Ensign*, November 1987; emphasis added.

Superstitious or geotic magic consists in the **invocation of devils or demons**, and supposes some tacit or express agreement between them and human beings.[14]

Moving forward to our own time, the meaning has not changed dramatically. For example, the *Encyclopedia Britannica* explains:

❚❚ Practices classified as magic include divination, astrology, incantations, alchemy, sorcery, spirit mediation, and necromancy....

The purpose of magic is to acquire knowledge, power, love, or wealth; to heal or ward off illness or danger; to guarantee productivity or success in an endeavour; to cause harm to an enemy; to reveal information; to induce spiritual transformation; to trick; or to entertain. The effectiveness of magic is often determined by the condition and performance of the magician, who is thought to have access to unseen forces and special knowledge of the appropriate words and actions to manipulate those forces.[15]

Joseph Smith and the Occult

To claim that the Prophet Joseph Smith involved himself with magical practices is to suggest that the Prophet engaged in occultic rituals or that he practiced some form of the dark arts to conjure evil spirits. *Rough Stone Rolling* promotes the following view of Joseph Smith:

- "... exact compliance with prescribed rituals was required" and "magic might have prepared him [Joseph Smith] to believe in a revelation of gold plates and translation with a stone."[16]

- The Prophet is a "boy who gazed into stones and saw treasure [that] grew up to become a translator who looked in a stone and saw words."[17]

---

14   Noah Webster, *An American Dictionary of the English Language*; emphasis added.

15   "Magic," Encyclopædia Britannica, accessed January 6, 2017, https://www.britannica.com/.

16   Richard L. Bushman, *Joseph Smith: Rough Stone Rolling* (New York: Alfred A. Knopf, 2005), 54.

17   Ibid, 73.

- "In addition to rod and stone divining, the Smiths probably believed in the rudimentary astrology found in the ubiquitous almanacs," and "Magical parchments handed down in the Hyrum Smith family may have originally belonged to Joseph Sr.."[18]

- Oliver Cowdery is accused of having "engaged in treasure-seeking and other magical practices in Vermont, and like others in this culture, melded magic with Christianity."[19]

- By 1828, the Prophet's "language was Biblical rather than occult"[20] as it had previously been.

These allegations also target the Smith family including the Prophet's father (Joseph Smith Sr.) and mother (Lucy Mack Smith). Can you imagine the family of the prophet returning from a day of labor on their farm to draw magic circles and practice rituals? Can you imagine Lucy Mack Smith, the faithful, consecrated, and religiously devout mother of the Prophet, whispering enchantments, or perhaps you might imagine a young Joseph Smith setting aside his Bible to study magical parchments?

Progressives do not seem to find this contradictory image of the Smiths problematic. "Magic," according to *Rough Stone Rolling*, "had served its purpose in [Joseph Smith's] life. In a sense, it was a preparatory gospel."[21]

Magic prepared Joseph Smith to serve the Lord? Magic was a forerunner of the Restoration? Did Joseph Smith dabble with occultic language, rudimentary astrology, or magic rituals during his early and even later life? If the answer is "yes," this places the faithful in a state of cognitive dissonance.

"Not Suffer a Witch to Live."

How does the Lord view magic, witchcraft, the occult, necromancy, astrology, and other deviant practices? These questions can be best answered by turning to the pages of holy writ upon which the Smiths

---

18   Ibid, 50.
19   Ibid, 73.
20   Ibid, 69.
21   Ibid, 54.

placed great importance. In our own day, the scriptures are the standard by which we should test Joseph Smith and his teachings.

The Son of God has been clear and decisive when it comes to witchcraft. The *Book of Mormon* explains that it was the Lord who gave the Law of Moses.[22] The "Mosaic law" Jesus Christ revealed to ancient Israel decrees:

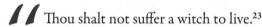 Thou shalt not suffer a witch to live.[23]

> A man also or woman that hath a familiar spirit, or that is a wizard, shall surely be put to death: they shall stone them with stones: their blood shall be upon them.[24]

From this we can conclude that the Lord does not celebrate, condone, or even tolerate this intensely serious sin. In Deuteronomy, He refers to tampering with dark forces as "abominations":

When thou art come into the land which the Lord thy God giveth thee, thou shalt not learn to do after the abominations of those nations.

> There shall not be found among you any one that maketh his son or his daughter to pass through the fire, or that useth **divination**, or an **observer of times**, or an **enchanter**, or a **witch**, Or a **charmer**, or a **consulter with familiar spirits**, or a **wizard**, or a **necromancer**.

> For all that do these things are an **abomination unto the Lord**: and because of these abominations the **Lord thy God doth drive them out from before thee**.[25]

Are we to accept the premise that Joseph Smith was an "abomination unto the Lord" just prior to, or even during the translation of the *Book of Mormon*? Scripture declares that the Son of God "is the same yesterday, today, and forever."[26] The same God who unequivocally and unmistakably condemned witchcraft during ancient times is the same

---

22   3 Nephi 15:5.

23   Exodus 22:18.

24   Leviticus 20:27.

25   Deuteronomy 18:9-12; emphasis added.

26   1 Nephi 10:18, Mormon 9:9, Hebrews 13:8.

God who appeared to Joseph Smith in the Sacred Grove. Therefore, while our modernist, "politically correct" culture may condone occultic activity and promote the dark arts in literature, fashion, film, music, games, holidays, and other "diversions," the Lord has never changed His position.

In the last days, the Lord revealed to the prophet Micah that He would "...cut off witchcrafts out of thine hand; and thou shalt have no more soothsayers..."[27]

Not only was this law given by commandment to both ancient and modern Israel, the Lord reiterated the law and its consequences to the New World Lehites. During His personal visit to the ancient Nephites in the Promised Land of America, after his resurrection, our Lord warned:

// And I [Jesus Christ] will cut off witchcrafts out of thy land, and thou shalt have no more soothsayers... And I will pluck up thy groves out of the midst of thee...[28]

Magic is Satanism

Furthermore, the prophet Mormon saw our day in vision. He knew the principles, doctrines, revelations, events, and the history that we need to know to navigate our world today. He compiled most of the *Book of Mormon*, including the two-thirds sealed portion we have yet to receive. In other words, Mormon was already familiar with at least a portion of the additional scripture, the greater light and knowledge we will enjoy during the Millennium, during his mortal life.[29] Based on his insight and knowledge, what did Mormon teach regarding magic and sorceries in his abridgment?

---

27   Micah 5:12.

28   3 Nephi 21:16-18.

29   Elder Bruce R. McConkie commented, "When, during the Millennium, the sealed portion of the Book of Mormon is translated, it will give an account of life in the premortal existence; of the creation of all things; of the Fall and the Atonement and the Second Coming; of temple ordinances, in their fulness; of the ministry and mission of translated beings; of life in the spirit world, in both paradise and hell; of the kingdoms of glory to be inhabited by resurrected beings; and many such like things. As of now, the world is not ready to receive these truths." Bruce R. McConkie, "The Bible, a Sealed Book," CES Symposium, August 1984, 1.

❦❦ And it came to pass that there were **sorceries**, and **witchcrafts**, and **magics**; and the **power of the evil one** was wrought upon all the face of the land, even unto the fulfilling of all the words of Abinadi, and also Samuel the Lamanite.[30]

For those who did **not belong to their church** did indulge themselves in **sorceries**, and in **idolatry** . . .[31]

Mormon associates magic with "the power of the evil one" and only those not belonging to the Church indulged themselves in this wickedness. The "evil one" is the adversary, whom we also know as Satan, or the devil.

Testimony of "a Spirit of Divination"

In the *New Testament*, the apostle Paul would not allow a woman involved in witchcraft to testify of the Gospel:

❦❦ And it came to pass, as we went to prayer, a certain damsel possessed with a **spirit of divination** met us, which brought her masters much gain by **soothsaying**:

The same followed Paul and us, and cried, saying, These men are the servants of the most high God, which shew unto us the way of salvation.

And this did she many days. But Paul, being **grieved**, turned and said to the spirit, I command thee in the name of Jesus Christ to come out of her. And he came out the same hour.[32]

How reasonable is it that the Lord would choose a man delving into spiritualism, divination, and possession, even if by so-called "folk magic," to bring forth His everlasting Gospel?

---

30   Mormon 1:19; emphasis added.

31   Alma 1:32; emphasis added.

32   Acts 16:16-18; emphasis added.

Joseph Smith's "Sins"

Was Joseph Smith perfect? The Prophet clarified:

❝ ... when did I ever teach any thing wrong from this stand? when was I ever confounded? ... I never told you I was perfect— but there is no error in the revelations which I have taught ... [33]

According to scripture, engaging in witchcraft ranks in seriousness within the realm of murder and adultery. Was the Prophet guilty of the most serious crimes a mortal can commit? The Prophet Joseph explained the degree to which he erred, clarifying in his own words:

❝ I frequently fell into many foolish errors [while growing up], and displayed the weakness of youth, and the foibles of human nature; which, I am sorry to say, led me into divers temptations, offensive in the sight of God. In making this confession, **no one need suppose me guilty of any great or malignant sins. A disposition to commit such was never in my nature.**

But I was guilty of levity, and sometimes associated with jovial company, etc., not consistent with that character which ought to be maintained by one who was called of God as I had been. But this will not seem very strange to any one who recollects my youth, and is acquainted with my native cheery temperament.[34]

Joseph Smith pointed out clearly that he was *not* "guilty of any great or malignant sins." By his own admission, Joseph confessed that he was guilty of "levity, and ... sometimes associated with jovial company." In other words, he was at times, while a young man, overly exuberant, boisterous or trifling in his conversation or temperament. However, he was certainly not guilty of sins justifying death, either temporally or spiritually. The "disposition to commit such was never in [his] nature."

In 1834, the Prophet Joseph Smith composed a letter to Oliver Cowdery wherein he clarified that while he had admitted to falling into "vices and follies," the worst transgression he had ever committed in his life "was light, and too often, vain mind, exhibiting a foolish and trifling conversation":

---

33   Joseph Smith, Discourse, 12 May 1844, as Reported by Thomas Bullock, p. 2, The Joseph Smith Papers; emphasis added.

34   Joseph Smith—History 1:28; emphasis added.

❝ During this time [growing-up years], as is common to most, or all youths, I fell into many vices and follies; but as my accusers are, and have been forward to accuse me of being guilty of gross and outragious [*sic*] violations of the peace and good order of the community, I take the occasion to remark, that, though, as I have said above, "as is common to most, or all youths, I fell into many vices and follies," I have **not**, neither can it be sustained, in truth, been **guilty** of **wronging or injuring any man** or society of men; and those imperfections to which I alude [*sic*], and for which I have often had occasion to lament, were a light, and too often, vain mind, exhibiting a foolish and trifling conversation.

This being **all**, and the **worst**, that my accusers can substantiate against my moral character . . .[35]

Keep in mind that Joseph Smith was raised in Puritan New England. "Trifling" and "vain" were not trifling and vain as they are today. In Puritan New England, the terms "trifling" and "vain" did not mean what they mean in our modern culture. Society was far more sober-minded, far more devoted to God. "Teenage" attitudes and behaviors, as we know them today, would have been essentially unknown.[36]

If we are to accept that Joseph Smith and his ancestors practiced "folk magic," including the use of peep stones, rods, crystals, rituals, etc., then one must conclude that Joseph Smith was either a deceiver or he was involved in Satanism. Joseph Smith on the other hand made it very clear that:

1. He had never lied or deceived anyone in his life, and he never "wronged" a human being.

2. The Prophet made it abundantly clear that he was never involved in any gross sins such as witchcraft or the occult.

From our experience, any faithful minded person will revolt at the very suggestion that the Prophet Joseph was ever a liar or an occultist.

---

35   Joseph Smith to Oliver Cowdery, *Messenger and Advocate* 1 (December 1834): 40; emphasis added.

36   Ezra Taft Benson, *The Teachings of Ezra Taft Benson* (Salt Lake City, UT: Bookcraft, 1988), 406.

Magic: "a Preparatory Gospel"

The new progressive narrative seems to picture magic as a version of, or a partner with the Gospel. In fact, *Rough Stone Rolling* refers to magic as a "preparatory gospel":

▌▌ When he [Joseph Smith] married Emma Hale in 1827, Joseph was on the eve of realizing himself as a prophet. He **may still have been involved in magic,** but he was sincere when he told Emma's father that his treasure-seeking days were over. **Magic had served its purpose** in his life. In a sense, it was a **preparatory gospel.**[37]

According to the new progressive narrative, Joseph Smith Sr. and Lucy Mack Smith encouraged Joseph's attentiveness to the Angel Moroni's instructions because the Smiths had learned to obey and comply precisely with "prescribed rituals." In the progressive mind, obeying Satanic rituals apparently prepared the Smiths to follow the Lord and His messengers:

▌▌ Traces of a **treasure-seeking mentality** still appeared in the family's reactions to the angel. His parents admonished Joseph to be rigorously obedient to the messenger's instructions, **just as exact compliance with prescribed rituals was required for successful money-digging.**[38]

Rough Stone Rolling's interpretation further suggests that magic enabled the Smith family's receptiveness to the coming of the Angel Moroni:

▌▌ After 1828, Joseph could no longer see that magic might have prepared him to believe in a revelation of gold plates and translation with a stone. It did not occur to him that **without magic his family might have scoffed** at his story of Moroni, as did the minister who rejected the First Vision. Magic had **played its part** and now could be cast aside.[39]

---

37   Richard L. Bushman, *Joseph Smith: Rough Stone Rolling* (New York: Alfred A. Knopf, 2005), 54; emphasis added.

38   Ibid, 53; emphasis added.

39   Ibid, 69; emphasis added.

It seems apparent that a growing number of progressives confuse the difference between a spiritual experience from the Lord and magical rituals involving Satanic spirits. For modernists, spiritual knowledge is not accepted. When describing a crisis of faith Bushman experienced while pursuing a degree at Harvard, Bushman explained, "[I am] not someone who has a 'simple faith' where just everything is absolutely true beyond any doubt." During an interview with *Mormon Stories*, John Dehlin asked how Bushman "became a believer again" or rediscovered his "believingness." Bushman responded:

/ / Well, ummm, I probably never recovered it all. Ummmm, I'm not someone who has a "simple faith" that where just everything is absolutely true beyond any doubt."[40]

In the progressive mind, spiritual knowledge is "simple faith." Spiritual knowledge, however, is not faith but actual experience. Spiritual knowledge comes from advanced experience and sacrifice. For someone who has never experienced spiritual knowledge from God, there may not be a great difference between the power of the adversary and the power of the Lord. As we consider the progressive premise, perhaps a slight hyperbole may help. Do we prepare our young men for the Priesthood by introducing the occult? Should we invite the deacon's quorum to a seance, or should we teach the young men to use a ouija board or tarot cards in preparation for their futures?

In some incomprehensible way, a growing number of our scholars seem to confuse the occult with the Gospel of Jesus Christ, associating the two as if they are interdependent and complementary. For those who are confused, here is clarification. Magic, witchcraft, and other forms of ritual occult constitute varying degrees of Satanism. Satan has power to mimic, impersonate, counterfeit, and deceive. The occult is not merely in conflict with the Lord and His gospel, it is directly and diametrically opposed. Magic is an inversion, a blatant mockery of the Kingdom of God.

The Lord's Kingdom and the devil's kingdom are not conjoined playgrounds upon which one can simply alternate between depending

---

40   "047: Richard Bushman Part 1 — Experiences as a Mormon Historian," January 22, 2007, Mormon Stories, accessed September 30, 2016, http://www. mormonstories.org/richard-bushman-and-rough-stone-rolling-part-1-experiences-as-a-mormon-historian.

upon one's mood. President Brigham Young drove this point home while instructing the Saints:

❙❙ It is **impossible to unite Christ and Baal**—their spirits **cannot unite**, their objects and purposes are **entirely different**; the one leads to eternal life and exaltation, the other to death and final destruction.[41]

Christ and Baal are **not reconciled**; the Lord will **hold no fellowship with the Devil**. But Satan will contend until he is driven from the earth. He is the adversary, the opposer, and accuser of the brethren. He opposes the Son of God in the **great struggle** between truth and error.[42]

Magic is not a tool of the Lord, nor is it neutral ground. In the Book of Exodus, Moses and Aaron faced a contest with Pharaoh and his Egyptian magicians. The Lord commanded Moses and Aaron to throw down Aaron's staff before Pharaoh whereupon it would turn into a serpent. When Moses and Aaron performed this miracle, Pharaoh was unfazed. He simply called his "wise men," "magicians," and "sorcerers" to cast down their own rods, which also became serpents. However, in a show of superiority, the Lord's serpent swallowed up the serpents of Pharaoh's magicians:

❙❙ And the Lord spake unto Moses and unto Aaron, saying, When Pharaoh shall speak unto you, saying, Shew a miracle for you: then thou shalt say unto Aaron, Take thy rod, and cast it before Pharaoh, and it shall become a serpent.

And Moses and Aaron went in unto Pharaoh, and they did so as the Lord had commanded: and Aaron cast down his rod before Pharaoh, and before his servants, and it became a serpent. Then Pharaoh also called the wise men and the sorcerers: now the magicians of Egypt, they also did in like manner with their enchantments. For

---

41   Brigham Young, "Union. Persecution. The Nature of the Kingdom of God.," in *Journal of Discourses*, vol. 11 (Liverpool, 1867), 274; emphasis added. Discourse given on December 23, 1866.

42   Brigham Young, "Character of God and Christ—Providences of God—Self-Government, &c," in *Journal of Discourses*, vol. 8 (Liverpool, 1861), 116; emphasis added. Discourse given on July 8, 1860.

they cast down every man his rod, and they became serpents: but Aaron's rod swallowed up their rods.[43]

When Moses confronted the Egyptian magicians in Pharaoh's court, it was not a contest between the Lord's prophet and "preparatory Gospel" prophets. It was a struggle between the power of Lucifer and the power of God, a battle between the servants of God and the servants of the devil. Magic is not simply a "force," it is a hostile power that is diametrically opposed to the authority of the Son of God. The two are incompatible and irreconcilable.

Magical Culture Stayed to the End?

Progressives make another accusation. *Rough Stone Rolling* claims that Joseph Smith employed magical rituals and that "remnants of the magical culture stayed with him to the end":

//   **Magic and religion melded in the Smith family** culture. . . . It may have taken four years for Joseph to purge himself of **his treasure-seeking greed**. Joseph Jr. never repudiated the stones or denied their power to find treasure. **Remnants of the magical culture stayed with him to the end.**[44]

What does *Rough Stone Rolling* mean in accusing Joseph Smith of maintaining a magical worldview "to the end"? The new narrative suggests that during the events leading up to Carthage, and in Carthage Jail, the Prophet Joseph may have still sympathized with and engaged in ancient "prescribed rituals." Interesting picture painted with the progressive brush: The Prophet Joseph Smith, the man we look to for nearly every revelation and doctrine in this dispensation, is confused by magic to his last day. Is Bushman alluding to the Prophet's alleged wearing of a Jupiter Talisman in Carthage? Some have suggested that the endowment produced by Joseph Smith toward the end of his life has occultic connections.[45] The Prophet has difficulty discerning and

---

43   Exodus 7:8-12.

44   Richard L. Bushman, *Joseph Smith: Rough Stone Rolling* (New York: Alfred A. Knopf, 2005), 51; emphasis added.

45   There is no real evidence that Joseph Smith was involved in any way in the occult. For Joseph Smith's Masonic involvement and the endowment see *Statesmen & Symbols: Prelude to the Restoration* (2014). The Jupiter Talisman will be addressed

therefore mixes the occult or Satanism with the power and influence of God throughout his life.

Why would anyone place their confidence in someone so confused, deluded and dark? Progressive historians suggest that, as a people, we should put our trust in a man who could not decipher between the Lord and the devil. A man who "melded" magic and religion throughout his life.

When all the ancient prophets looked to our day, they all uniformly agreed that during our era, our time in mortality, the world languished under the most foolish, dark, and literally apostate situation.[46] Nephi summarized it well when he said that in many instances even the humble followers of Christ, in our day, are deceived and led astray by false philosophies because we turn to the learning of men for our understanding as opposed to relying upon the arm of the Lord.[47] In our day, the Lord has covered the seers and the prophets while we blindly allow the blind to lead us as we grope for the wall.[48]

---

in a later work.

46   Elder Marlin K. Jensen (Church Historian and Recorder at the time) commented during a November 2011 fireside, ". . . the fifteen men that are above me [Marlin K. Jensen] in the hierarchy of the Church . . . realize that, maybe, since Kirtland we've never had a period of—I'll call it apostasy—like we're having right now, largely over these issues." Peter Henderson and Kristina Cooke, "Special Report: Mormonism Besieged by the Modern Age," Reuters, January 31, 2012, accessed March 2019, https://www.reuters.com/article/us-mormonchurch/special-report-mormonism-besieged-by-the-modern-age-idUSTRE80T1CM20120131; Stephen Smoot, "LDS Church Essays Tackle Controversial Issues," FairMormon, February 19, 2014, accessed March 2019, https://www.fairmormon.org/blog/2014/02/19/lds-church-essays-tackle-controversial-issues.

See also Isaiah 3, 10, 13; Mormon 8:35-41; 2 Nephi 27:1, 28:11-16, 30:1; JST Matthew 21:53-56; Ether 2:11, 8:23-25; D&C 35:7, 45:28-31.

47   2 Nephi 28:14.

48   2 Nephi 27:5. The Prophet Joseph Smith commented, "It is my meditation all the day, and more than my meat and drink, to know how I shall make the Saints of God comprehend the visions that roll like an overflowing surge before my mind. Oh! how I would delight to bring before you things which you never thought of!" Joseph Smith History, volume D-1, 16 April 1843, 1534, The Joseph Smith Papers.

"I [Joseph Smith] could explain a hundred fold more than I ever have, of the glories of the Kingdoms manifested to me in the vision, were I permitted, and were the people prepared to receive it, the Lord deals with this people as a tender parent with a child, communicating light and intelligence and the knowledge of his ways, as they can hear it." Joseph Smith History, volume D-1, 16 April 1843, 1556, The Joseph Smith Papers.

"Brother Brigham, if I [Joseph Smith] was to reveal to this people what the Lord has revealed to me, there is not a man or a woman would stay with me." Brigham Young,

As the Servant and Prophet of the Lord Jesus Christ, Joseph Smith and Lucifer are eternally grappling enemies. Not only was the sin of dabbling with Satan's power "never in [his] nature,"[49] but from his youth he was "destined to prove a disturber and an annoyer of his [Satan's] kingdom."[50] Joseph Smith and "Baal" were not friends at any time during his life. In the Prophet's own words:

" It seems as though the adversary was aware, at a very early period of my life, that I was destined to prove a **disturber** and an **annoyer** of his kingdom; else why should the powers of darkness combine against me? Why the opposition and persecution that arose against me, almost in my infancy?[51]

Here Joseph Smith makes it very clear that God has a Kingdom and the devil has an opposing kingdom. The devil's kingdom is not

---

"Endless Variety of Organizations—Blessings that Await the Faithful," in *Journal of Discourses*, vol. 9 (Liverpool, 1862), 294. Discourse given on May 25, 1862.

President Wilford Woodruff remembered, "The fact is, there are a great many things taught in the building up of this kingdom which seem strange to us, being contrary to our traditions, and are calculated to try men. Brother Joseph used a great many methods of testing the integrity of men; and he taught a great many things which, in consequence of tradition, required prayer, faith, and a testimony from the Lord, before they could be believed by many of the Saints. His mind was opened by the visions of the Almighty, and the Lord taught him many things by vision and revelation that were never taught publicly in his days; for the people could not bear the flood of intelligence which God poured into his mind." Wilford Woodruff, "Necessity of Adhering to the Priesthood in Preference to Science and Art," in *Journal of Discourses*, vol. 5 (Liverpool, 1858), 83-84. Discourse given on April 9, 1857.

President Brigham Young likewise observed, "In the due time of the Lord, the Saints and the world will be privileged with the revelations that are due to them. They now have many more than they are worthy of, for they do not observe them. The Gentile nations have had more of the revelations of God than is their just due. And I will say, as I have before said, if guilt before my God and my brethren rests upon me in the least, it is in this one thing—that I have revealed too much concerning God and his kingdom, and the designs of our Father in heaven. If my skirts are stained in the least with wrong, it is because I have been too free in telling what God is, how he lives, the nature of his Providences and designs in creating the world, in bringing forth the human family on the earth, his designs concerning them, &c. If I had, like Paul, said—"But if any man be ignorant, let him be ignorant," perhaps it would have been better for the people." Brigham Young, "Privileges of the Sabbath—Duty of Living Our Religion—Human Longevity, &c," in *Journal of Discourses*, vol. 8 (Liverpool, 1861), 58. Discourse given on May 20, 1860.

49   Joseph Smith—History 1:28.

50   Joseph Smith—History 1:20.

51   Ibid; emphasis added.

a "preparer" for, or a stepping stone into God's Kingdom. The devil's servants and followers are not preparers of the Lord's people. The Prophet was not a follower, at any time, in the devil's kingdom. Throughout the Prophet's life, there was animosity between himself and the devil's kingdom—not friendship—and certainly not preparation.

Claims Involving Joseph Smith and Magic

When anyone encounters material claiming Joseph Smith or his family dabbled in magical practices, the answers can be found generally in one of the two following categories:

1. **Dishonest, questionable or even nonexistent sources** – It is often the case that claims made by progressive historians, anti-Mormon literature, and other material are not based in credible, primary sources. Do your own research, and investigate their claims!

2. **Counterfeits of the Priesthood** – Satan delights in creating a mockery of sacred symbols, principles, ordinances, and teachings. Each must answer whether Joseph Smith worked with the Lord's version of the principles and ordinances or the counterfeit. In one remarkable example, accusers point to Joseph Smith's involvement in Satanism because the inverted pentagram can be found on the Nauvoo Temple. Studying the history of this particular symbol reveals that it is an historical icon, a pure and holy symbol long predating the relationship with the occult. As is too often the case, Lucifer hijacked this symbol for his own perverted purposes.[52] Another example involves Joseph Smith's interest in Freemasonry. Perhaps you have wondered why Joseph Smith was a Freemason. Or why there was a Masonic lodge in Nauvoo. The Joseph Smith Foundation produced a feature length documentary entitled, *Statesmen & Symbols: Prelude to the Restoration* (2014), which delves into Joseph Smith's involvement with Freemasonry.[53]

---

52   "Why Are Inverted Pentagrams on LDS Mormon Temples?" Latter-day Answers, May 31, 2018, accessed March 2019, http://ldsanswers.org/why-are-inverted-pentagrams-on-lds-mormon-temples/.

53   *Statesmen & Symbols: Prelude to the Restoration*, dir. L. Hannah Stoddard and James F. Stoddard, III (Joseph Smith Foundation, 2014), DVD. *Statesmen & Symbols: Prelude to the Restoration* is a feature length documentary produced by the

Joseph Smith and Jesus Christ

A common argument posited by scholars, anti-Mormons, and those confused because of claims made by these two groups, comes from a profusion of sources suggesting Joseph Smith's involvement in magic. Critics and progressive apologists combine in the belief that there must be some substance behind these arguments, just as the "learned" Scribes, the progressive Sadducees, and the pious religionist Pharisees in the Lord's day argued that He cast out devils by Beelzebub or the prince of devils. Was there substance to the arguments behind the accusations leveled at the Son of God during His mortal ministry? Was the Lord a product of his paganized, Hellenistic, Rabbinical culture? Should we give equal weight to the statements of Judas, Herod, Caiaphas, Pilot, Peter, and John? Or should we "meld" all of their statements together? Consider these questions as you read the following passages:

/ / And the scribes which came down from Jerusalem said, **He hath Beelzebub, and by the prince of the devils casteth he out devils.** And he called them unto him, and said unto them in parables, How can Satan cast out Satan? And if a kingdom be divided against itself, that kingdom cannot stand. And if a house be divided against itself, that house cannot stand. And if Satan rise up against himself, and be divided, he cannot stand, but hath an end.[54]

It may be interesting, but it certainly is no coincidence, that the accusations leveled against Joseph Smith demonstrate an incredible parallel to those leveled against the Son of God during his mortal sojourn or ministry. Do many of the scribes of our day accuse Joseph Smith of the very same crimes as the scribes of the Lord's day accused the Master? Perhaps we can view the accusations and aspersions cast at Joseph Smith as evidence that he was indeed a true prophet of God.

Darkness and lies always combine against true prophets, and those who have the spirit of sin and darkness always rise up to oppose those enlightened by the spirit of God. Darkness and light are locked eternally in conflict, one against the other. The Prophet Joseph Smith taught:

Joseph Smith Foundation® exploring temple symbolism. Discover the reason behind Joseph Smith's involvement with Masonry, the purpose of inverted pentagrams on LDS temples, the use of sacred symbols by the Founding Fathers and more.

54   Mark 3:22-26; emphasis added.

// ... false prophets **always arise to oppose** the true prophets, and they will prophesy so very **near the truth** that they will deceive almost the very chosen ones ... in relation to the Kingdom of God —the devil always **sets up his Kingdom at the very same time in opposition** to God ...[55]

In previous chapters we learned that many of the Prophet's closest associates apostatized and then involved themselves in the occult, later accusing Joseph Smith of using occultic means to translate the *Book of Mormon*. It is a true principle that the wicked view the righteous through their own eyes:

// Cursed are all those that shall lift up the heel against mine anointed, saith the Lord, and **cry they have sinned when they have not sinned** before me, saith the Lord, but have done that which was meet in mine eyes, and which I commanded them.

But those who cry transgression do it because they are the **servants of sin**, and are the **children of disobedience themselves**.[56]

William E. McLellin, a former member of the Twelve who became one of Joseph Smith's most bitter opponents, became deeply involved in Satanic revelations, while David Whitmer, one of the Three Witnesses later apostatized and consorted with a witch. Both were complicit in the deaths, persecution, and the driving of the Saints from Missouri. Whitmer also claimed to receive "revelations" denouncing The Church of Jesus Christ of Latter-day Saints.

Progressive scholars claim our history is in a transitional period. They would have us move away from the traditional, long-standing foundation established by prophets of God to take on a so-called "enlightened" and "educated" approach. To do so, they require that we disregard countless testimonies, including this counsel, taken from an appropriately entitled talk delivered by President Gordon B. Hinckley, "Lord, Increase Our Faith":

---

55   Joseph Smith, Discourse, 12 May 1844, as Reported by Thomas Bullock, p. 1, The Joseph Smith Papers; emphasis added.

56   Doctrine and Covenants 121:16-17; emphasis added.

❝ I have no doubt there was folk magic practiced in those days. Without question there were superstitions and the superstitious. I suppose there was some of this in the days when the Savior walked the earth. There is even some in this age of so-called enlightenment. For instance, some hotels and business buildings skip the numbering of floor thirteen. Does this mean there is something wrong with the building? Of course not. Or with the builders? No.

Similarly, the fact that there were superstitions among the people in the days of Joseph Smith is **no evidence whatever** that the Church came of such superstition.

Joseph Smith himself wrote or dictated his history. It is his testimony of what occurred, and he sealed that testimony with his life. It is written in language clear and plain and unmistakable. From an ancient record he translated the Book of Mormon by the gift and power of God. It is here for all to see and handle and read. Those who have read with faith and inquired in prayer have come to a certain knowledge that it is true. The present effort of trying to find some other explanation for the organization of the Church, for the origin of the Book of Mormon, and for the priesthood with its keys and powers will be similar to other anti-Mormon fads which have come and blossomed and faded. Truth will prevail. A knowledge of that truth comes by effort and study, yes. But it comes primarily as a gift from God to those who seek in faith.[57]

In the end, will we allow the anti-Mormonism of the past to continue to hijack mainstream Latter-day Saint history, or will we heed President Hinckley's warning? The recurring question throughout this book, one that each Latter-day Saint must answer is, "Where do I stand"?

---

57   Gordon B. Hinckley, "Lord, Increase Our Faith," The Church of Jesus Christ of Latter-day Saints, accessed December 2016, https://www.lds.org/general-conference/1987/10/lord-increase-our-faith?lang=eng; emphasis added.

16

NO ONE WAS BETRAYED

When Jana Riess, a popular religion and history editor, conducted the "Next Mormons Survey" in 2016, she asked former members why they decided to leave The Church of Jesus Christ of Latter-day Saints. She expected past historical issues to arise as a primary factor, but was surprised to find that:

> **//** ... the third most common reason overall (and tied for first among Millennials) was "I did **not trust the Church leadership to tell the truth** about controversial issues." And that's the core problem right there. It's a **trust gap.**[1]

One of, if not the primary issue prompting this "trust gap" is the new "seer stone narrative." As progressive historians publish their historical revisions, they maintain that past Church leaders were either misinformed or deceptive and that our history needs to be rewritten. Not surprisingly, vulnerable Latter-day Saints respond with feelings of intense hurt and betrayal. In 2013, Hans Mattsson, a member of the 3rd Quorum of the Seventy and a leader in Sweden went public with his own concerns, becoming one of "the highest-ranking church official[s] who has gone public with deep concerns."[2] When asked why

---

1   Jana Riess, "Mormon Leaders Have Trust Issues," Religion News Service, April 19, 2017, accessed March 2019, https://religionnews.com/2017/04/19/mormon-leaders-have-trust-issues/; emphasis added.

2   This description of Hans Mattsson by Greg Prince was quoted in Laurie Goodstein in the *New York Times*. Laurie Goodstein, "Some Mormons Search the Web and Find Doubt," *The New York Times*, July 20, 2013, accessed July 2018, https://www.nytimes.com/2013/07/21/us/some-mormons-search-the-web-and-find-doubt.html.

he left the Church, he echoed sentiments now common among many members. He, like other members, felt "betrayed":

❙❙ The first doubts filtered up to him from members who had turned to the Internet to research a Sunday school talk. There are dozens of Web sites other than the Mormons' own that present critical views of the faith. The questions were things like: **Why does the church always portray Joseph Smith translating the Book of Mormon from golden plates, when witnesses described him looking down into a hat at a "peep stone," a rock that he believed helped him find buried treasure?** . . . "Sometimes people are furious because they feel they haven't been told the truth growing up," he said. "They feel like they were tricked or betrayed."[3]

Around the time Mattsson went public with his concerns, Jeremy Runnells, a seventh generation Latter-day Saint, was experiencing his own faith crisis. He composed a detailed letter to a CES director where he outlined his concerns with recent discoveries surrounding Latter-day Saint history, doctrine, and so forth. One of the primary concerns Runnells listed was the method of translation responsible for the *Book of Mormon*:

❙❙ BOOK OF MORMON TRANSLATION Concerns & Questions ... Unlike the story I've been taught in Sunday School, Priesthood, General Conferences, Seminary, EFY, *Ensigns*, Church history tour, Missionary Training Center, and BYU ... Joseph Smith used a rock in a hat for translating the Book of Mormon.

In other words, Joseph used the same magic device or "Ouija Board" that he used during his treasure hunting days. He put a rock – called a "peep stone" – in his hat and put his face in the hat to tell his customers the location of buried treasure on their property. He also used this same method for translating the Book of Mormon, while the gold plates were covered, placed in another

---

3   Laurie Goodstein, "Some Mormons Search the Web and Find Doubt," *The New York Times*, July 20, 2013, accessed February 2019, https://www.nytimes.com/2013/07/21/us/some-mormons-search-the-web-and-find-doubt.html; emphasis added.

room, or even buried in the woods. . . . The gold plates were not used for the Book of Mormon we have today.[4]

Understandably frustrated, Jeremy Runnells had grown up being told that Joseph Smith translated the *Book of Mormon* from ancient Nephite plates using the Urim and Thummim. Jeremy compiled examples of popular Latter-day Saint art he had seen for years when reading the *Ensign, Preach My Gospel,* or in films produced by the Church—each one depicting Joseph Smith intently studying characters on plates or using a breastplate and spectacles called the "Urim and Thummim." Children have grown up since Primary with the teaching that Joseph Smith translated the *Book of Mormon* by studying the characters directly, translating them into English using the Urim and Thummim.[5] There was no seer stone, no peep stone in a hat. Now Jeremy was learning from prestigious historians, authors, and researchers that this "dominant narrative" never took place. Instead, he was told, Joseph Smith translated the *Book of Mormon* using a treasure hunting peep stone in a hat.

After receiving no response, Jeremy released his *CES Letter* online where it went viral. In less than three years, it was downloaded an estimated 600,000 times.[6] It is our opinion that Jeremy Runnells has not received a satisfactory answer to his letter in regard to the translation of the *Book of Mormon*, despite a number of "responses" from Latter-day Saint apologists. The answers he did receive served

---

4   Jeremy Runnells, "CES Letter - My Search for Answers to My Mormon Doubts," PDF file, October 2017, accessed December 2016, https://cesletter.org/CES-Letter.pdf.

5   For example, the *Primary 5: Doctrine and Covenants and Church History* manual published in 1997 and used for years states, "Once Joseph and Emma Smith were settled in Harmony, Pennsylvania, Joseph began to translate the gold plates. At first Joseph spent a lot of time becoming familiar with the plates and the language in which they were written. As he studied and prayed, the Urim and Thummim helped him understand the characters on the plates. Joseph learned that the process of translation requires faith, hard work, worthiness, patience, and obedience." "Lesson 6: Joseph Smith Begins to Translate the Gold Plates," The Church of Jesus Christ of Latter-day Saints, accessed July 2018, https://www.lds.org/manual/primary-5-doctrine-and-covenants-and-church-history/lesson-6.

See also the children's reader produced by the Church, *Book of Mormon Stories (Beginning Reader).*

6   "Jeremy Runnells, Author of CES Letter, Faces LDS Church Excommunication," CES Letter Foundation. February 9, 2016. Accessed February 27, 2019. https://cesletter.org/jeremy-runnells-faces-lds-excommunication.html.

only to aggravate his conflict. The high-profile apologists and historians had in essence said, "You are right; the story you were told was false. Joseph Smith dictated the *Book of Mormon* using a treasure-digging peep stone in a hat. But that isn't all, Joseph Smith and his family were led by a sordid, indolent, and unmoored character, and they participated in ritual magic, alcoholism, and treasure-seeking greed." Can anyone blame Jeremy Runnells for feeling "upset," "desperate,"[7] and betrayed? Today, Jeremy Runnells subscribes to "no gods or religions."[8] Our hearts go out to him and to the many hundreds of thousands, if not millions, who have and will find themselves in similar shoes.

Richard Bushman, in promoting his "seer stone narrative," only added fuel to the fire for many struggling Latter-day Saints when he responded to a participant's question regarding whether the traditional understanding of Church history is accurate during a 2016 fireside. He advised the questioner, and the audience at large:

> I think that for the Church to remain strong it has to **reconstruct its narrative**. The **dominant narrative is not true**; it **can't be sustained**. The Church has to absorb all this new information or it will be on very shaky grounds and that's what it is trying to do and it will be a **strain for a lot of people**, older people especially. But I think it has to change.[9]

The following month, Bushman elaborated on his meaning:

> I consider *Rough Stone Rolling* a **reconstructed narrative**. It was **shocking** to some people. They could not bear to have the old story disrupted in any way. What I was getting at in the quoted passage is that we must be willing to modify the account according to newly authenticated facts. If we don't we will weaken our position. Unfortunately, not everyone can adjust to this new material. Many think they were deceived and the church was lying. That is not a fair judgment in my opinion. The whole church, from top to

---

7   "CES Letter 2.0 Launched," CES Letter Foundation, December 3, 2017, accessed February 27, 2019, https://cesletter.org/updates/CES-Letter-2.0.html.

8   "Frequently Asked Questions," CES Letter Foundation, accessed February 27, 2019, https://cesletter.org/faq/#religion.

9   "Richard and Claudia Bushman," YouTube video, 1:56:30, "Blake Bishop," June 12, 2016, https://www.youtube.com/watch?v=MA0YS8LWWX4; emphasis added.

bottom, has had to adjust to the findings of our historians. We are all having to reconstruct.[10]

The proposed "reconstructed narrative" of our Church history, as well as the "reconstructed" life and character of the Prophet Joseph Smith, is admittedly a departure from the traditional or "dominant narrative" inherited from past Church leaders and historians including Willard Richards (who was present at the Carthage martyrdom), George A. Smith (a cousin to the Prophet Joseph Smith who knew him well), President Wilford Woodruff, President Joseph F. Smith (nephew of the Prophet through his closest brother, Hyrum), and President Joseph Fielding Smith.

Bushman and other seer stone proponents claim the "dominant narrative" is "not true" and needs to be rewritten. Said another way, the history and the accounts of sacred events that we have been teaching Church membership for 200 years is suddenly false and misleading. Understandably, members who have been taught that this is the "true Church" begin to question their faith when progressive historians tell them that the Church isn't so "true" after all.

It is a serious charge to suggest that Latter-day Saints have been betrayed by our dominant historical narrative given to us by our past leaders. Especially disconcerting is the suggestion that past Presidents of the Church lied to the members. The question is, does the "reconstructed narrative" promoted by Richard Bushman, Michael MacKay, Mark Ashurst-McGee, Brant Gardner, and a growing number of others hold up when scrutinized against primary sources, credible history, and the scriptures? When it comes to the translation of the *Book of Mormon*, if one believes the testimonies of the Lord Jesus Christ, the Prophet Joseph Smith, and Oliver Cowdery, the answer is a resounding, no! Joseph Smith did *not* translate the *Book of Mormon* using a seer stone; his translation was genuine. He used ancient plates and the Nephite Urim and Thummim. He studied and exerted faith and his character was pure and honorable.

The battle in which we are currently engaged is a battle for the very heart of our faith. What was done to American history is now being done to the history of the Restoration of the Gospel of Jesus Christ.

10   "Richard and Claudia Bushman," YouTube video, 1:56:30, "Blake Bishop," June 12, 2016, https://www.youtube.com/watch?v=MA0YS8LWWX4; emphasis added.

The late 19th and 20th centuries saw progressive historians rewriting United States history and laudatory biographies of the early Founding Fathers (including George Washington, Thomas Jefferson, John Adams, etc.). The revisionists wrote a "new narrative" that included sordid accusations such as Thomas Jefferson having an affair with his black slave, Sally Hemings,[11] or the allegation that George Washington was arrogant, vain, and ambitious,[12] followed by other claims disparaging Benjamin Franklin as a womanizer[13] and Samuel Adams as a violent anarchist.[14] The "new narrative" of the Founding Fathers asserts these men were atheists, agnostics, and deists. What has been the result? Today, our Constitution hangs by a thread.[15] Our country is in severe decline, wracked with political division, and is collapsing from within. When progressive historians maligned the character of the Founding Fathers, they dishonestly eradicated our country's righteousness and purity, degrading our heritage until there was nothing left to defend, nothing to stand for, nothing to be proud of. The foundation we abandoned has left our country crumbling.

---

11   See David Barton, *The Jefferson Lies: Exposing the Myths You've Always Believed About Thomas Jefferson* (Nashville: Thomas Nelson, 2012), 1-30. See Chapter 1, "Thomas Jefferson Fathered Sally Hemings' Children.". "So many things that we are told today about our Founding Fathers simply aren't true – such as that Thomas Jefferson fathered the child of his slave girl, that he was an anti-Christian secularist who rewrote the Bible to his liking, and that he was just another racist, bigoted colonial. But historical fact proves otherwise – that Jefferson was a visionary, an innovator, a man who revered Jesus, and a man whose pioneering stand for liberty and God-given inalienable rights fostered a better world for this nation and its posterity." (Description from WallBuilders.com)

12   See Jay A. Parry and Andrew M. Allison, *The Real George Washington* (National Center for Constitutional Studies, 1991), and Peter A. Lillback, *George Washington's Sacred Fire* (Providence Forum Press, 2006).

13   Andrew M. Allison, W. Cleon Skousen, and M. Richard Maxfield, *The Real Benjamin Franklin* (Freemen Institute, 1982), 229-233.

14   Rod Gragg, *Forged in Faith: How Faith Shaped the Birth of the Nation*, 1607-1776 (New York: Howard Books, a Division of Simon & Schuster, 2011).

15   "31) HANG BY A THREAD: What Have Latter-day Prophets Taught concerning the Prophecy of Joseph Smith That the United States Constitution Would Hang by a Thread and Be Saved, If Saved at All, through the Efforts of the Elders of Israel?" Joseph Smith Foundation, accessed March 2019, https://josephsmithfoundation.org/faqs/government/31-hang-by-a-thread-what-have-latter-day-prophets-taught-concerning-the-prophecy-of-joseph-smith-that-the-united-states-constitution-would-hang-by-a-thread-and-be-saved-if-saved-at-all-through-the/.

Today, progressive historians have initiated the same attack against our Church history.[16] Instead of heralding our early leaders as men of integrity, honor, and virtue—men worthy of respect—the revisionists have repackaged them into racist, chauvinist, treasure-digging, occultic, magic-dabbling, wicked men who were given "extraordinary callings." Yes, "ordinary men with extraordinary callings." Even the seemingly innocuous statement, "ordinary man," transforms Joseph Smith from a holy prophet of God to a magician and "village seer," dictating what may be only a heart-warming, parable-filled, literary tome from his treasure-hunting rock in a hat.

What are the fruits of this "new narrative"? There are many thousands of men and women, returned missionaries, teens, and even ecclesiastical leaders who are abandoning their faith, losing their testimonies and finally, leaving the Church. And what of the millions more who now question their faith, who are confused and who cannot find the answers they are looking for?

Testify That Joseph Smith is a Prophet of God

The authors have been queried continuously as to why they devote so much time to Joseph Smith. They have been asked, "What is the big deal?" Some seem to think, "Who cares if Joseph Smith was good or bad? Why do we need to learn about him today? Does he really matter?"

---

16   Ezra Taft Benson, "God's Hand in Our Nation's History" (Devotional, Brigham Young University, March 28, 1977), accessed March 2019, https:// speeches.byu.edu/talks/ezra-taft-benson_gods-hand-nations-history/. "Today we are almost engulfed by this tide of self-criticism, depreciation, and defamation . . . . I know the philosophy behind this practice—"to tell it as it is." All too often those who subscribe to this philosophy are not hampered by too many facts. . . . Some have termed this practice as "historical realism" or moderately call it "debunking." I call it slander and defamation. I repeat, those who are guilty of it in their writing or teaching will answer to a higher tribunal. . . . This humanistic emphasis on history is not confined only to secular history; there have been and continue to be attempts made to bring this philosophy into our own Church history. Again the emphasis is to underplay revelation and God's intervention in significant events . . . It is a state of mind and spirit characterized by one history buff, who asked: "Do you believe the Church has arrived at a sufficient state of maturity where we can begin to tell our *real* story?" Implied in that question is the accusation that the Church has not been telling the truth. Unfortunately, too many of those who have been intellectually gifted become so imbued with criticism that they become disaffected spiritually. . . . To those who have not sought after or received a testimony of Joseph Smith's divine calling, he will ever remain what one called 'the enigma from Palmyra.' . . . My purpose further is to forewarn you about a humanistic emphasis which would tarnish our own Church history and its leaders."

When President David O. McKay's father was serving a mission in Scotland, he discovered that if we fail to teach the truth about the life, character, and teachings of the Prophet Joseph Smith, we will lose the Spirit of God:

❮❮ When [my father] began preaching in his native land and bore testimony of the restoration of the gospel of Jesus Christ, he noticed that the people turned away from him. They were bitter in their hearts against anything [related to the Church], and the name of Joseph Smith seemed to arouse antagonism in their hearts.

One day he concluded that the best way to reach these people would be to preach **just the simple principles**, the atonement of the Lord Jesus Christ, the first principles of the gospel, and **not bear testimony of the restoration.**

Some have advised the authors of this book to do the same. But President McKay explains why we cannot do so, while relating his father's experience:

❮❮ In a month or so he became **oppressed** with a **gloomy, downcast feeling**, and he **could not enter into the spirit of his work**. He did not really know what was the matter, but his **mind** became **obstructed**; his spirit became **depressed**; he was **oppressed** and **hampered**; and that feeling of **depression** continued until it **weighed him down** with such **heaviness** that he went to the Lord and said, "Unless I can get this feeling removed, I shall have to go home. I can't continue having my work thus hampered."

This same spirit plagues many today. Members are questioning their direction, they are questioning their heritage, they are questioning their faith. President McKay's father struggled with a spirit of "gloom," "depression," and "heaviness" after choosing to overlook Joseph Smith and focus only on "Christ" and the "Atonement." A transformation occurred when, through inspiration, he discovered the answer.

❮❮ The discouragement continued for some time after that, when, one morning before daylight, following a sleepless night, he decided to retire to a cave, near the ocean, where he knew he would be shut off from the world entirely, and there pour out his soul to God and ask why he was oppressed with this feeling, what he had done, and what he could do to throw it off and continue his work. He started out in the dark toward the cave. He became so eager to get to it that he started to run. As he was leaving the town, he was hailed by an officer who wanted to know what was the matter. He gave some noncommittal but satisfactory reply and was permitted to go on. Something just seemed to drive him; he had to get relief.

He entered the cave or sheltered opening, and said, "Oh, Father, what can I do to have this feeling removed? I must have it lifted or I cannot continue in this work"; and he heard a voice, as distinct as the tone I am now uttering, say, **"Testify that Joseph Smith is a prophet of God."** Remembering then what he tacitly had decided six weeks or more before, and becoming overwhelmed with the thought, the whole thing came to him in a realization that he was there for a special mission, and **he had not given that special mission the attention it deserved.** Then he cried in his heart, "Lord, it is enough," and went out from the cave.[17]

President McKay's father discovered an intrinsic truth, a key to weathering the storms of our day, a day when even "the humble followers of Christ . . . are led, that in **many instances** they do err because they are taught by the precepts of men."[18]

First, learn the *real* Joseph Smith and then "testify that Joseph Smith is a prophet of God." While some today suggest the Prophet Joseph Smith is no longer needed, that we have the *Book of Mormon* and that is enough or that we should focus only on "Christ" and His "Atonement," the teachings of prophets both ancient and modern insist:

❧❧ Joseph Smith holds the keys of this last dispensation, and is **now engaged** behind the veil in the great work of the last days. . . . It is his mission to see that all the children of men in this last dispensation are saved, that can be . . . [19] (President Brigham Young)

---

17   David O. McKay, *Cherished Experiences from the Writings of President David O. McKay*, comp. Clare Middlemiss (Salt Lake City: Deseret Book, 1976), 11-12; emphasis added.

18   2 Nephi 28:14; emphasis added.

19   Brigham Young, "Intelligence, Etc," in *Journal of Discourses*, vol. 7 (Liverpool,

> The **greatest activity** in this world or in the world to come is **directly related** to the **work and mission of Joseph Smith**—man of destiny, prophet of God. . . . The Prophet Joseph Smith was not only "one of the noble and great ones," but he gave and continues to give attention to important matters here on the earth even today from the realms above.[20] (President Ezra Taft Benson)

Bruce R. McConkie taught that "the measure of a person's spiritual **maturity** is found in his or her **loyalty** to the **Prophet Joseph Smith**."[21] Are we loyal to him?

Today, there are many who desire to move the Church and its members away from our foundational moorings. While many progressives labor to take Joseph Smith from off "the pedestal" to which past Presidents of the Church and faithful members have placed him, we have the opportunity, like our forebearers, to obtain a witness of his righteous character and divine mission for ourselves.

If our history is changed, our doctrine will change also. If Joseph Smith was a "bitter fountain," and true prophets of God are not examples of character, or are not "pure fountains," the landscape of our faith changes. The "new narrative" places the Restoration, the restored Gospel of Jesus Christ under attack. Margaret Young, an adjunct faculty member at BYU-Provo, has been perhaps more honest and clear than others in stating the charted course or direction of the progressive "new narrative." In a 2015 blog post entitled "The Future of Mormonism (the Next Five Years)," she stated:

> **//** . . . the future of Mormonism is bright. We are on a **bridge**. . . . Change comes slowly in the Church, but to those seeking to find miracles, the changes over the past fifty years have been monumental. . . . **We will become a church known for exactly the opposite reasons it was known for in the nineteenth century.**[22]

1860), 289; emphasis added. Discourse given on October 9, 1859.

20   Ezra Taft Benson, *God, Family, Country: Our Three Great Loyalties* (Salt Lake City: Deseret Book, 1974), 30-31; emphasis added.

21   Joseph Fielding McConkie, *The Bruce R. McConkie Story: Reflections of a Son* (Salt Lake City: Deseret Book, 2003), 256. See also Bruce R. McConkie, "Joseph Smith: A Revealer of Christ", BYU Devotional Address, 3 September 1978, 6; emphasis added.

22   Margaret Blair Young, "The Future of Mormonism (the Next Five Years)," The Welcome Table, August 05, 2015, accessed March 13, 2019, https://www.patheos.

If the new progressive narrators have their way, what will this new Church—which is precisely the opposite of what it was nearly two hundred years ago—look like? Has God changed or were our previous leaders, as they imply, simply leading in the wrong direction?

There are two opposing forces: the Truth vs the lie, the Light vs the darkness. Will we allow the loss of the faith expressed by Joseph and Hyrum for which they bled and died, the loss of the pure truth and history of the Restoration?

No one was betrayed! But now that you know, the millions who are searching for the truth but "know not where to find it"[23] need your voice, your testimony of the Prophet Joseph Smith. President Heber C. Kimball, one of the two faithful of the original Quorum of the Twelve Apostles, prophetically warned:

> You **imagine** . . . that **you would have stood** by him [Joseph Smith] when persecution raged and he was assailed by foes within and without [the Church]. You would have **defended** him and been **true to him** in the midst of every trial. **You think** you would have been delighted to have **shown your integrity** in the days of mobs and traitors.
>
> Let me say to you, that **many** of you will see the time when you will have **all the trouble, trial and persecution that you can stand**, and **plenty of opportunities** to show that you are true to God and his work. This Church has before it **many close places** through which it will have to pass before the work of God is crowned with victory.
>
> **To meet the difficulties** that are coming, it will be **necessary** for you to have a **knowledge of the truth** of this work **for yourselves**. The **difficulties** will be of such character that the man or woman who does **not possess** this **personal knowledge or witness will fall**. If you have not got the testimony, **live right** and **call upon the Lord** and **cease not till you obtain it**. If you do not you **will not stand**. . . .
>
> The **time will come** when **no man nor woman will be able to endure on borrowed light**. Each will have to be **guided by the**

---

com/blogs/welcometable/2015/07/the-future-of-mormonism-the-next-five-years/; emphasis added.

23   Doctrine and Covenants 123:12.

light within himself. If you do not have it, **how can you stand?** Do you believe it?[24]

When Joseph Smith languished in the bitter cold of Liberty Jail, he was promised that "his people" would never turn against him "by the testimony of traitors,"[25] but would stand to defend his name, his character, his doctrine, and his mission. President Heber C. Kimball also prophesied that while many of the Prophet's "boys" are asleep, they will one day rise up and "bear testimony" to the "true character of Joseph [Smith]":

> At present the Prophet Joseph's boys lay apparently in a state of slumber, everything seems to be perfectly calm with them, but by and by God will wake them up, and they will roar like the thunders of Mount Sinai.
>
> There is much work to be done: God is not asleep, and He will wake up our children and they will bear off this kingdom to the nations of the earth, and will bear testimony to the truth of this work, and of the **integrity** and **true character** of Joseph . . .[26]

Brothers and sisters, it is time to wake up! Who will rise up and "stand by [the Lord's] servant Joseph, faithfully, in whatsoever difficult circumstances he may be for the word's sake"[27]?

We, the authors, declare the Prophet Joseph Smith the greatest, most holy, most righteous, most faithful man—even the most humble leader ever to have lived—excepting the Son of God.[28] We know with unequivocal certainty that he lives, just as we know his Master, Jesus Christ lives.

---

24   Orson F. Whitney, *Life of Heber C. Kimball* (Salt Lake City, 1888), 461; emphasis added. Reported by John Nicholson; emphasis added.

25   Doctrine and Covenants 122:3.

26   Heber C. Kimball, "The Saints Should Prepare for Future Emergencies," in *Journal of Discourses*, vol. 4 (Liverpool, 1860), 6; emphasis added. Discourse given on June 29, 1857.

27   Doctrine and Covenants 6:18.

28   Many early leaders also testified of this: "I am bold to say that, Jesus Christ excepted, no better man ever lived or does live upon this earth. I am his witness." Brigham Young, "A Knowledge of God Obtained Only Through Obedience to the Principles of Truth," *Journal of Discourses*, vol. 9 (Salt Lake City: Deseret Book, 1974), 332. "I look upon Joseph Smith as the greatest prophet that ever breathed the breath of life, excepting Jesus Christ." Wilford Woodruff, *The Deseret Weekly* 38, no. 1 (March 23, 1889): p. 389, https://books.google.com/books?id=vKsUAAAA YAAJ&pg=PA389).

Topics in Upcoming Volumes

William E. McLellin's "New Narrative"

Translation Accounts:
Martin Harris, Emma Hale Smith Bidamon, William Smith

Joseph Smith as a Translator:
The Bible, The Book of Abraham, The Kinderhook Plates

"Study it Out in Your Mind" vs. a Free Gift

Textual Changes in the Book of Mormon Manuscripts

Urim and Thummim or Seer Stone?

Mark Hoffman: The Salamander & the "New Narrative"

Restoration of Biblical Urim & Thummim

The 1826 & 1830 Trial

Joseph Smith: Alleged "Village Seer," Seer Stones, Rods

Lucy Mack Smith & Magic Rituals

Alleged Smith Family Magical Parchments

Treasure Digging

And more!

Index

L. Hannah Stoddard, author

L. Hannah Stoddard is the lead author of *Seer Stone v. Urim & Thummim: Book of Mormon Translation on Trial.* She is the executive director of the Joseph Smith Foundation, and producer or director of seven documentary feature films.

- Nephites in Europe (Episodes 1 & 2, Quest for the Nephite Remnant) (2019)
- Hidden Bloodlines: The Grail & the Lost Tribes in the Lands of the North (2017)
- Unlocking the Mystery of the Two Prophets: Revelation 11 (2017)
- The Prophet Joseph: More than we know (2015)
- Statesmen & Symbols: Prelude to the Restoration (2014)
- For Our Day: Divinely Sanctioned Governments (2013)
- For Our Day: Covenant on the Land (2013)

In addition to directing Joseph Smith Foundation projects for over a decade, she is often invited to speak on various radio and video programs. Hannah helped direct her first documentary film, beginning at age 16. She has worked as a history and literature teacher, graphic design artist, software developer, videographer, project manager, agriculturist and research assistant. Her work focuses on Church history and doctrine, answers to Latter-day Saint faith crisis questions, educational philosophy, culture, and defending the Prophet Joseph Smith. Hannah's research supports the writings and teachings of ancient and latter-day prophets.

JAMES F. STODDARD III, AUTHOR

James F. Stoddard is a film producer, author, entrepreneur, and father of 10 children. James is the executive strategist for the Joseph Smith Foundation. He is a direct descendant of Asael and Mary Duty Smith, the Prophet Joseph Smith's grandparents, and other LDS Church history figures. James is the co-author of *Seer Stone v. Urim & Thummim: Book of Mormon Translation on Trial* and the producer or executive producer of eight documentary films:

- Nephites in Europe (Episodes 1 & 2, Quest for the Nephite Remnant) (2019)
- Hidden Bloodlines: The Grail & the Lost Tribes in the Lands of the North (2017)
- Unlocking the Mystery of the Two Prophets: Revelation 11 (2017)
- The Prophet Joseph: More than we know (2015)
- Statesmen & Symbols: Prelude to the Restoration (2014)
- For Our Day: Divinely Sanctioned Governments (2013)
- For Our Day: Covenant on the Land (2013)
- Creation and Evolution: A Witness of Prophets (2007)

James has worked in private, public, religious, corporate and home education as well as engineering, videography, property development, and natural health. He has started and helps operate several family businesses and enjoys working with his kids. James spends any free moments working on Highland Cathedral Estate, a planned family retreat and learning facility with perennial gardens and walking trails specializing in experimental farming techniques and four-season food production. James has worked as a release time Seminary teacher and as an instructor at the Provo Missionary Training Center (MTC). His research supports the writings and teachings of ancient and latter-day prophets.

Joseph Smith Foundation Documentaries
www.JosephSmithFoundation.org

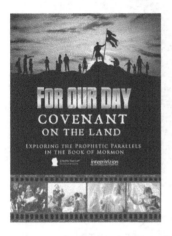

For Our Day: Covenant on the Land (DVD)

This film discusses the covenant on the Promised Land for both ancient and modern inhabitants, presenting inspiring history from the American colonization, paralleling the Puritans, Pilgrims and other righteous forebears with Lehi, Nephi and the first part of the Book of Mormon. Is latter-day history laid out and foreshadowed in the Book of Mormon?

For Our Day: Divinely Sanctioned Governments (DVD)

This film compares the Nephite and Latter-day governments of liberty. Covering principles of liberty including: Unalienable Rights, Oath of Office, Federalism, the U.S. and Israel connection and the Laws of Mosiah—this DVD adds an understanding of governmental principles as they are taught in the most correct book, the Book of Mormon.

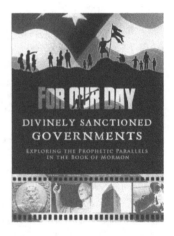

The Prophet Joseph: More than we know (DVD)

Ground-breaking research on latter-day prophecy! Is the Prophet Joseph the Angel in Revelation 14, the designator of Zion inheritances, the Messenger in Malachi, the Servant in Isaiah, the passport to Celestial glory, the Voice crying in the wilderness? Discover the Prophet Joseph Smith in a way you have never imagined!

CPSIA information can be obtained
at www.ICGtesting.com
Printed in the USA
LVHW051803060321
680755LV00007B/116

9 781644 670118